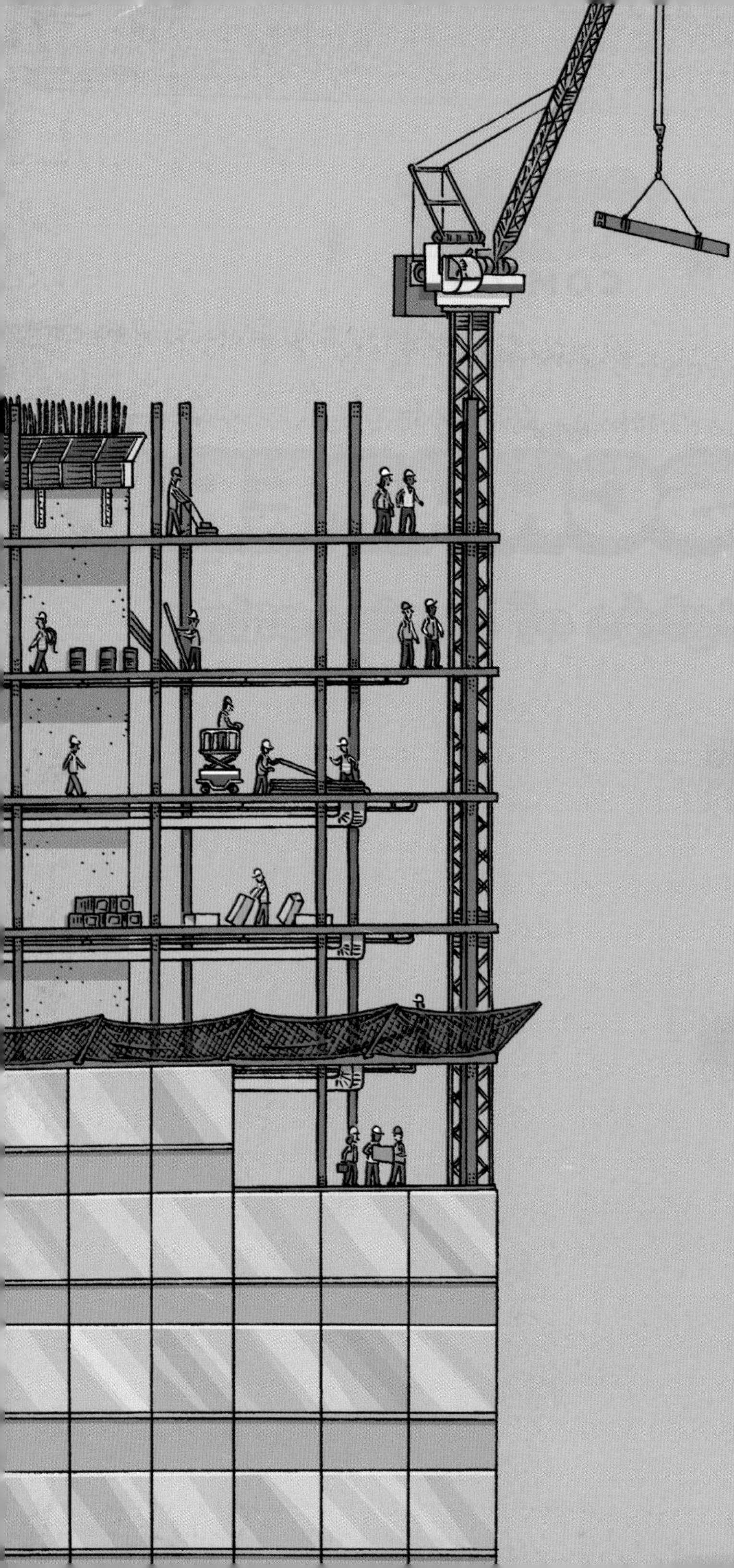

SKYSCRAPERS

The Heights of Engineering

John Kerschbaum

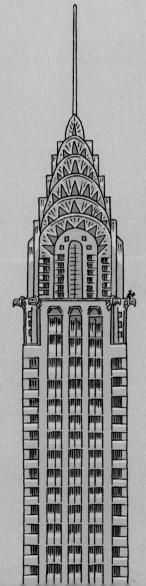

:01

First Second

New York

For Frances and Norah

First Second

Copyright © 2019 by John Kerschbaum

Published by First Second
First Second is an imprint of Roaring Brook Press,
a division of Holtzbrinck Publishing Holdings Limited Partnership
120 Broadway, New York, NY 10271

Don't miss your next favorite book from First Second! For the latest updates
go to firstsecondnewsletter.com and sign up for our enewsletter.

Library of Congress Control Number: 2018953663

Paperback ISBN: 978-1-62672-794-6
Hardcover ISBN: 978-1-62672-795-3

Our books may be purchased in bulk for promotional, educational, or business use. Please contact your local
bookseller or the Macmillan Corporate and Premium Sales Department at (800) 221-7945 ext. 5442 or by email
at MacmillanSpecialMarkets@macmillan.com.

First edition, 2019
Edited by Dave Roman
Skyscraper consultant: Donald Friedman, PE, F.APT, F.ASCE
Cover design by Andrew Arnold and Chris Dickey
Interior book design by Rob Steen
Printed in China by Toppan Leefung Printing Ltd., Dongguan City, Guangdong Province

Drawn with Derwent 2H and H pencils on Strathmore 100-lb. Bristol. Inked with various sized Pigma Micron pens.
Corrections were made with Copic Opaque White applied with a ten-year-old Winsor & Newton Series 7 watercolor
brush, size 00, that has only about a dozen hairs left in it. The art was then scanned and colored in Photoshop.

10 9 8 7 6 5 4 3 2 1

Since the dawn of mankind, people have dreamed of reaching the sky. Early civilizations built colossal monuments like the Great Pyramids of Giza and the Yongning Temple in China to showcase their great achievements. And while much has changed since the days of the ancient Egyptians, humanity's desire to build higher has only grown. Even today, cities compete to build ever-taller buildings as a sign of their importance and to mark their arrival on the world stage. Yet the massive skyscrapers of the modern world are more than just monuments—they're one of the keys to ensuring that we keep the Earth healthy and habitable for generations to come.

As the world's population continues to grow, more and more people will need to fit into the same amount of space that we have today; the Earth isn't getting any bigger, after all. In fact, the first skyscrapers were built to accommodate the great migration of people to cities like New York and Chicago during the Industrial Revolution around 1760–1830. Since then, skyscrapers have sprouted all over the globe as people flock to urban centers in search of better opportunities. With more people living and working in tall buildings, there's more room for farmers to grow their crops and less of a need to cut down forests to make way for human development.

And recently, the trend of people moving to cities to live and work in tall buildings has only accelerated. Each year, the Council on Tall Buildings and Urban Habitat studies the number of skyscrapers taller than 656 feet (200 meters) that are built. In 2008, there were 47 such skyscrapers completed; in 2017, that number jumped to a record-breaking 144 completions.

Not only are we building more skyscrapers, but these buildings continue to get taller and taller as well. Faster, more powerful elevators have allowed builders to grow their towers to new heights by transporting people hundreds of feet in the air in a matter of seconds. Technical advances in engineering have also made tall buildings more structurally sound. These factors, among others, have led to a seemingly endless competition to build the world's tallest building.

At the beginning of the 21st century, the Petronas Twin Towers in Kuala Lumpur held the title of world's tallest buildings, rising 1,483 ft (452 m) above the ground. In 2004, Taipei 101 in Taiwan took their crown, standing roughly 164 ft (50 m) taller than the Petronas Towers. By 2010, the Burj Khalifa in Dubai had taken the top spot—climbing to an incredible 2,719 ft (828 m). Yet the competition is far from over. Today, an even taller tower is being built in Jeddah, Saudi Arabia, that is expected to top out at 3,281 ft (1,000 m) above the Earth.

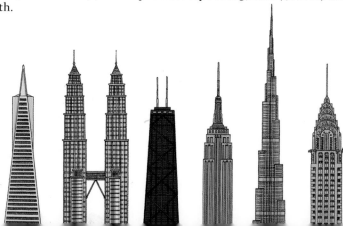

Looking toward the future, skyscrapers will continue to evolve in fascinating ways. We're just now beginning to see the implementation of skybridges—which connect tall buildings hundreds of feet in the air and allow cities to form new networks high above the ground. These "horizontal" skyscrapers are being made possible by inventions such as a new type of elevator that goes side to side as well as up and down.

New technologies are also making buildings smarter, allowing them to learn from their daily interactions with humans and provide services based on this information. As we speak, the newest generation of skyscrapers is helping to reduce the greenhouse gases that cause climate change by, for example, admitting optimal sunlight to reduce the need for artificial light.

These innovations—among many others—will dramatically change how cities look and operate in the near future. Around 2.5 billion people will be added to the world's cities by 2050, so it's important that we continue to think of new and creative ways for our cities to grow taller, smarter, and more connected. Clearly, skyscrapers are not simply a passing trend or a way for cities to boast their statuses; they are the future of humanity on our planet.

With your help, we can build the next generation of smart, sustainable cities. But first, explore the history and the inner workings of tall buildings with this dynamically illustrated introduction to skyscrapers!

—Antony Wood, Executive Director of the
Council on Tall Buildings and Urban Habitat

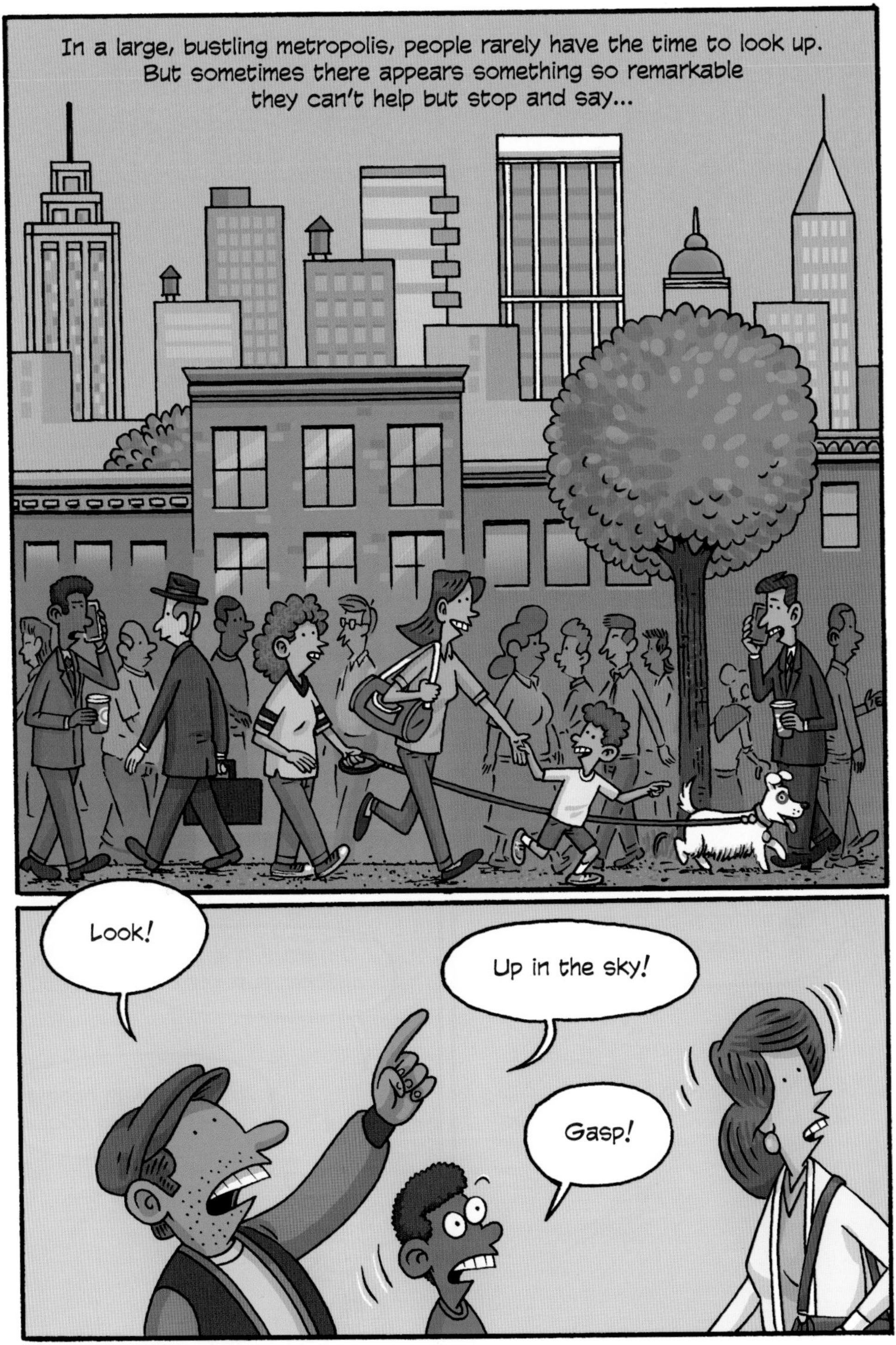
In a large, bustling metropolis, people rarely have the time to look up. But sometimes there appears something so remarkable they can't help but stop and say...
Look!
Up in the sky!
Gasp!

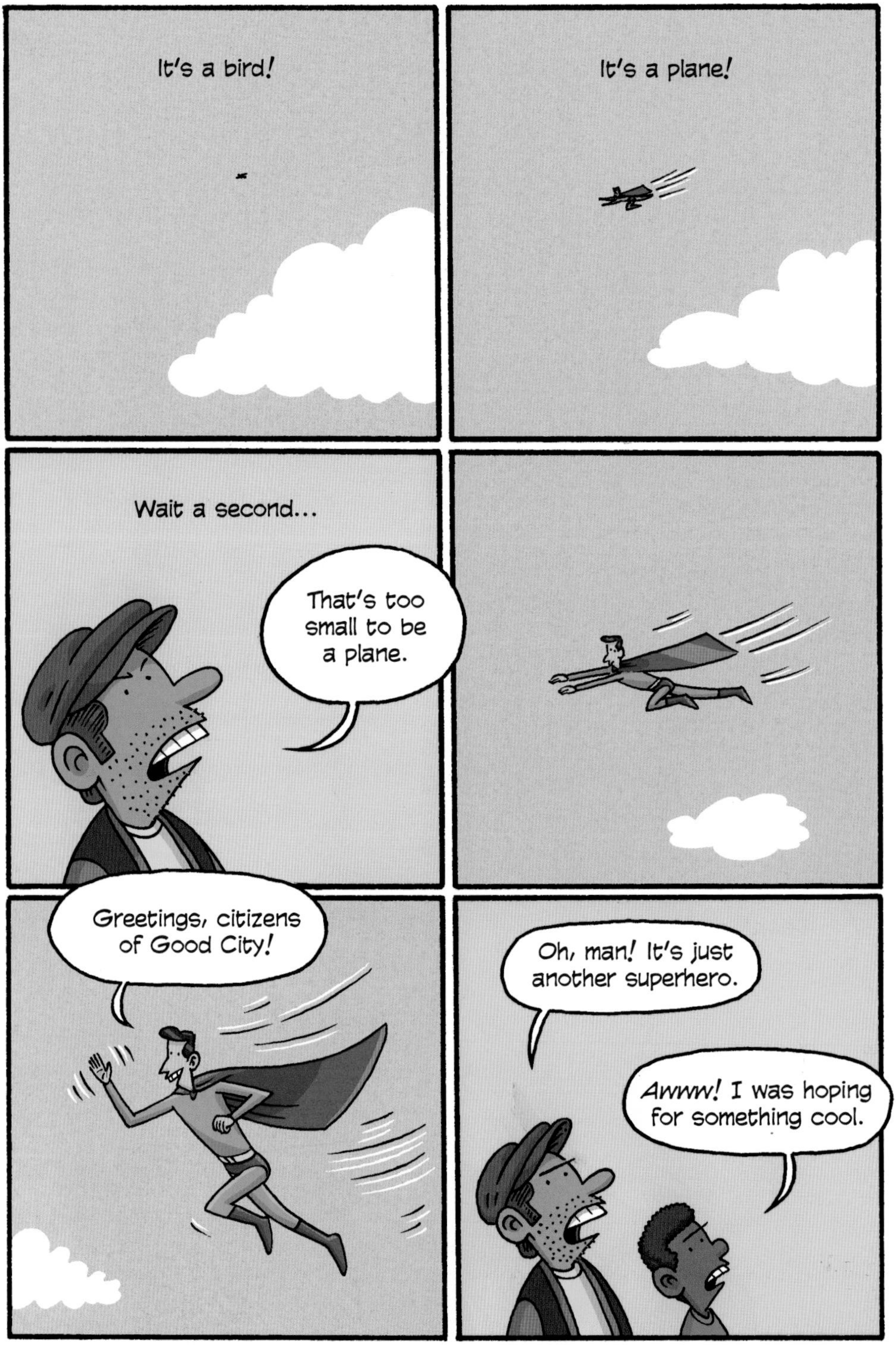
It's a bird!
It's a plane!
Wait a second...
That's too small to be a plane.
Greetings, citizens of Good City!
Oh, man! It's just another superhero.
Awww! I was hoping for something cool.

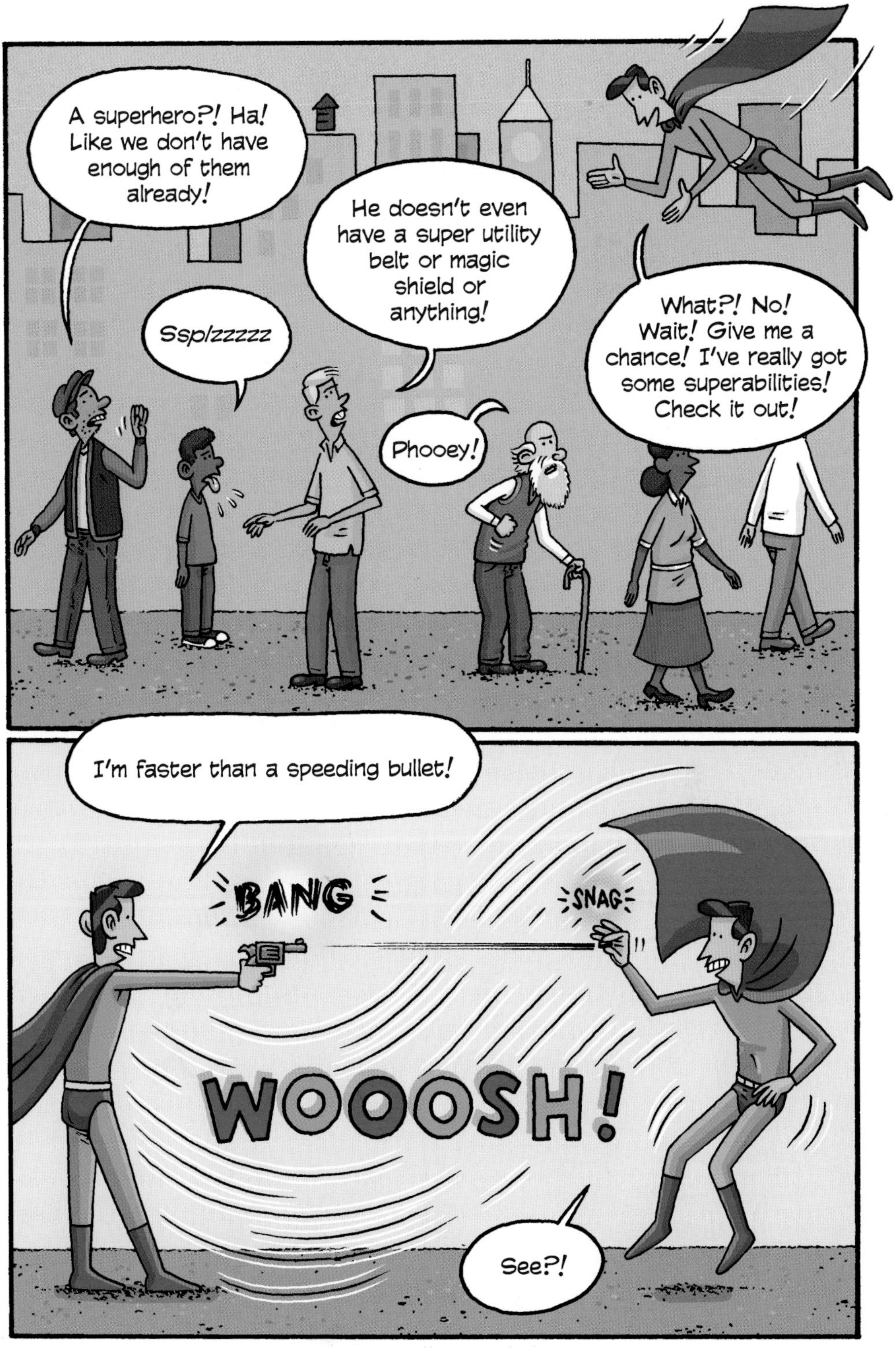
A superhero?! Ha! Like we don't have enough of them already!
Ssplzzzzz
He doesn't even have a super utility belt or magic shield or anything!
Phooey!
What?! No! Wait! Give me a chance! I've really got some superabilities! Check it out!
I'm faster than a speeding bullet!
BANG
SNAG
WOOOSH!
See?!

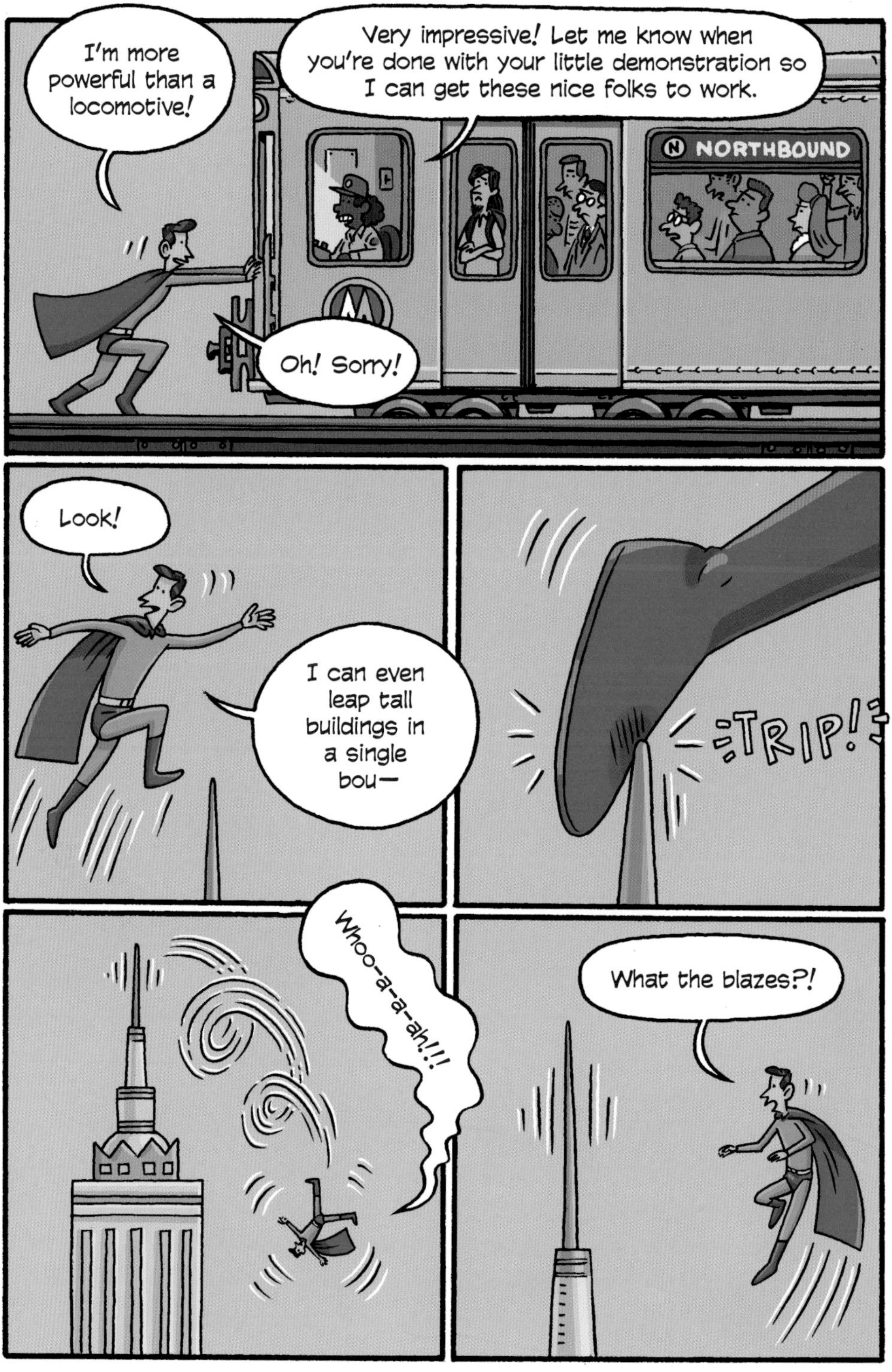
I'm more powerful than a locomotive!
Very impressive! Let me know when you're done with your little demonstration so I can get these nice folks to work.
NORTHBOUND
Oh! Sorry!
Look!
I can even leap tall buildings in a single bou—
TRIP!
Whoo-a-a-ah!!!
What the blazes?!

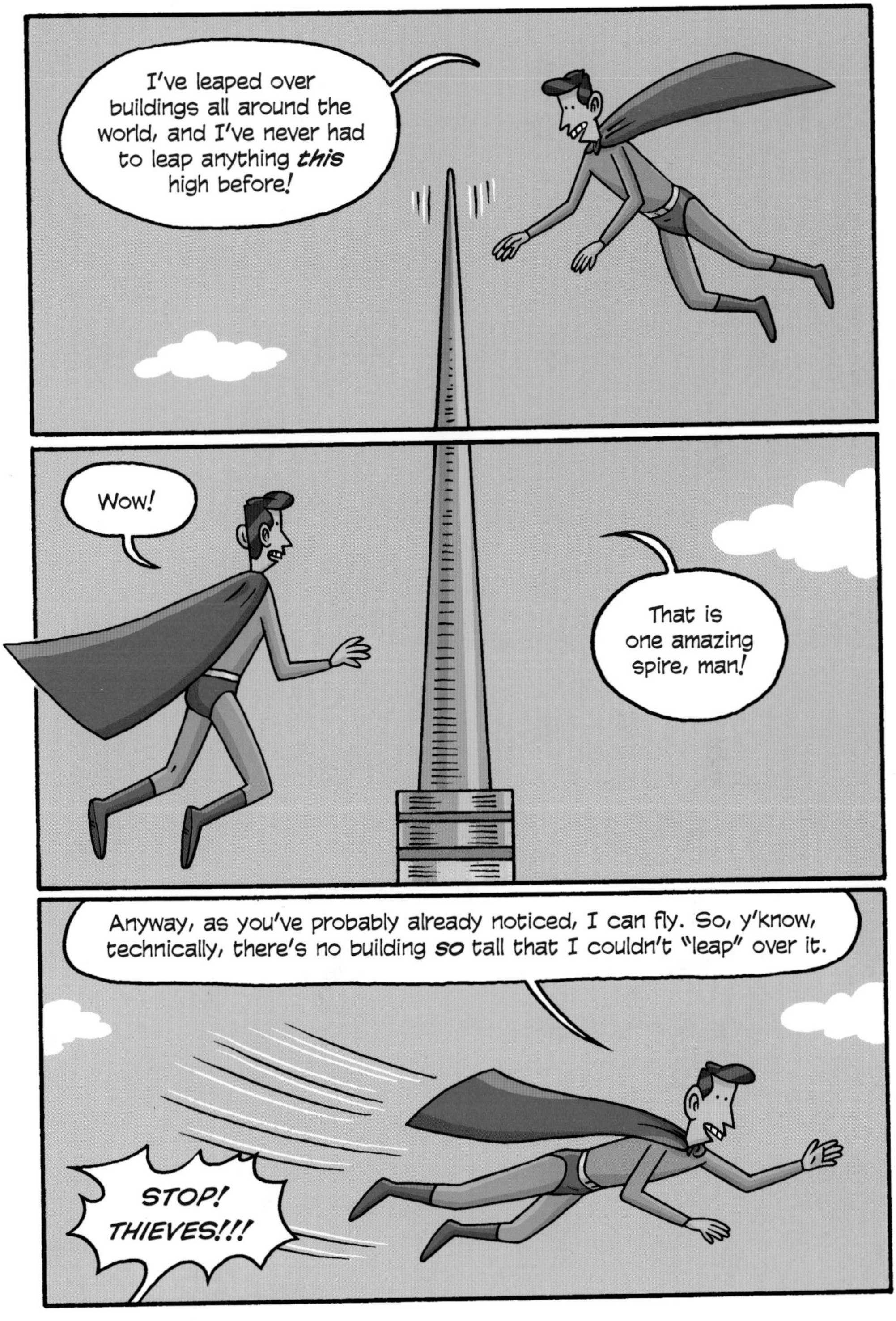
I've leaped over buildings all around the world, and I've never had to leap anything *this* high before!
Wow!
That is one amazing spire, man!
Anyway, as you've probably already noticed, I can fly. So, y'know, technically, there's no building *so* tall that I couldn't "leap" over it.
STOP! THIEVES!!!

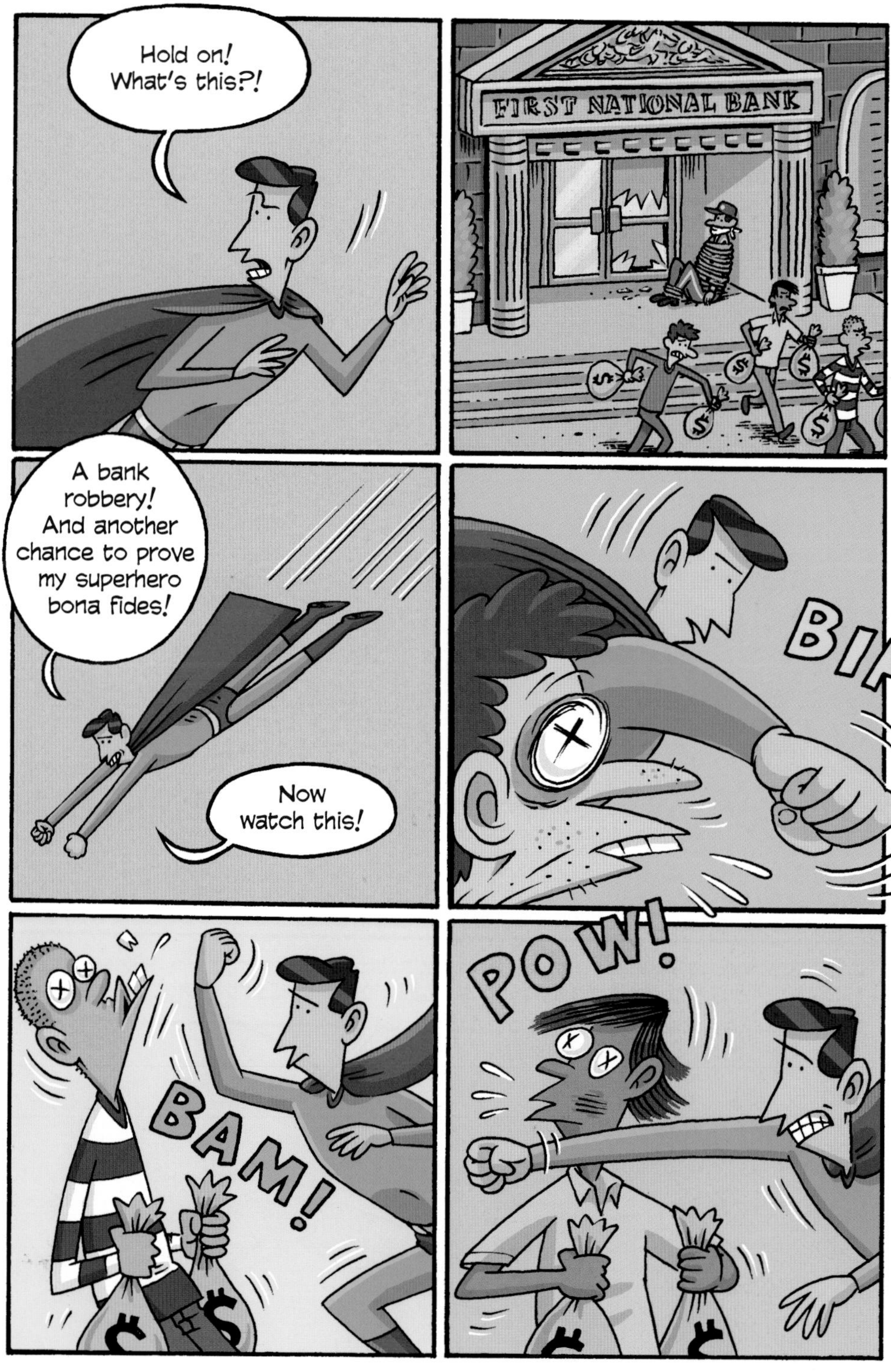
Hold on! What's this?!
FIRST NATIONAL BANK
A bank robbery! And another chance to prove my superhero bona fides!
Now watch this!
BIF!
BAM!
POW!

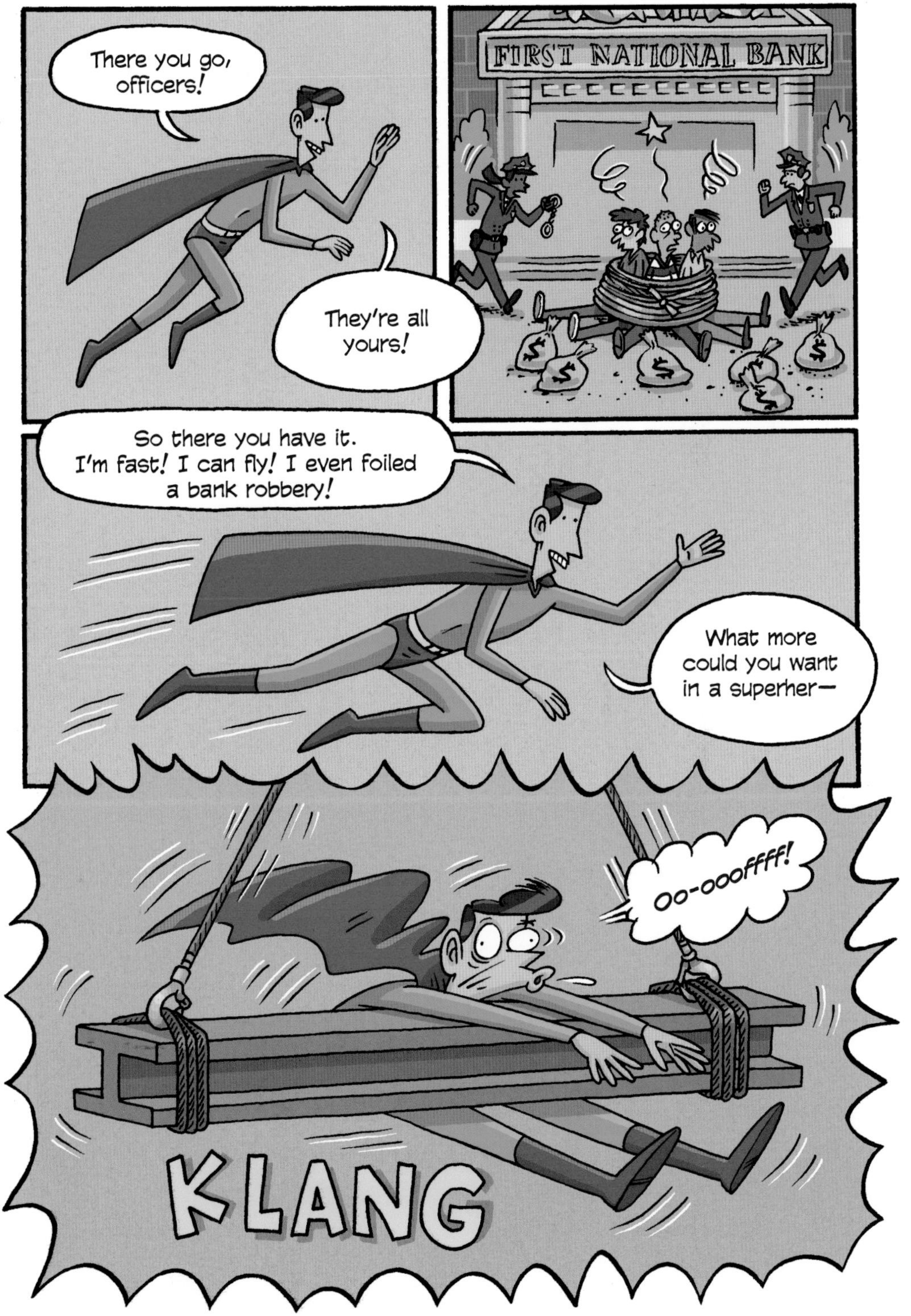
There you go, officers!
They're all yours!
FIRST NATIONAL BANK
So there you have it. I'm fast! I can fly! I even foiled a bank robbery!
What more could you want in a superher—
Oo-oooffff!
KLANG

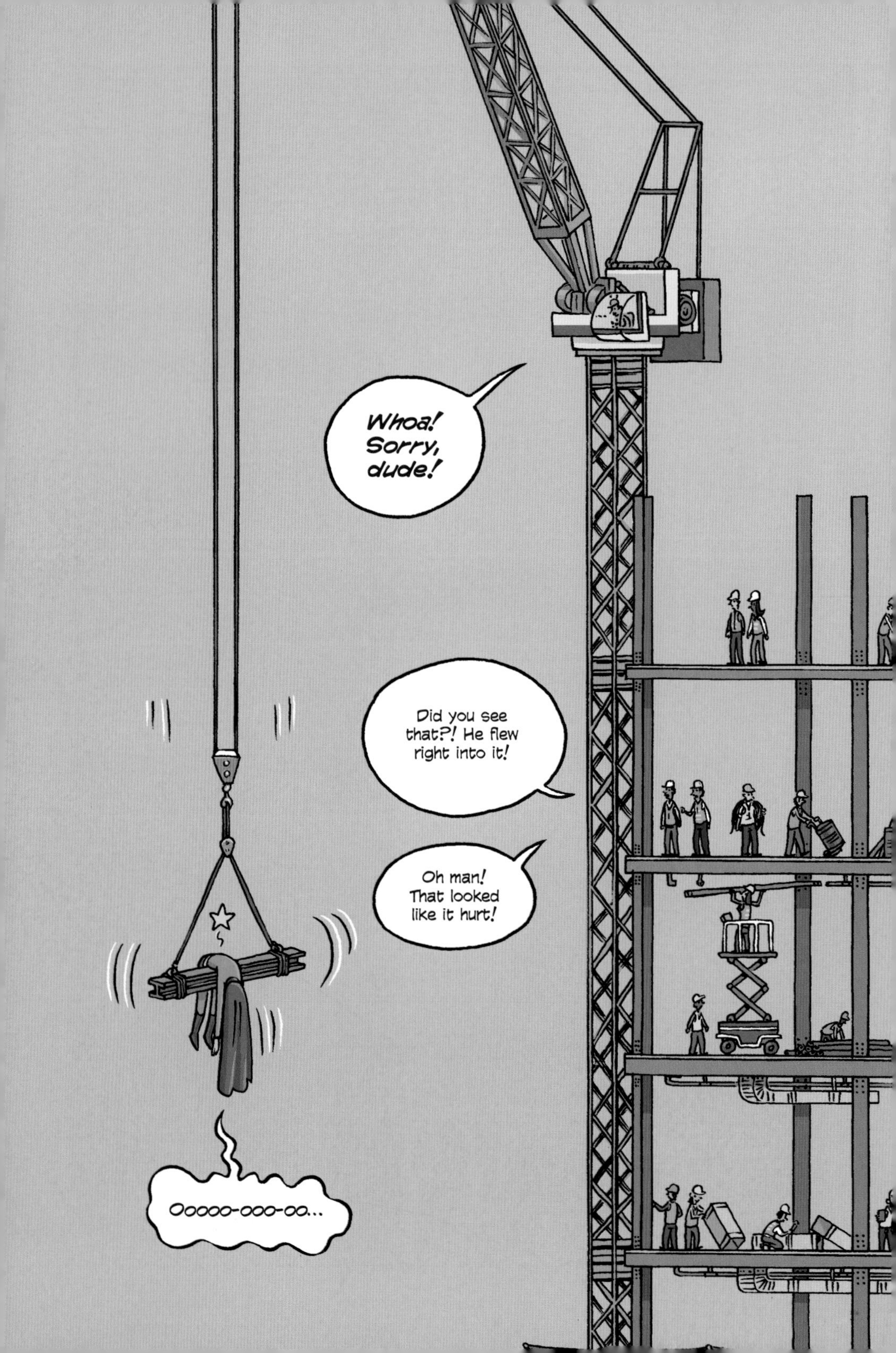
Whoa! Sorry, dude!
Did you see that?! He flew right into it!
Oh man! That looked like it hurt!
Ooooo-ooo-oo...

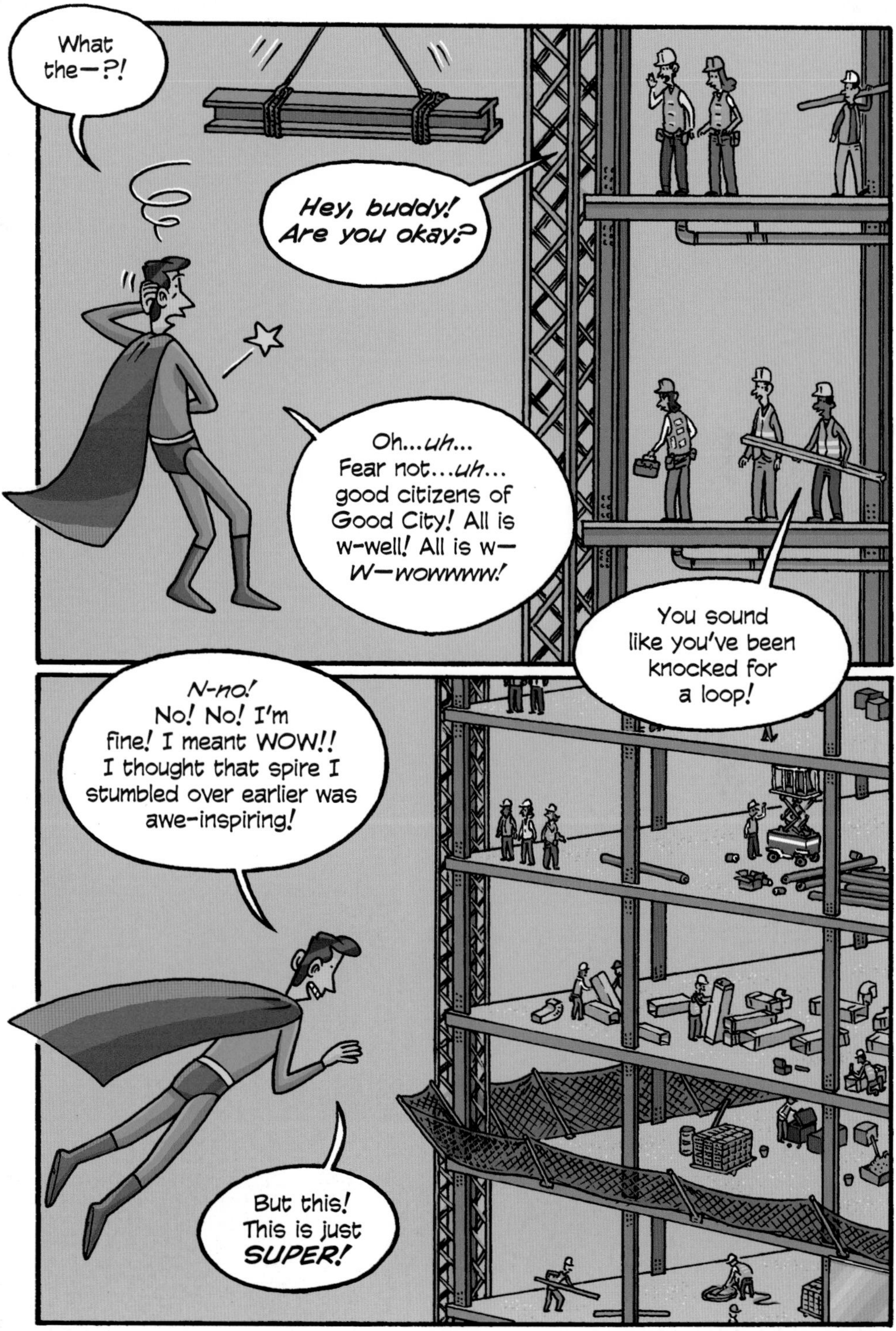

What the—?!
Hey, buddy! Are you okay?
Oh...uh... Fear not...uh... good citizens of Good City! All is w-well! All is w— W—wowwww!
You sound like you've been knocked for a loop!
N-no! No! No! I'm fine! I meant WOW!! I thought that spire I stumbled over earlier was awe-inspiring!
But this! This is just SUPER!

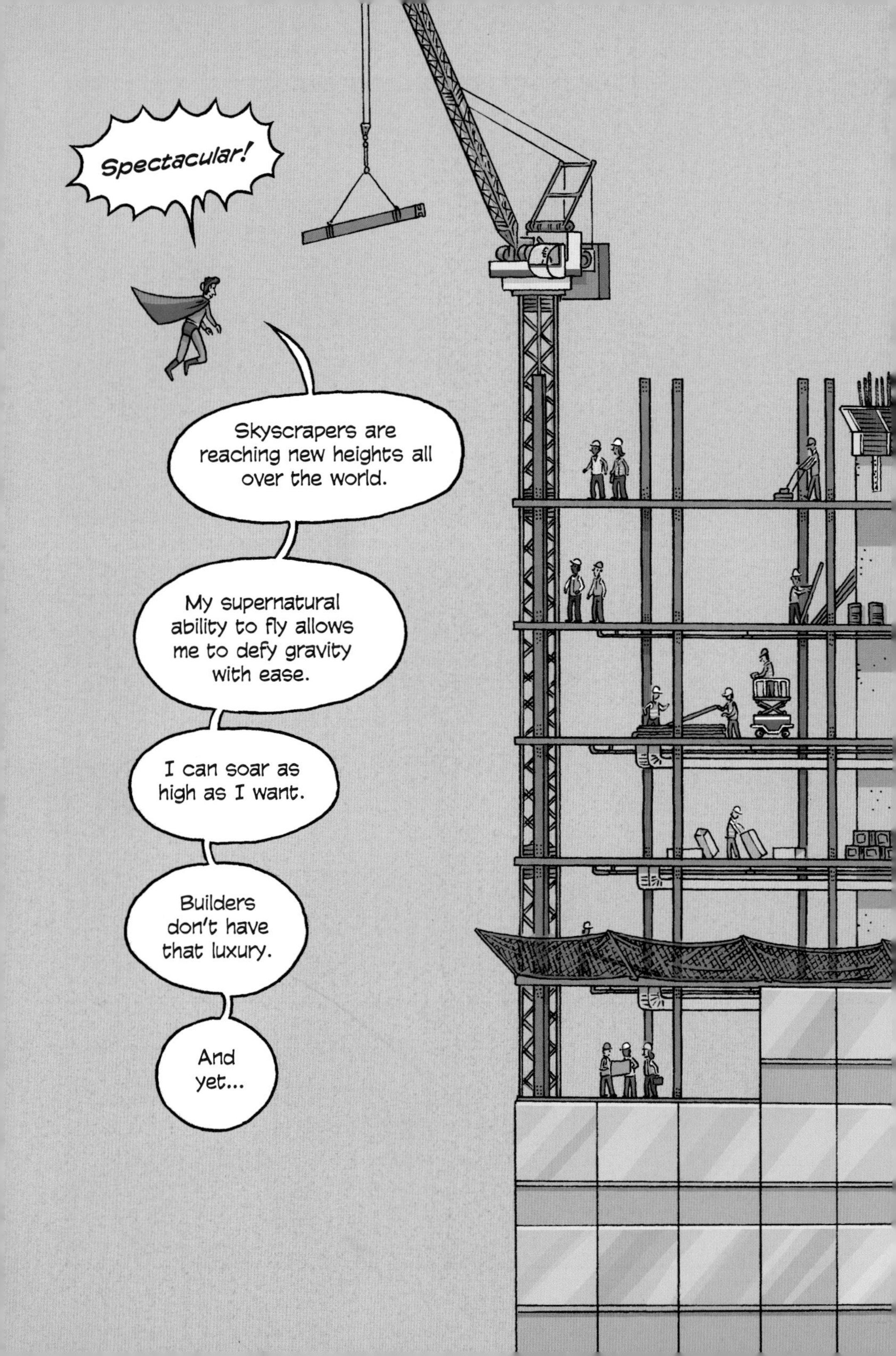
Spectacular!
Skyscrapers are reaching new heights all over the world.
My supernatural ability to fly allows me to defy gravity with ease.
I can soar as high as I want.
Builders don't have that luxury.
And yet...

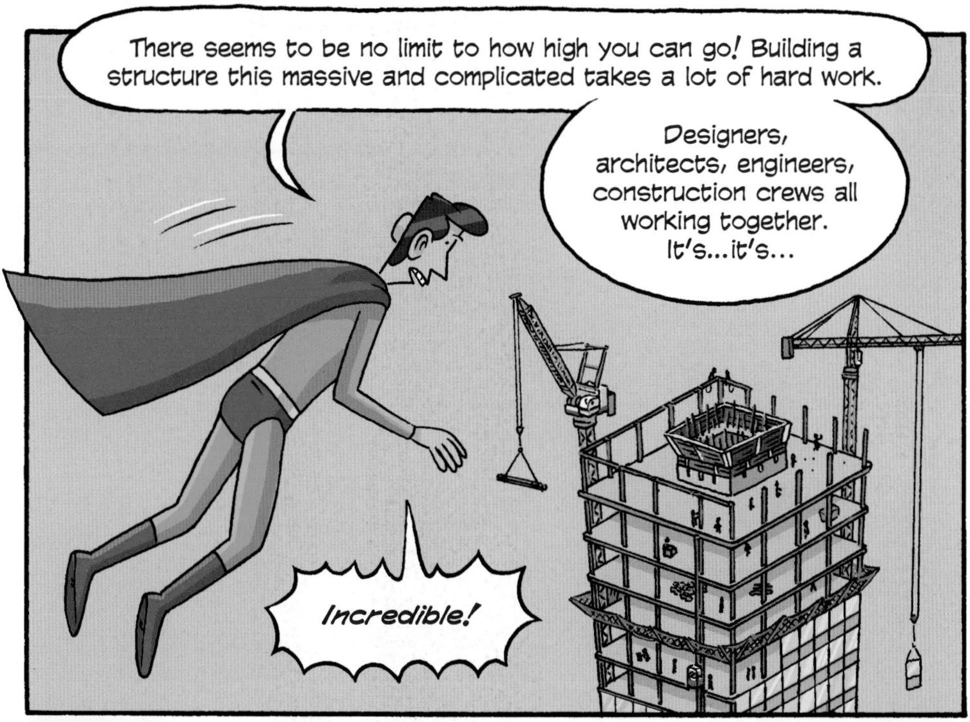
There seems to be no limit to how high you can go! Building a structure this massive and complicated takes a lot of hard work.
Designers, architects, engineers, construction crews all working together. It's...it's...
Incredible!

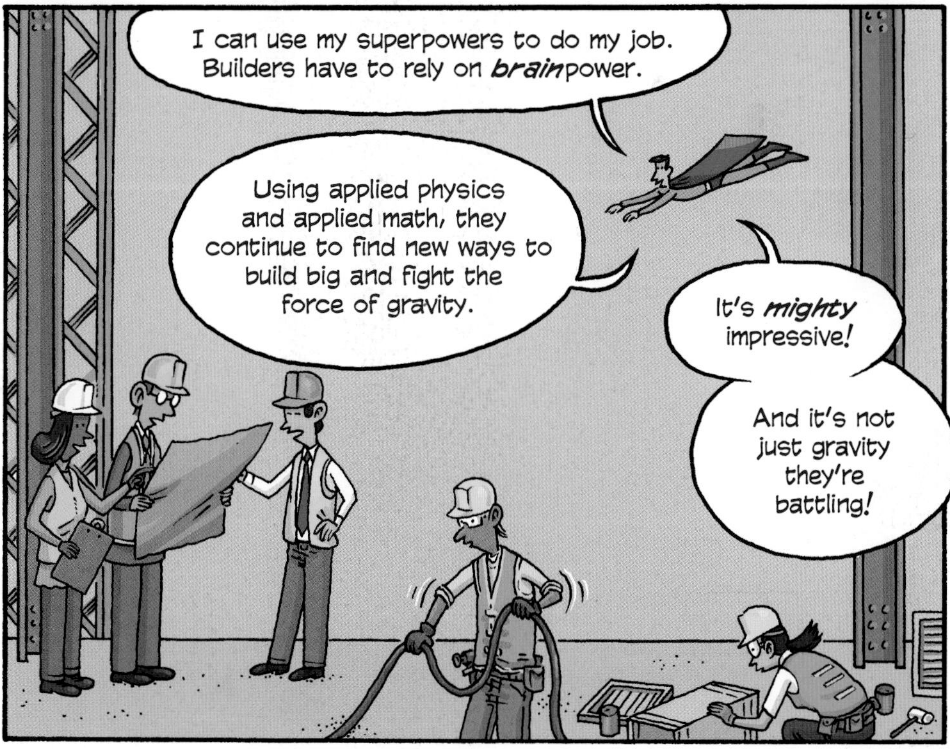
I can use my superpowers to do my job. Builders have to rely on ***brain***power.
Using applied physics and applied math, they continue to find new ways to build big and fight the force of gravity.
It's ***mighty*** impressive!
And it's not just gravity they're battling!

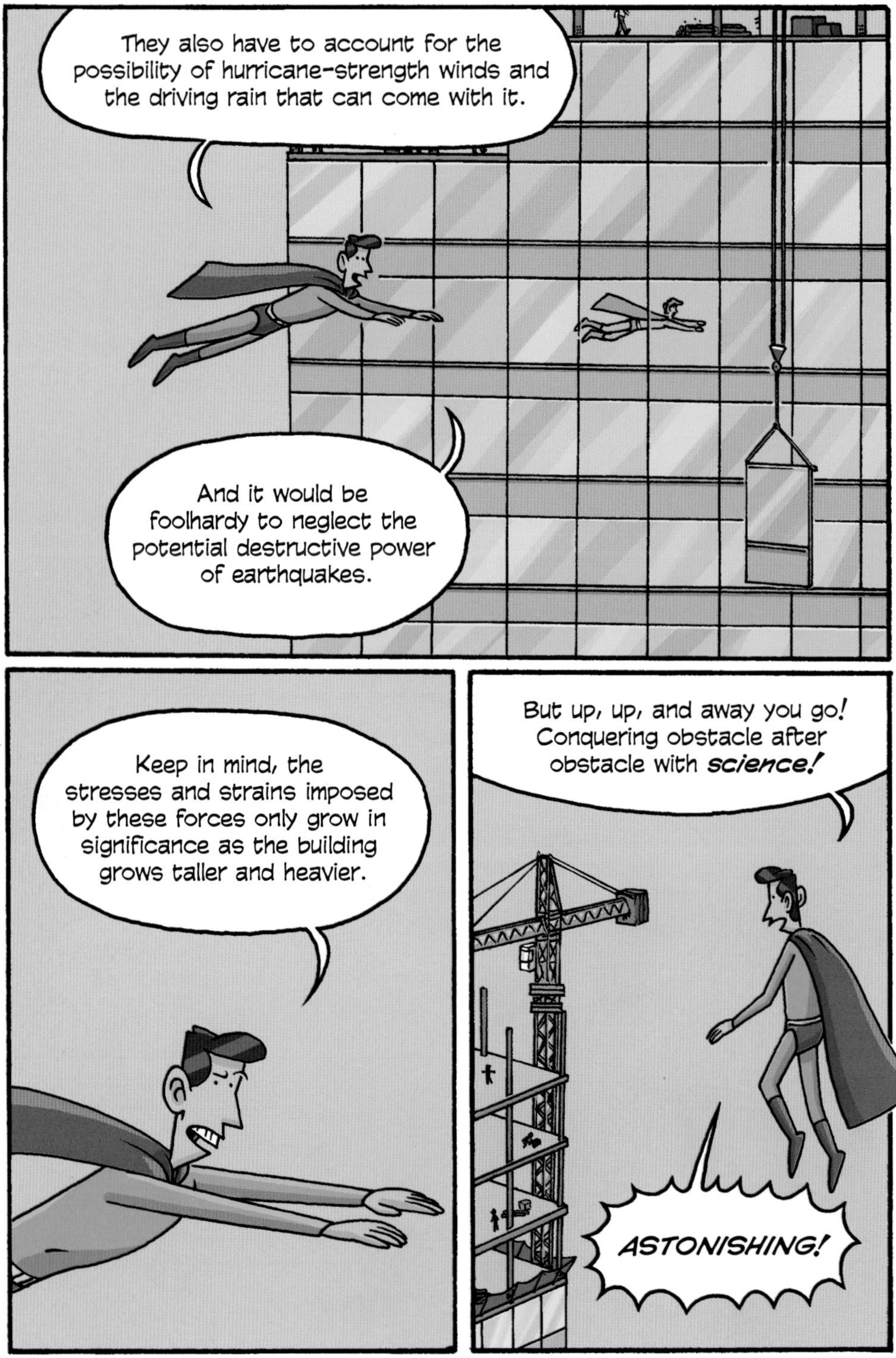
They also have to account for the possibility of hurricane-strength winds and the driving rain that can come with it.
And it would be foolhardy to neglect the potential destructive power of earthquakes.
Keep in mind, the stresses and strains imposed by these forces only grow in significance as the building grows taller and heavier.
But up, up, and away you go! Conquering obstacle after obstacle with *science!*
ASTONISHING!

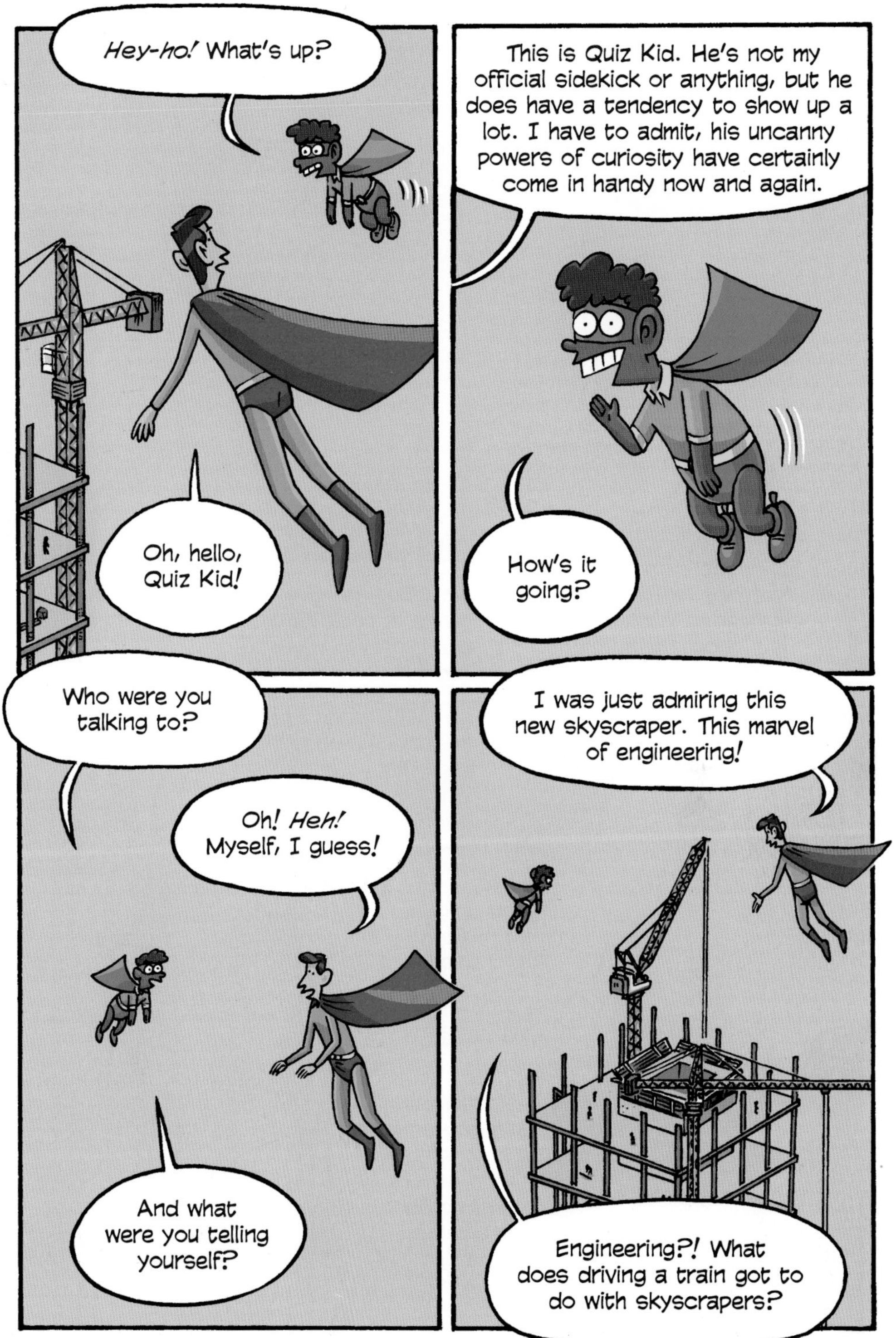

Hey-ho! What's up?
Oh, hello, Quiz Kid!
This is Quiz Kid. He's not my official sidekick or anything, but he does have a tendency to show up a lot. I have to admit, his uncanny powers of curiosity have certainly come in handy now and again.
How's it going?
Who were you talking to?
Oh! *Heh!* Myself, I guess!
And what were you telling yourself?
I was just admiring this new skyscraper. This marvel of engineering!
Engineering?! What does driving a train got to do with skyscrapers?

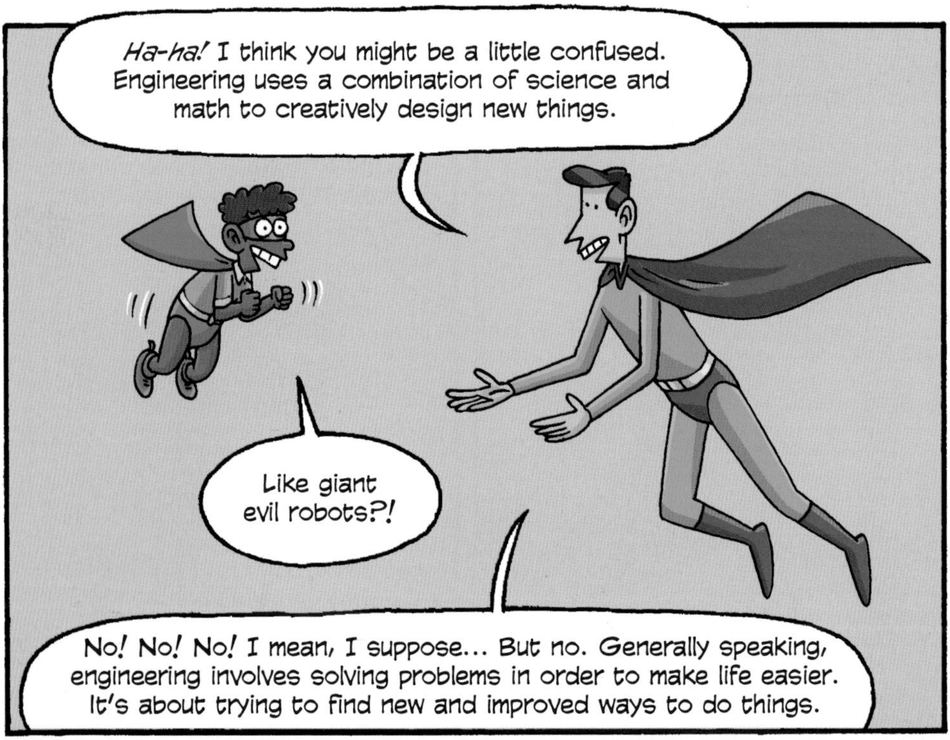
Ha-ha! I think you might be a little confused. Engineering uses a combination of science and math to creatively design new things.
Like giant evil robots?!
No! No! No! I mean, I suppose... But no. Generally speaking, engineering involves solving problems in order to make life easier. It's about trying to find new and improved ways to do things.

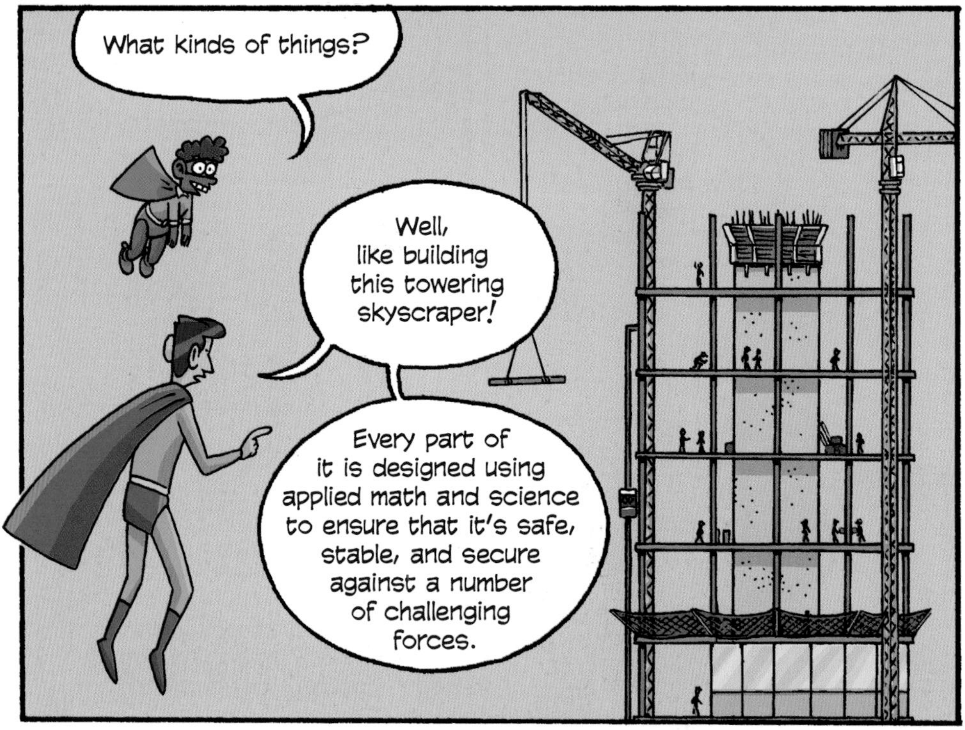
What kinds of things?
Well, like building this towering skyscraper!
Every part of it is designed using applied math and science to ensure that it's safe, stable, and secure against a number of challenging forces.

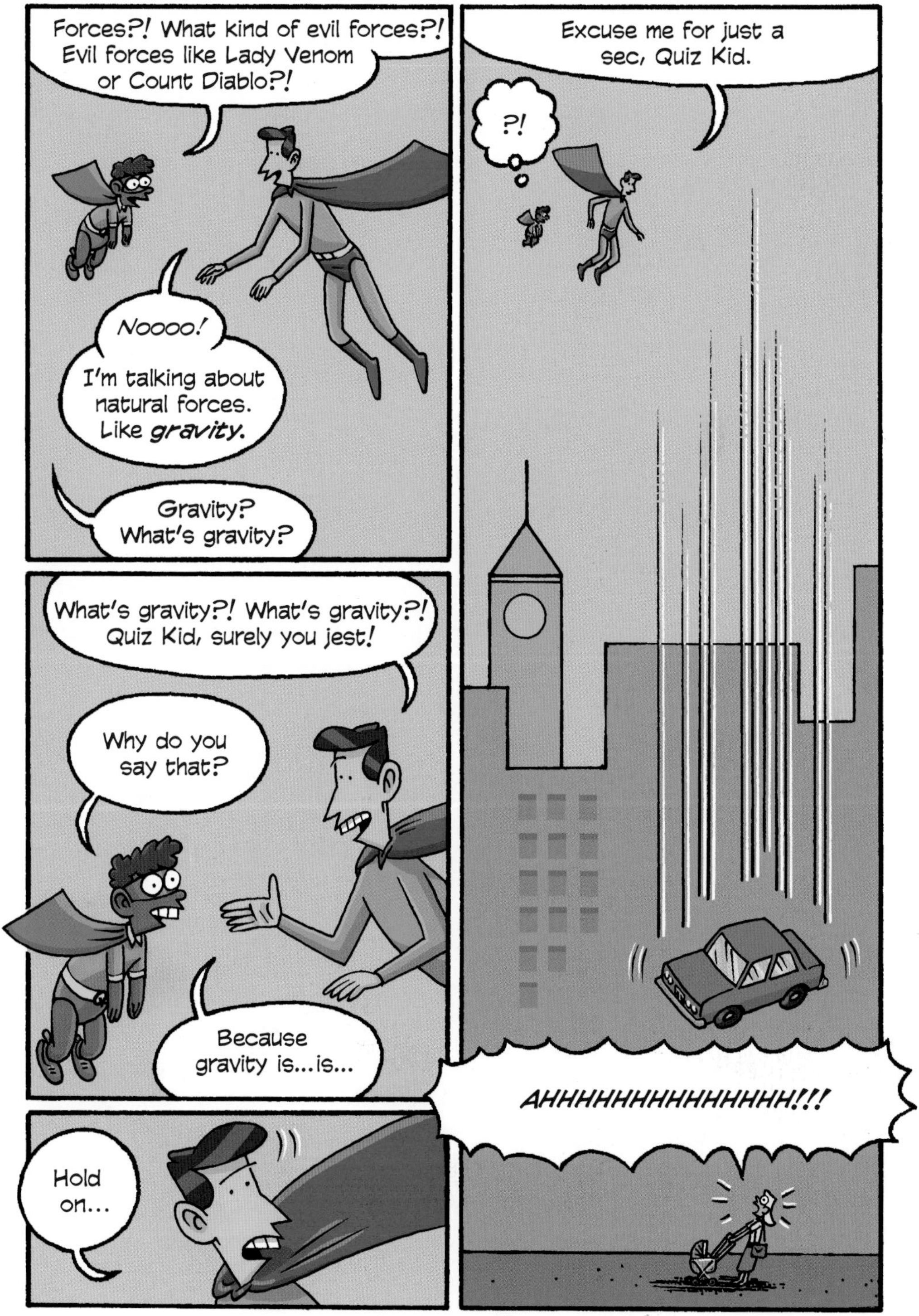
Forces?! What kind of evil forces?! Evil forces like Lady Venom or Count Diablo?!
Noooo!
I'm talking about natural forces. Like *gravity*.
Gravity? What's gravity?
What's gravity?! What's gravity?! Quiz Kid, surely you jest!
Why do you say that?
Because gravity is...is...
Hold on...
Excuse me for just a sec, Quiz Kid.
?!
AHHHHHHHHHHHHHH!!!

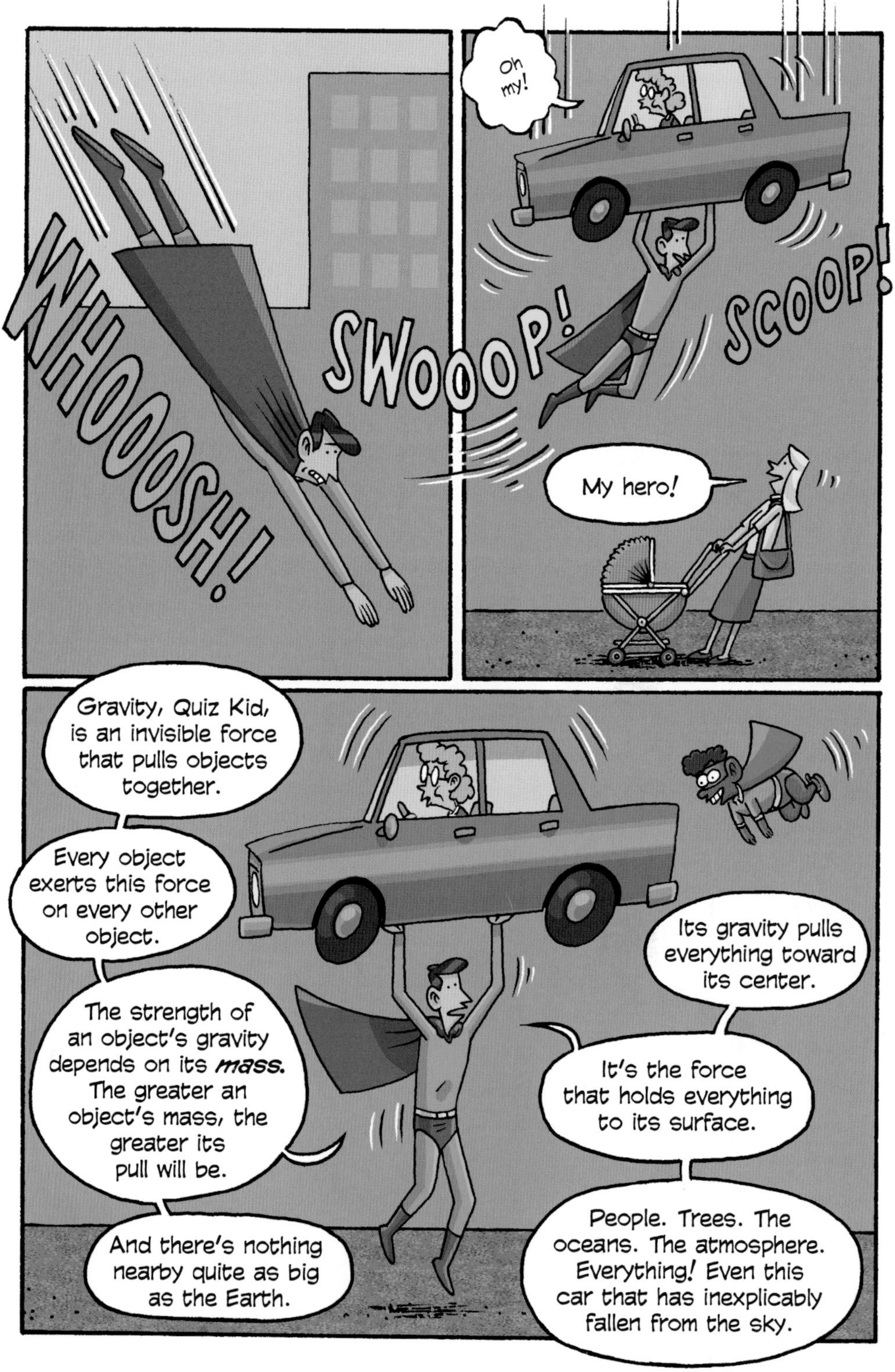
WHOOOSH!
Oh my!
SWOOOP!
SCOOP!
My hero!
Gravity, Quiz Kid, is an invisible force that pulls objects together.
Every object exerts this force on every other object.
The strength of an object's gravity depends on its *mass.* The greater an object's mass, the greater its pull will be.
And there's nothing nearby quite as big as the Earth.
Its gravity pulls everything toward its center.
It's the force that holds everything to its surface.
People. Trees. The oceans. The atmosphere. Everything! Even this car that has inexplicably fallen from the sky.

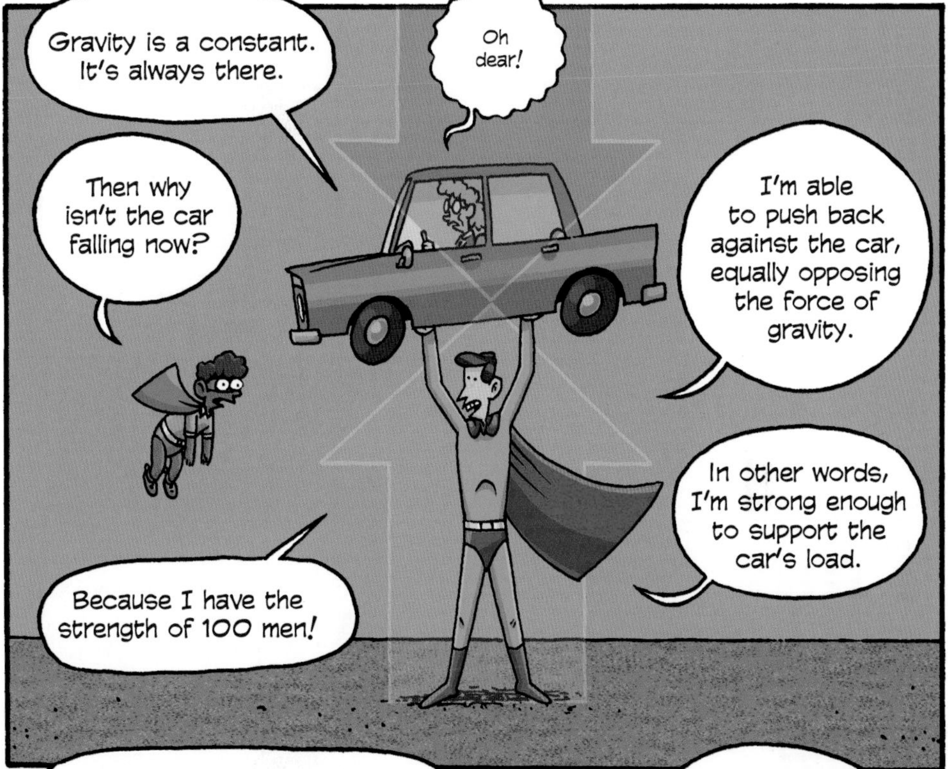
Gravity is a constant. It's always there.
Oh dear!
Then why isn't the car falling now?
I'm able to push back against the car, equally opposing the force of gravity.
In other words, I'm strong enough to support the car's load.
Because I have the strength of 100 men!

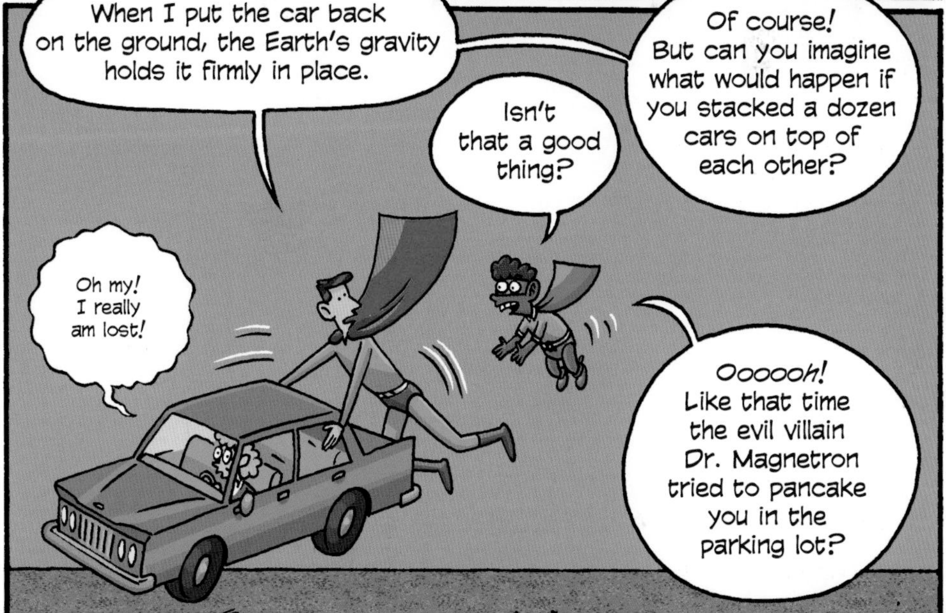
When I put the car back on the ground, the Earth's gravity holds it firmly in place.
Isn't that a good thing?
Of course! But can you imagine what would happen if you stacked a dozen cars on top of each other?
Oh my! I really am lost!
Oooooh! Like that time the evil villain Dr. Magnetron tried to pancake you in the parking lot?

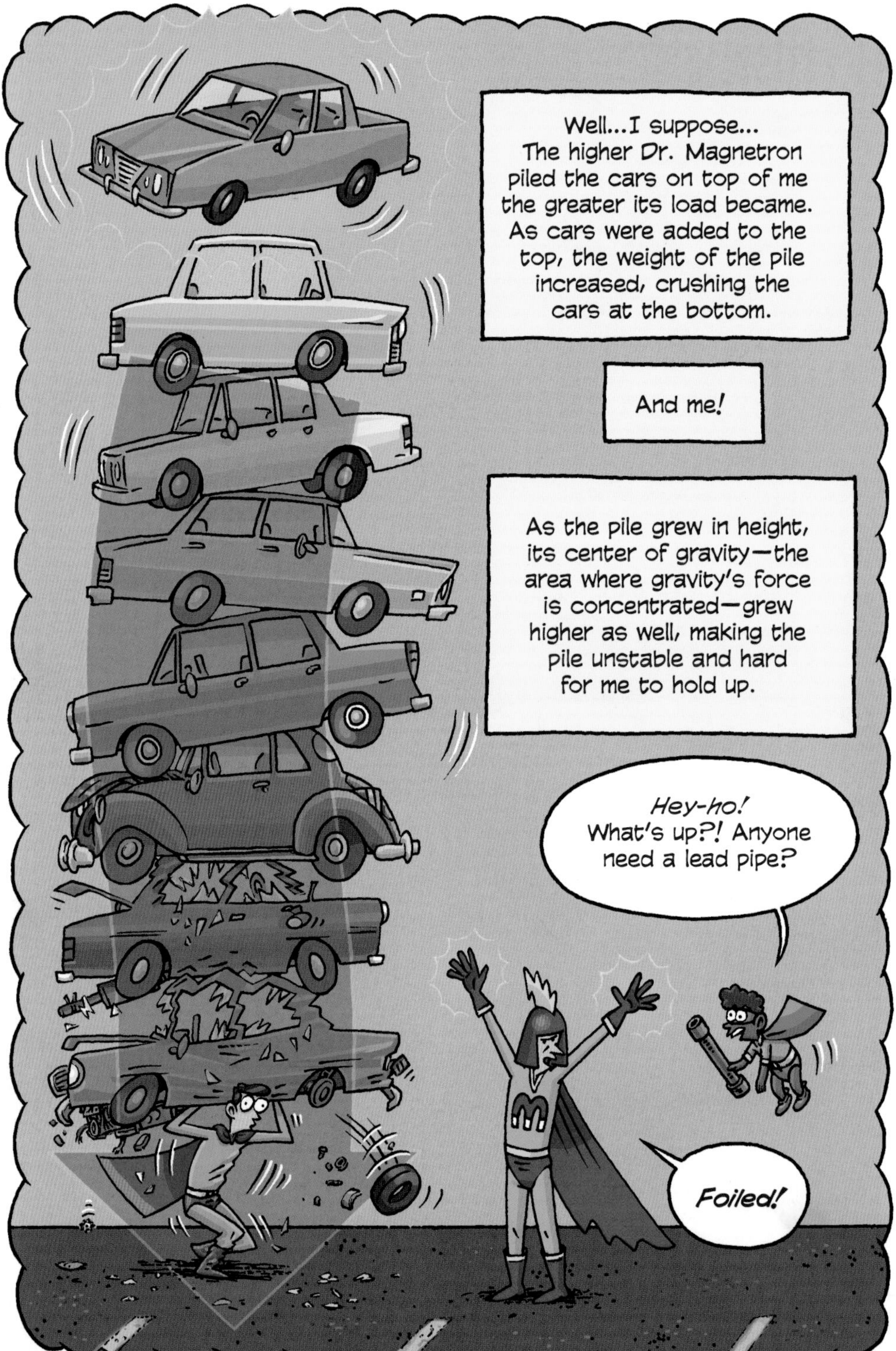
Well...I suppose...
The higher Dr. Magnetron piled the cars on top of me the greater its load became. As cars were added to the top, the weight of the pile increased, crushing the cars at the bottom.
And me!
As the pile grew in height, its center of gravity—the area where gravity's force is concentrated—grew higher as well, making the pile unstable and hard for me to hold up.
Hey-ho! What's up?! Anyone need a lead pipe?
Foiled!

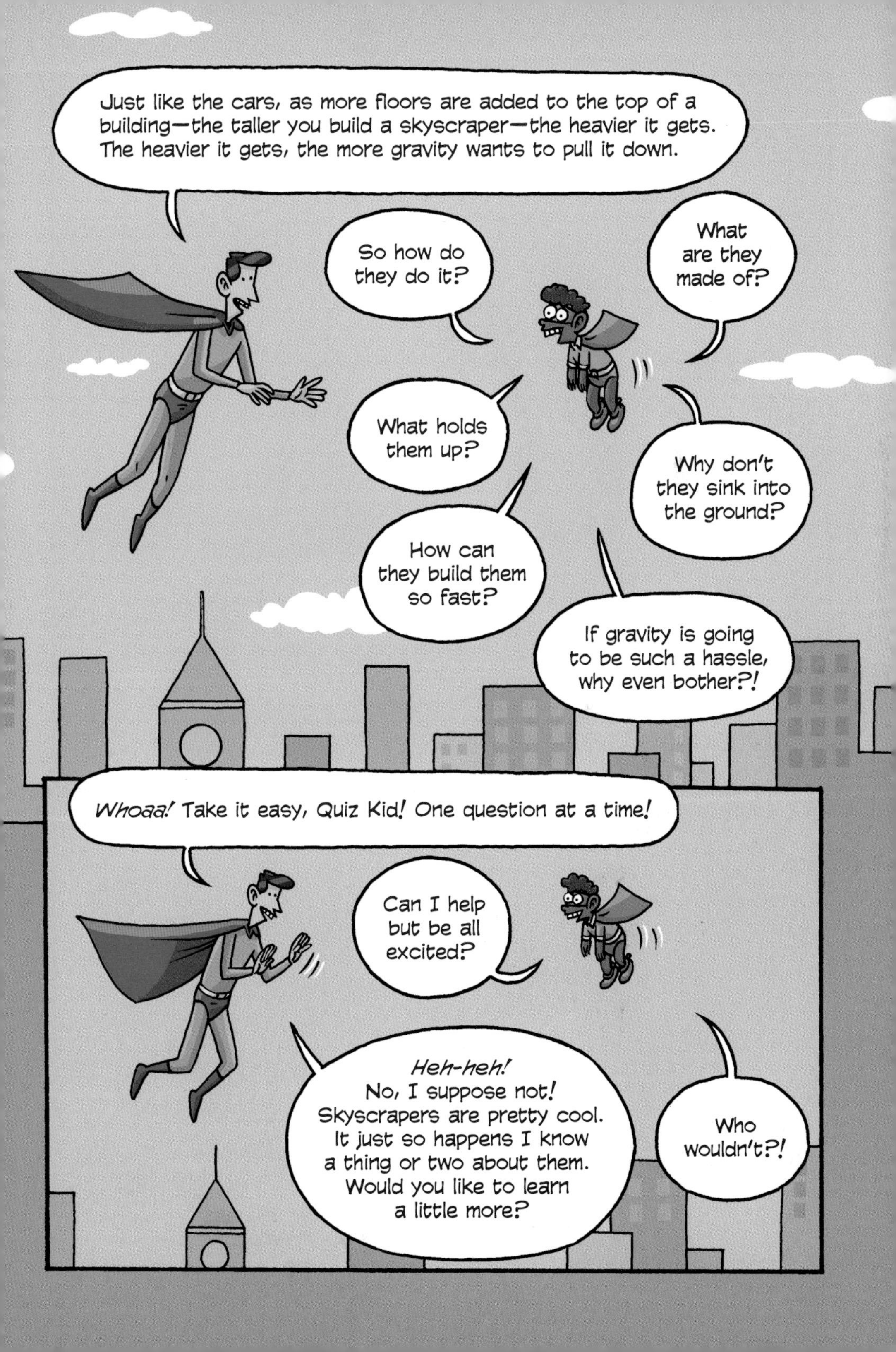

Just like the cars, as more floors are added to the top of a building—the taller you build a skyscraper—the heavier it gets. The heavier it gets, the more gravity wants to pull it down.
So how do they do it?
What are they made of?
What holds them up?
Why don't they sink into the ground?
How can they build them so fast?
If gravity is going to be such a hassle, why even bother?!
Whoaa! Take it easy, Quiz Kid! One question at a time!
Can I help but be all excited?
Heh-heh! No, I suppose not! Skyscrapers are pretty cool. It just so happens I know a thing or two about them. Would you like to learn a little more?
Who wouldn't?!

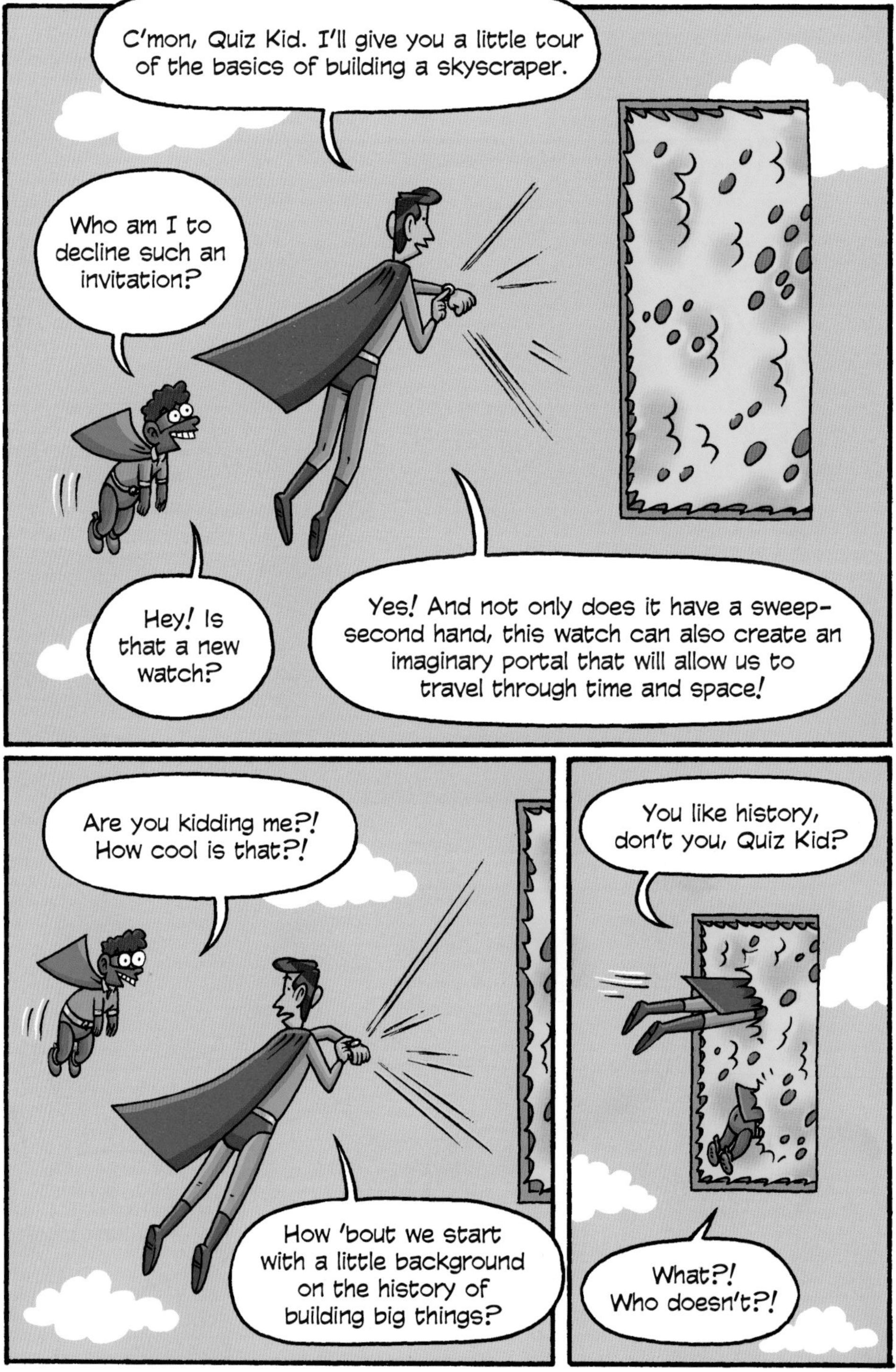
C'mon, Quiz Kid. I'll give you a little tour of the basics of building a skyscraper.
Who am I to decline such an invitation?
Hey! Is that a new watch?
Yes! And not only does it have a sweep-second hand, this watch can also create an imaginary portal that will allow us to travel through time and space!
Are you kidding me?! How cool is that?!
How 'bout we start with a little background on the history of building big things?
You like history, don't you, Quiz Kid?
What?! Who doesn't?!

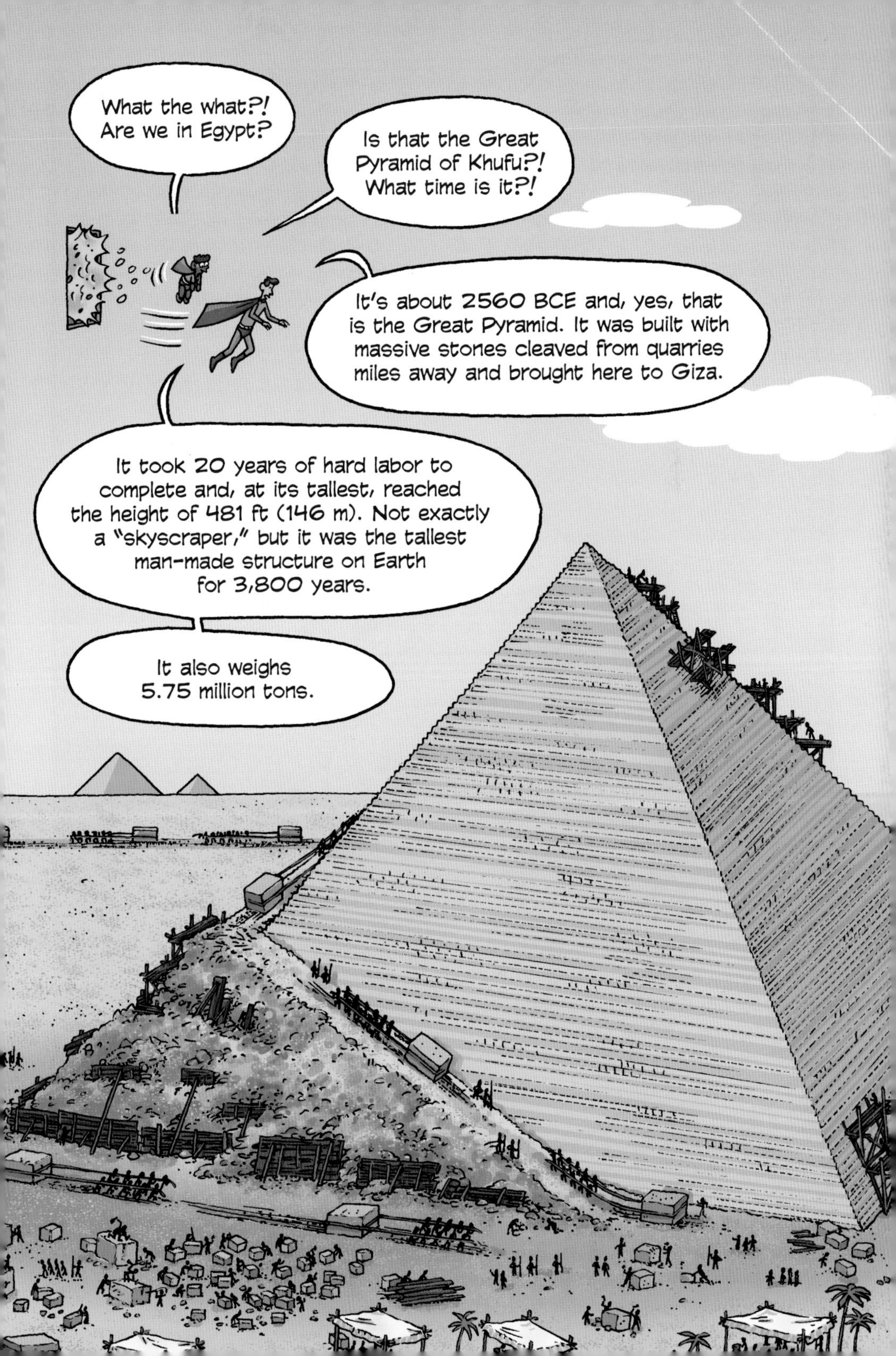
What the what?! Are we in Egypt?
Is that the Great Pyramid of Khufu?! What time is it?!
It's about 2560 BCE and, yes, that is the Great Pyramid. It was built with massive stones cleaved from quarries miles away and brought here to Giza.
It took 20 years of hard labor to complete and, at its tallest, reached the height of 481 ft (146 m). Not exactly a "skyscraper," but it was the tallest man-made structure on Earth for 3,800 years.
It also weighs 5.75 million tons.

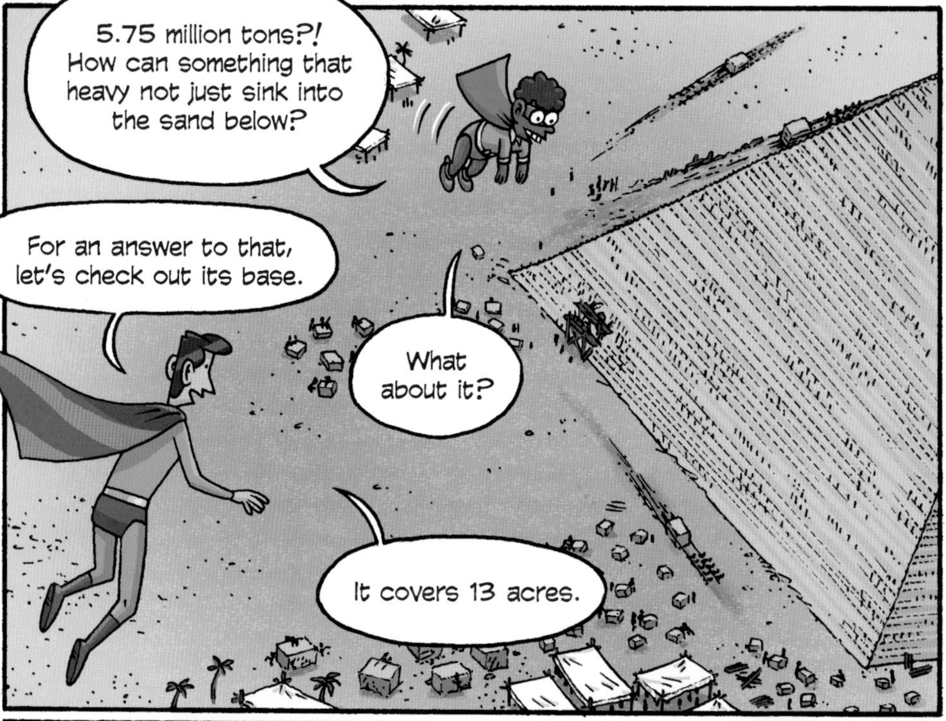
5.75 million tons?! How can something that heavy not just sink into the sand below?
For an answer to that, let's check out its base.
What about it?
It covers 13 acres.

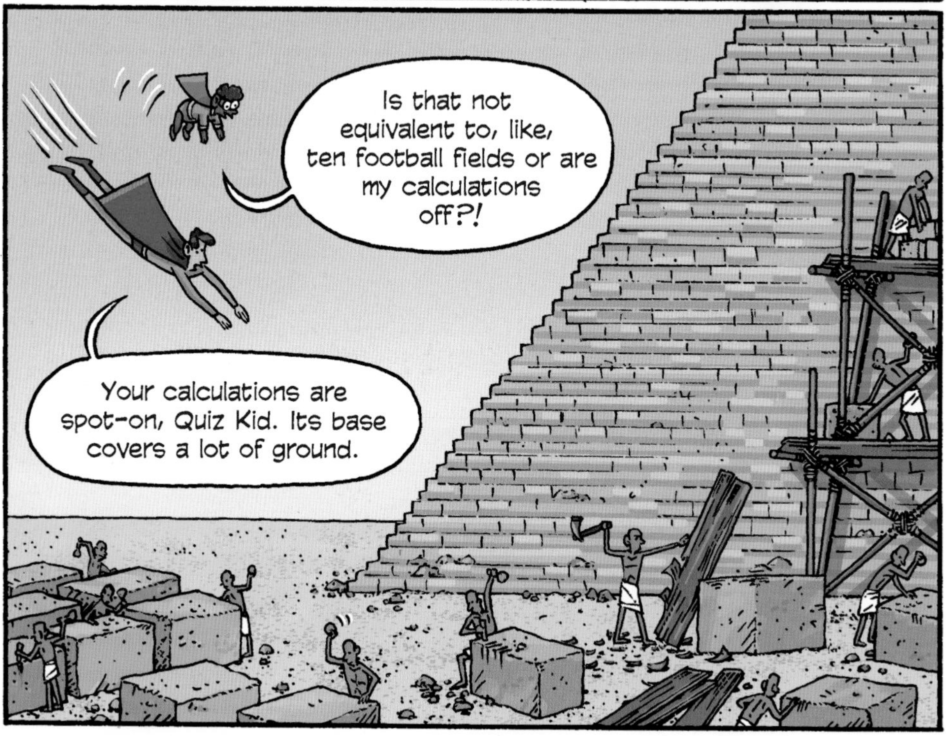
Is that not equivalent to, like, ten football fields or are my calculations off?!
Your calculations are spot-on, Quiz Kid. Its base covers a lot of ground.

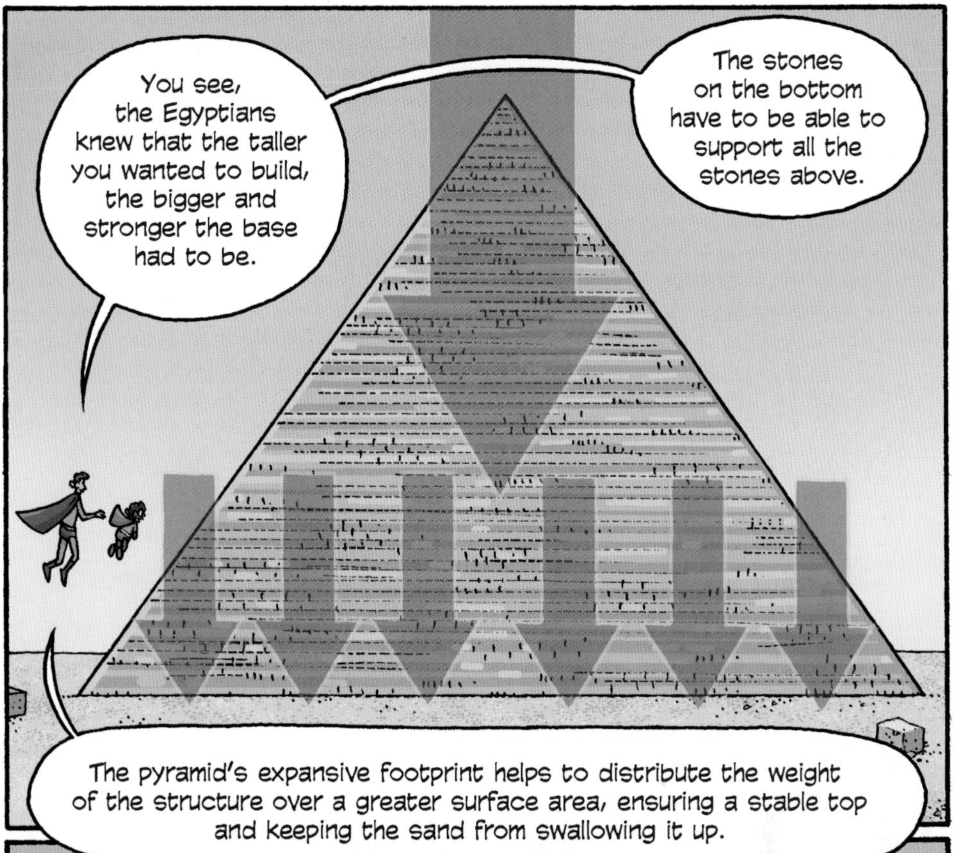
You see, the Egyptians knew that the taller you wanted to build, the bigger and stronger the base had to be.
The stones on the bottom have to be able to support all the stones above.
The pyramid's expansive footprint helps to distribute the weight of the structure over a greater surface area, ensuring a stable top and keeping the sand from swallowing it up.

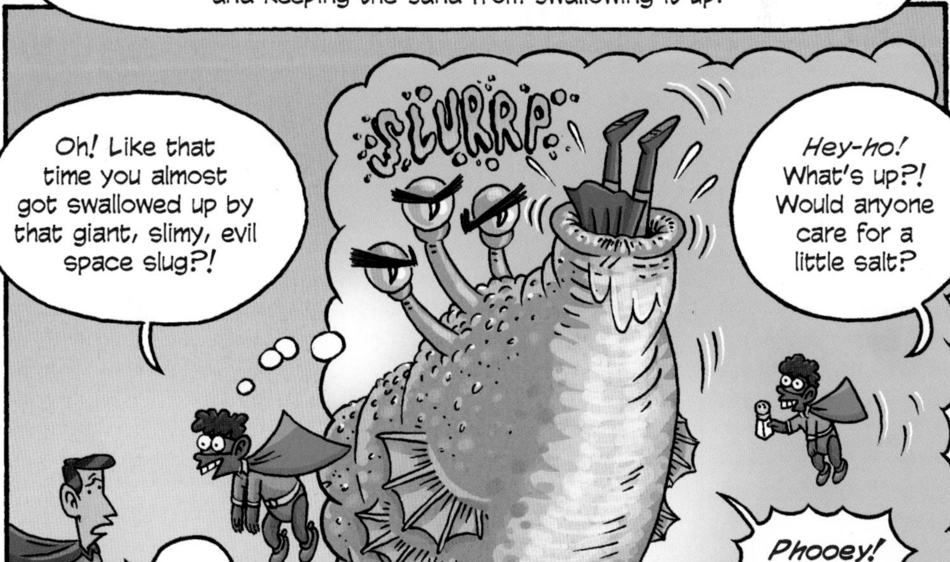
Oh! Like that time you almost got swallowed up by that giant, slimy, evil space slug?!
SLURRP
Hey-ho! What's up?! Would anyone care for a little salt?
Uh...
Phooey!

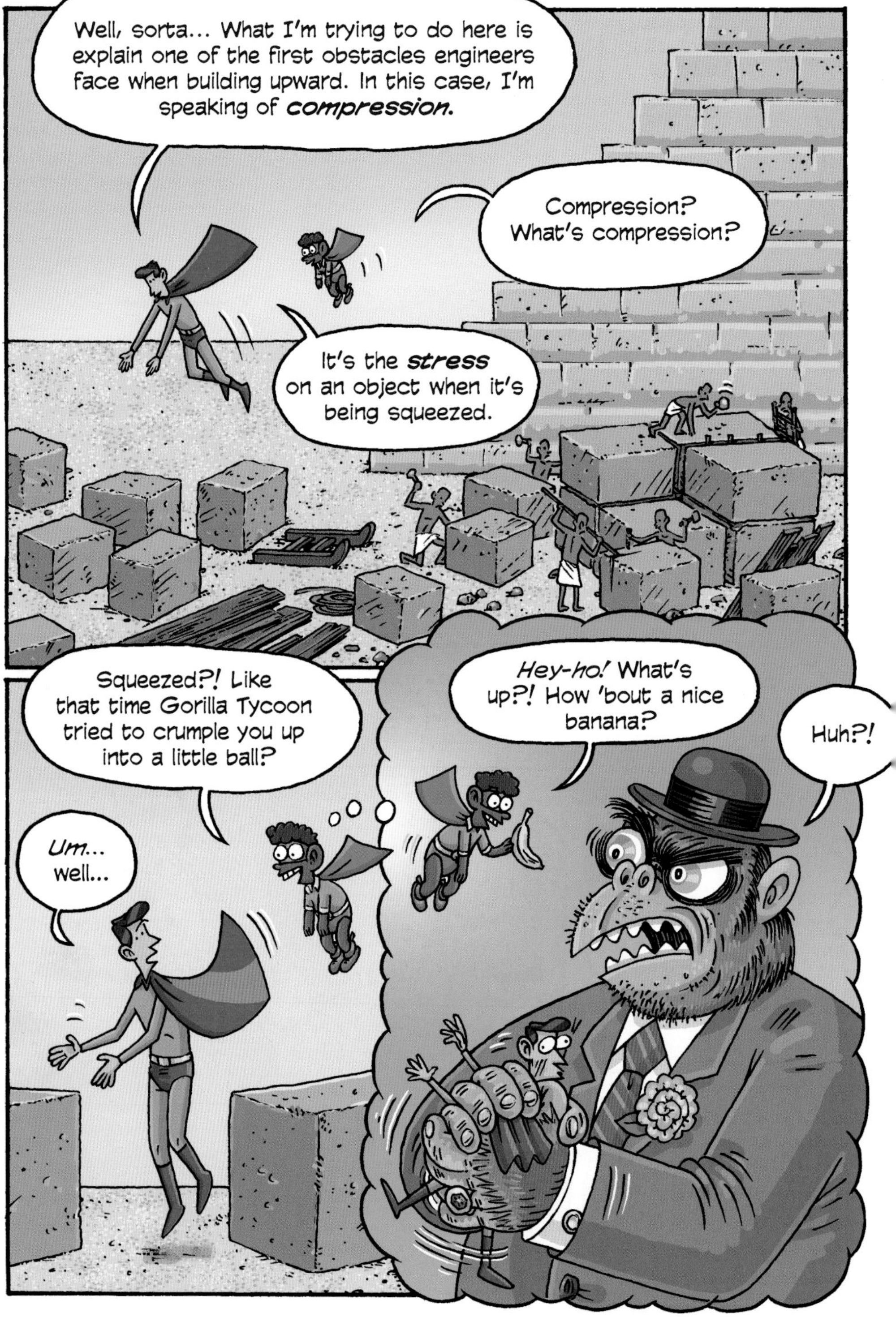
Well, sorta... What I'm trying to do here is explain one of the first obstacles engineers face when building upward. In this case, I'm speaking of ***compression.***
Compression? What's compression?
It's the ***stress*** on an object when it's being squeezed.
Squeezed?! Like that time Gorilla Tycoon tried to crumple you up into a little ball?
Hey-ho! What's up?! How 'bout a nice banana?
Huh?!
Um... well...

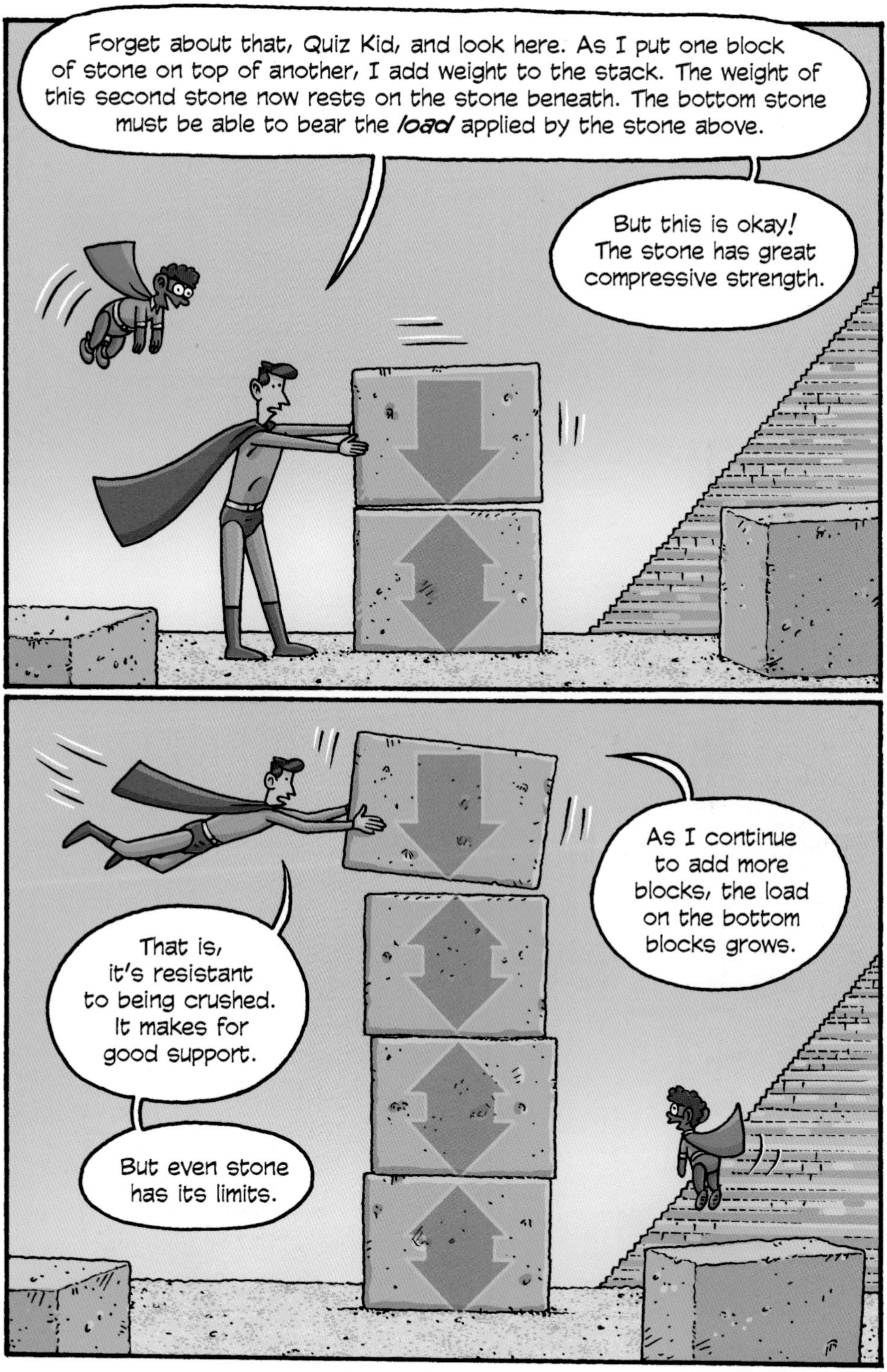
Forget about that, Quiz Kid, and look here. As I put one block of stone on top of another, I add weight to the stack. The weight of this second stone now rests on the stone beneath. The bottom stone must be able to bear the *load* applied by the stone above.
But this is okay! The stone has great compressive strength.
That is, it's resistant to being crushed. It makes for good support.
But even stone has its limits.
As I continue to add more blocks, the load on the bottom blocks grows.

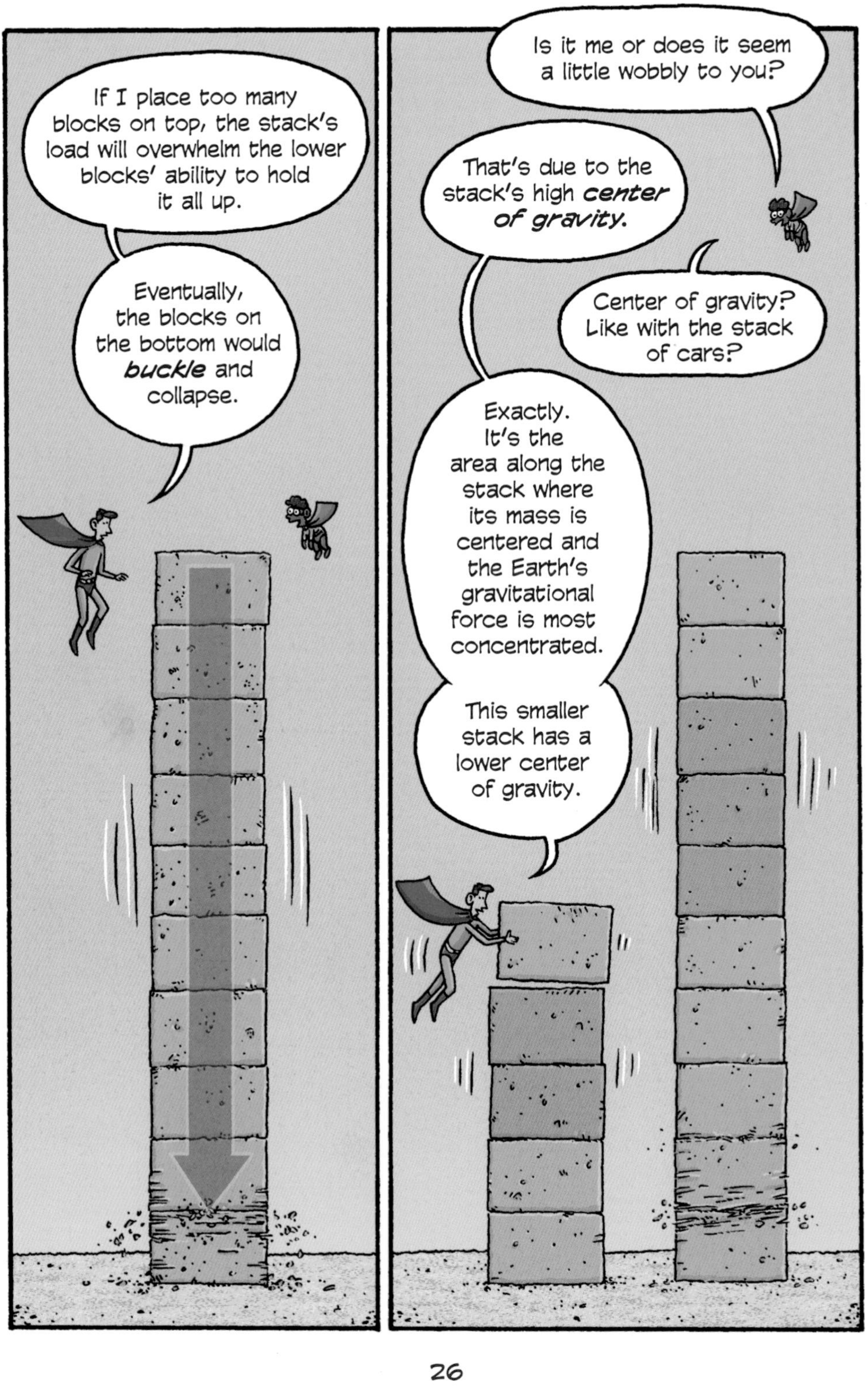
If I place too many blocks on top, the stack's load will overwhelm the lower blocks' ability to hold it all up.
Eventually, the blocks on the bottom would *buckle* and collapse.
Is it me or does it seem a little wobbly to you?
That's due to the stack's high ***center of gravity.***
Center of gravity? Like with the stack of cars?
Exactly. It's the area along the stack where its mass is centered and the Earth's gravitational force is most concentrated.
This smaller stack has a lower center of gravity.

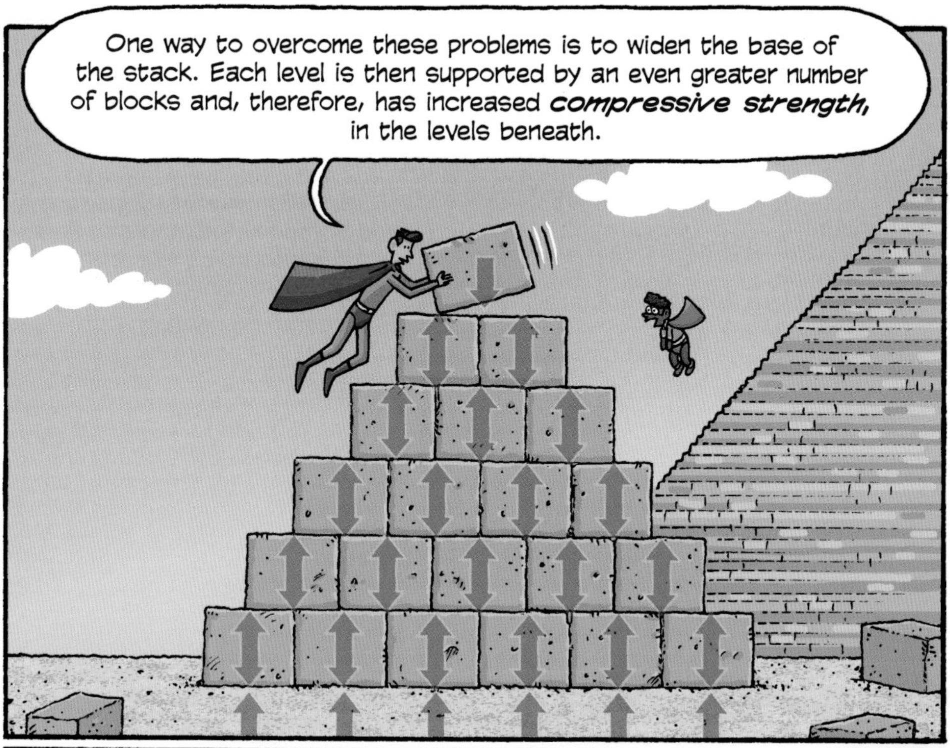
One way to overcome these problems is to widen the base of the stack. Each level is then supported by an even greater number of blocks and, therefore, has increased ***compressive strength,*** in the levels beneath.

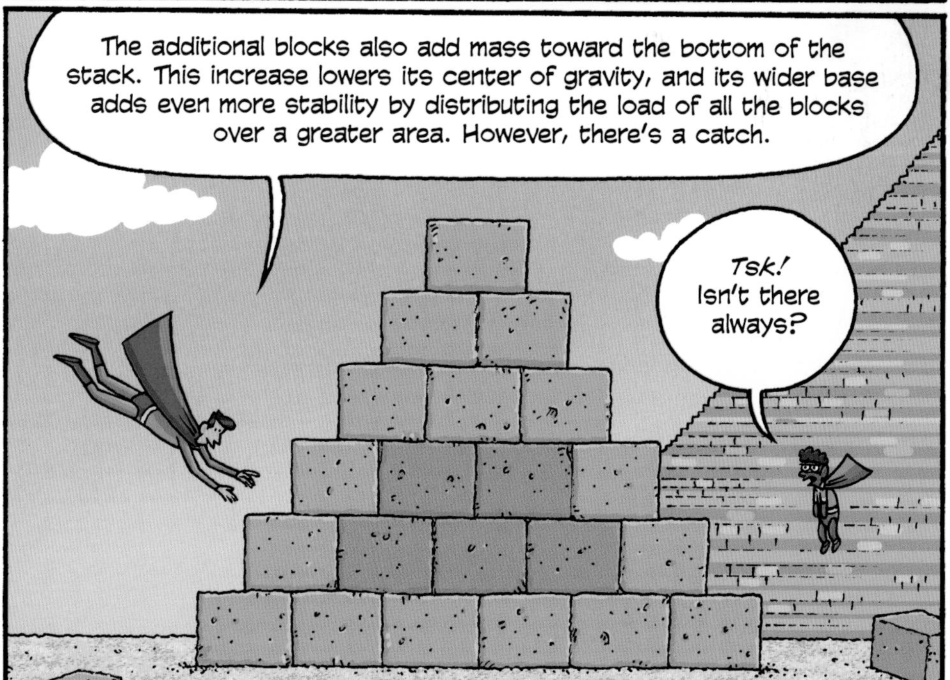
The additional blocks also add mass toward the bottom of the stack. This increase lowers its center of gravity, and its wider base adds even more stability by distributing the load of all the blocks over a greater area. However, there's a catch.
Tsk! Isn't there always?

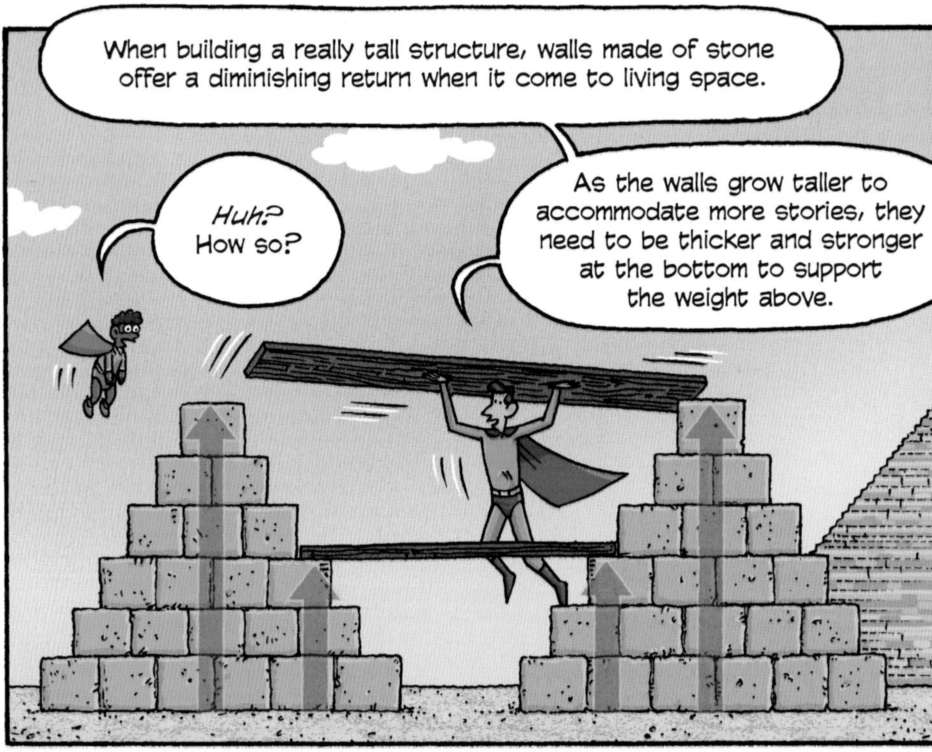
When building a really tall structure, walls made of stone offer a diminishing return when it come to living space.
Huh? How so?
As the walls grow taller to accommodate more stories, they need to be thicker and stronger at the bottom to support the weight above.

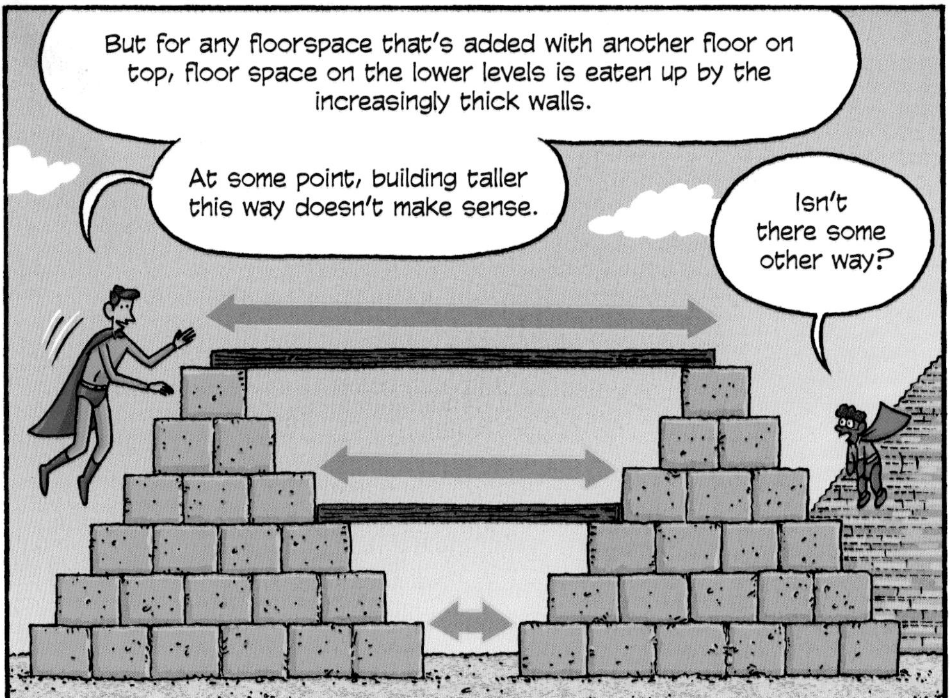
But for any floorspace that's added with another floor on top, floor space on the lower levels is eaten up by the increasingly thick walls.
At some point, building taller this way doesn't make sense.
Isn't there some other way?

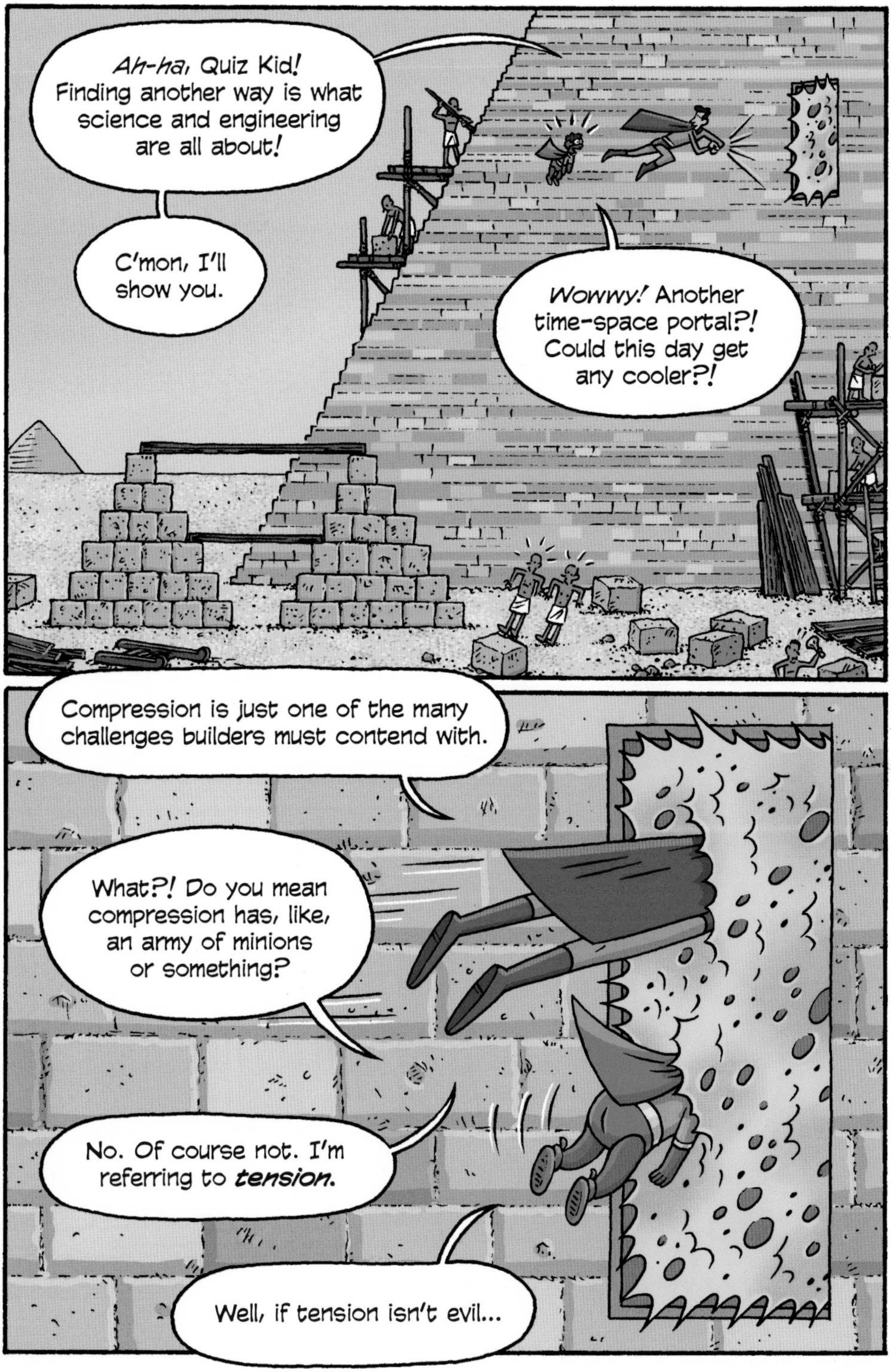
Ah-ha, Quiz Kid! Finding another way is what science and engineering are all about!
C'mon, I'll show you.
Wowwy! Another time-space portal?! Could this day get any cooler?!
Compression is just one of the many challenges builders must contend with.
What?! Do you mean compression has, like, an army of minions or something?
No. Of course not. I'm referring to tension.
Well, if tension isn't evil...

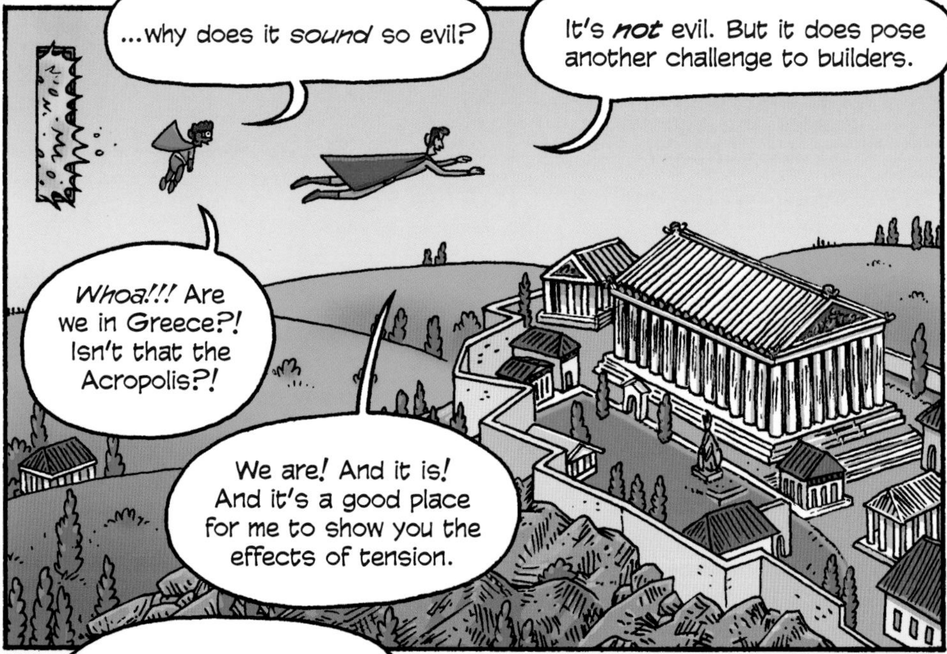
...why does it *sound* so evil?
It's ***not*** evil. But it does pose another challenge to builders.
Whoa!!! Are we in Greece?! Isn't that the Acropolis?!
We are! And it is! And it's a good place for me to show you the effects of tension.

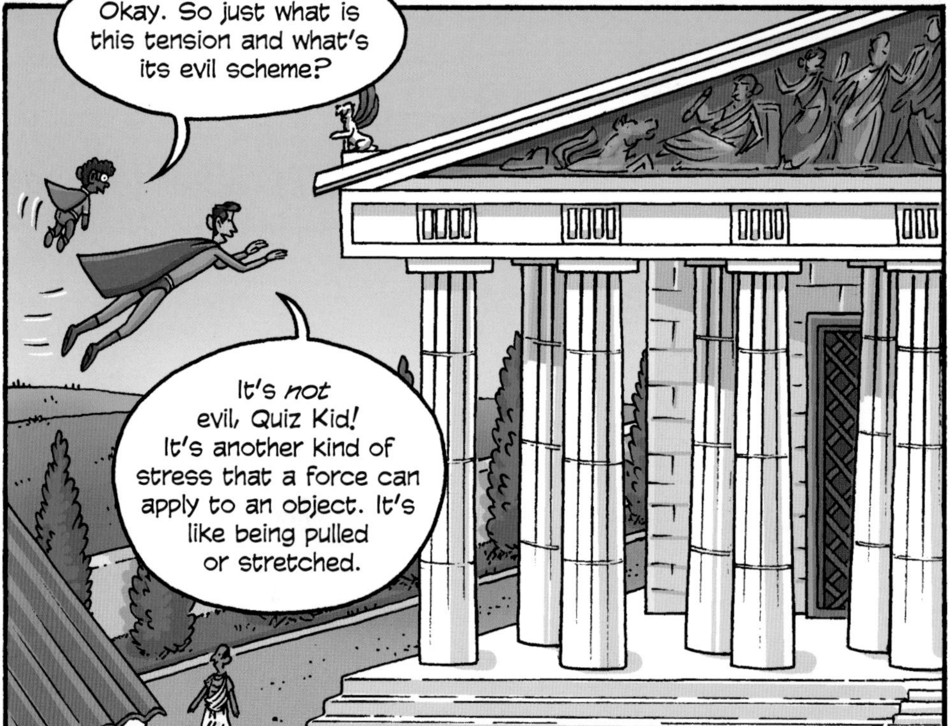
Okay. So just what is this tension and what's its evil scheme?
It's *not* evil, Quiz Kid! It's another kind of stress that a force can apply to an object. It's like being pulled or stretched.

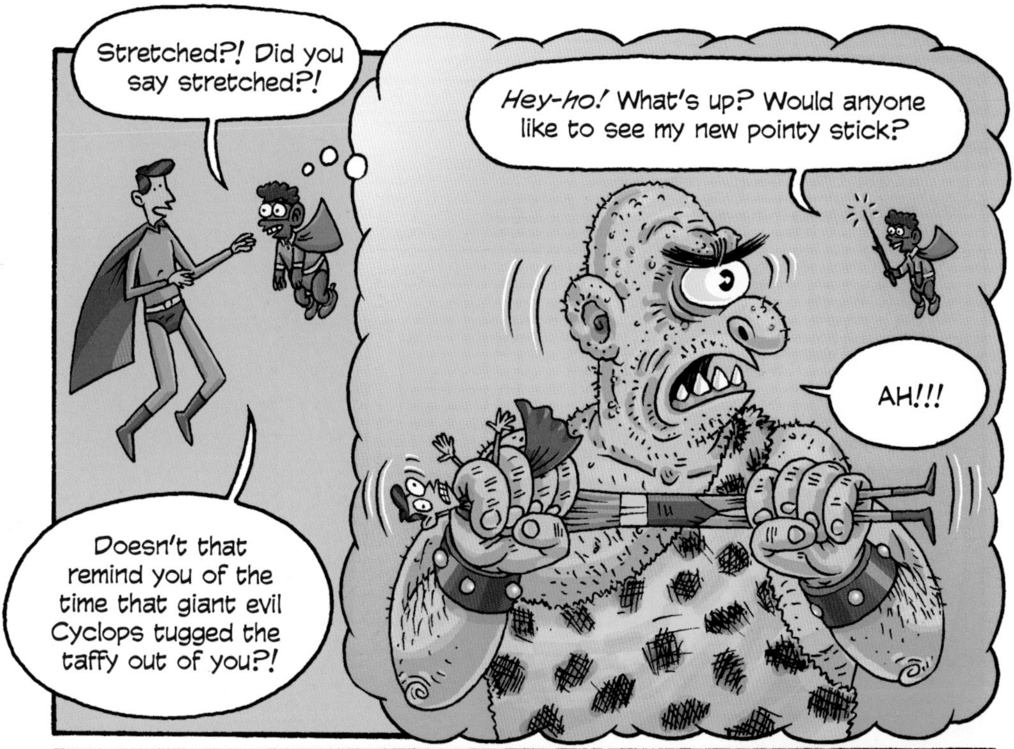
Stretched?! Did you say stretched?!
Hey-ho! What's up? Would anyone like to see my new pointy stick?
AH!!!
Doesn't that remind you of the time that giant evil Cyclops tugged the taffy out of you?!

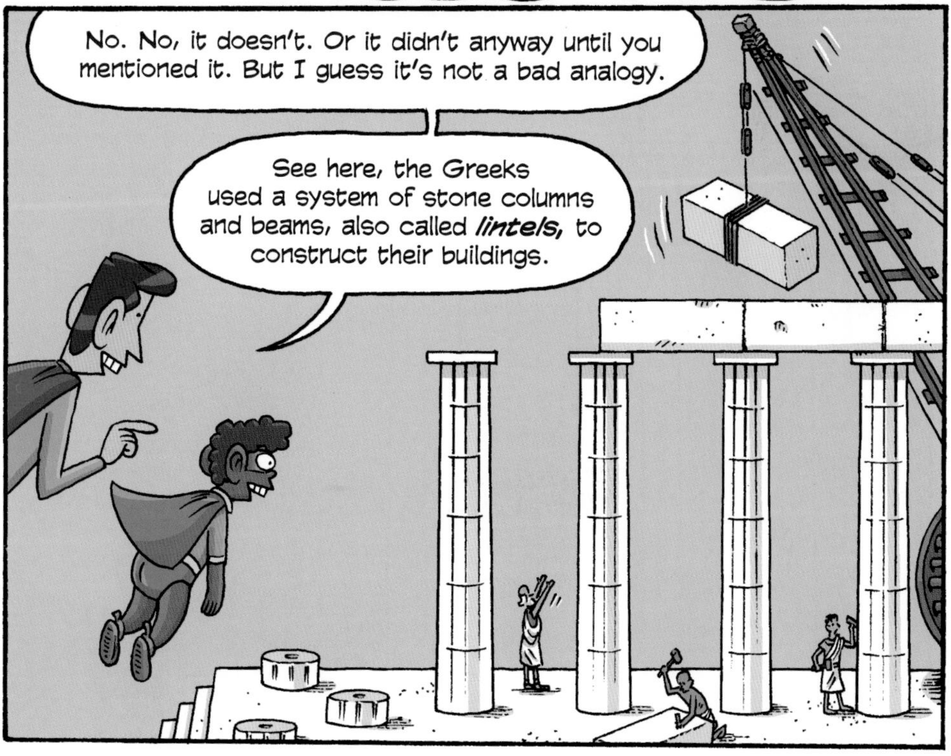
No. No, it doesn't. Or it didn't anyway until you mentioned it. But I guess it's not a bad analogy.
See here, the Greeks used a system of stone columns and beams, also called *lintels,* to construct their buildings.

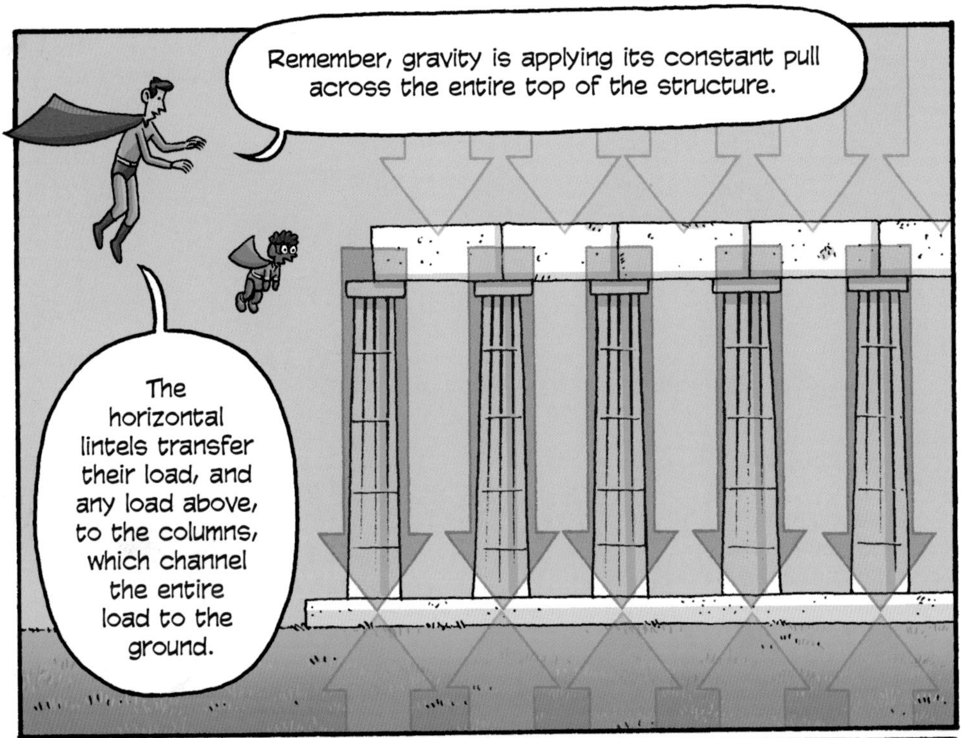
Remember, gravity is applying its constant pull across the entire top of the structure.
The horizontal lintels transfer their load, and any load above, to the columns, which channel the entire load to the ground.

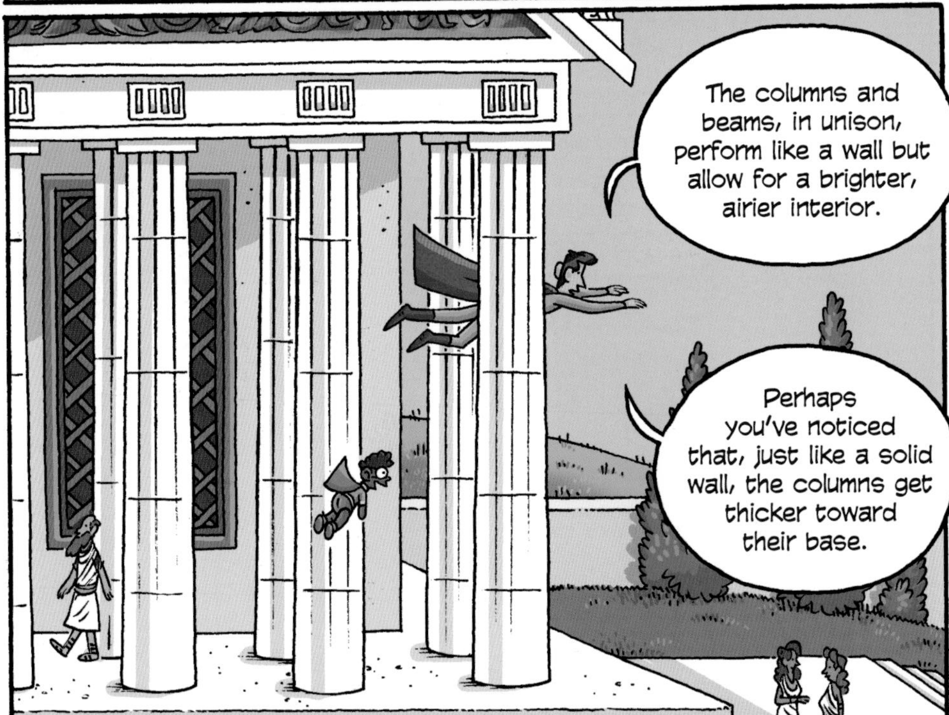
The columns and beams, in unison, perform like a wall but allow for a brighter, airier interior.
Perhaps you've noticed that, just like a solid wall, the columns get thicker toward their base.

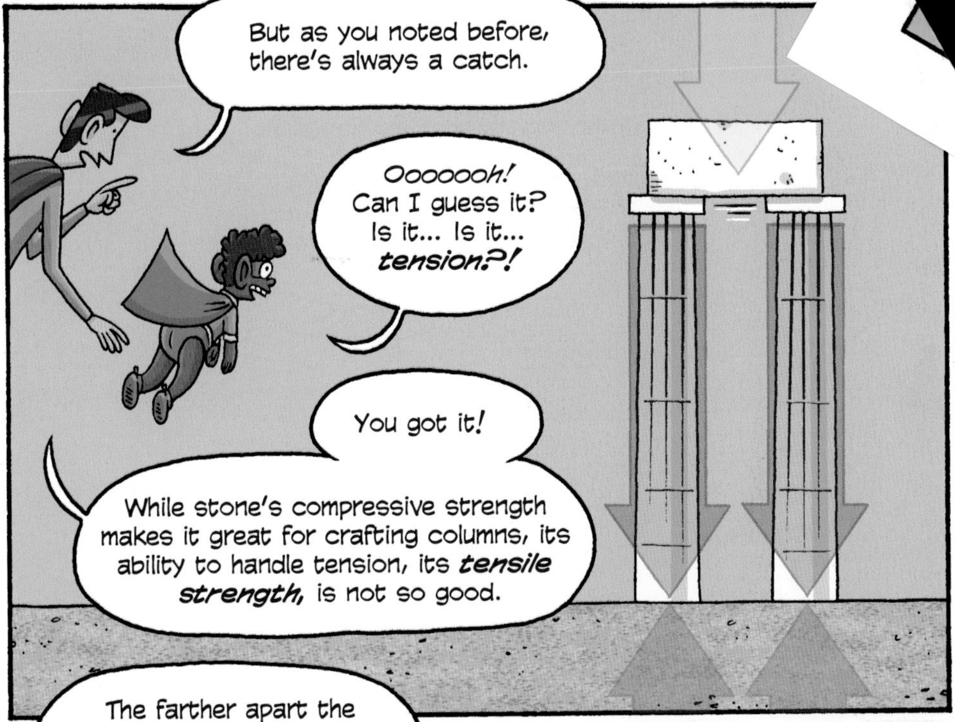

But as you noted before, there's always a catch.
Ooooooh! Can I guess it? Is it... Is it... ***tension?!***
You got it!
While stone's compressive strength makes it great for crafting columns, its ability to handle tension, its ***tensile strength,*** is not so good.

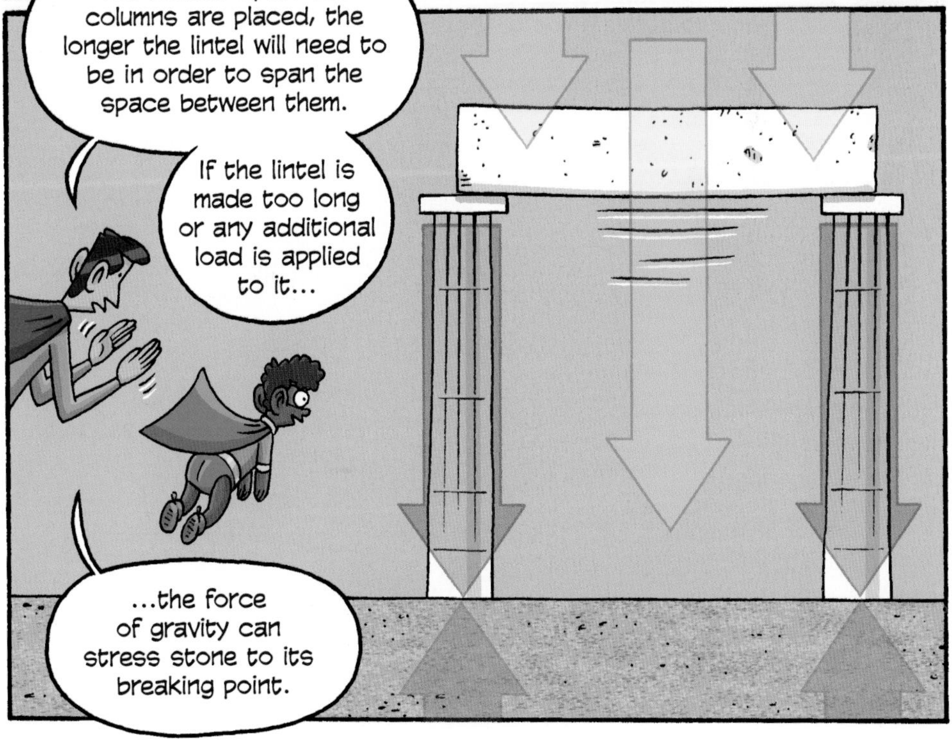

The farther apart the columns are placed, the longer the lintel will need to be in order to span the space between them.
If the lintel is made too long or any additional load is applied to it...
...the force of gravity can stress stone to its breaking point.

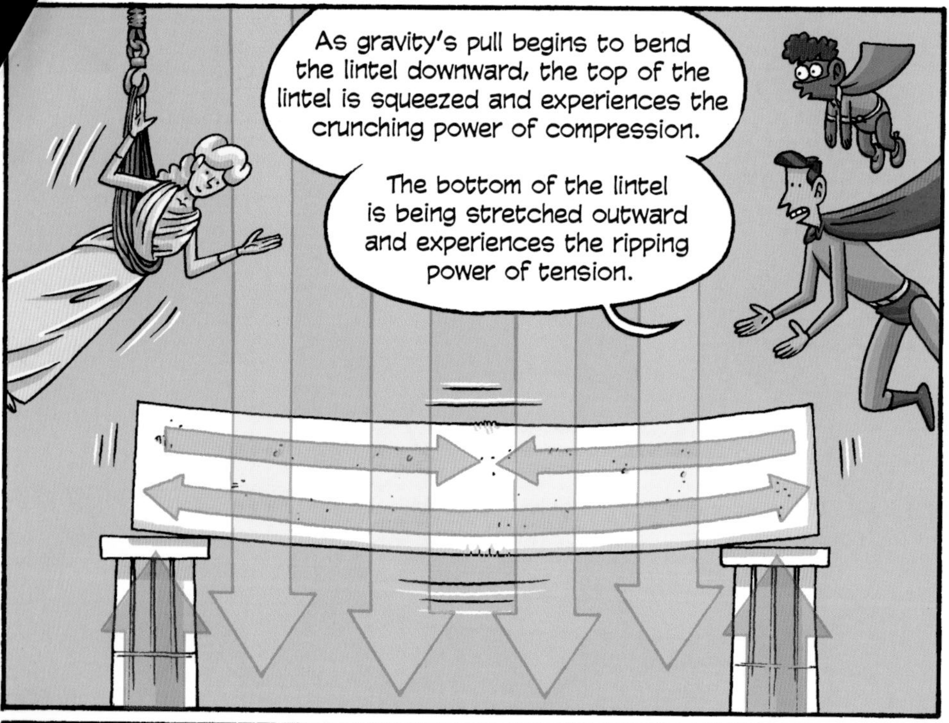
As gravity's pull begins to bend the lintel downward, the top of the lintel is squeezed and experiences the crunching power of compression.
The bottom of the lintel is being stretched outward and experiences the ripping power of tension.

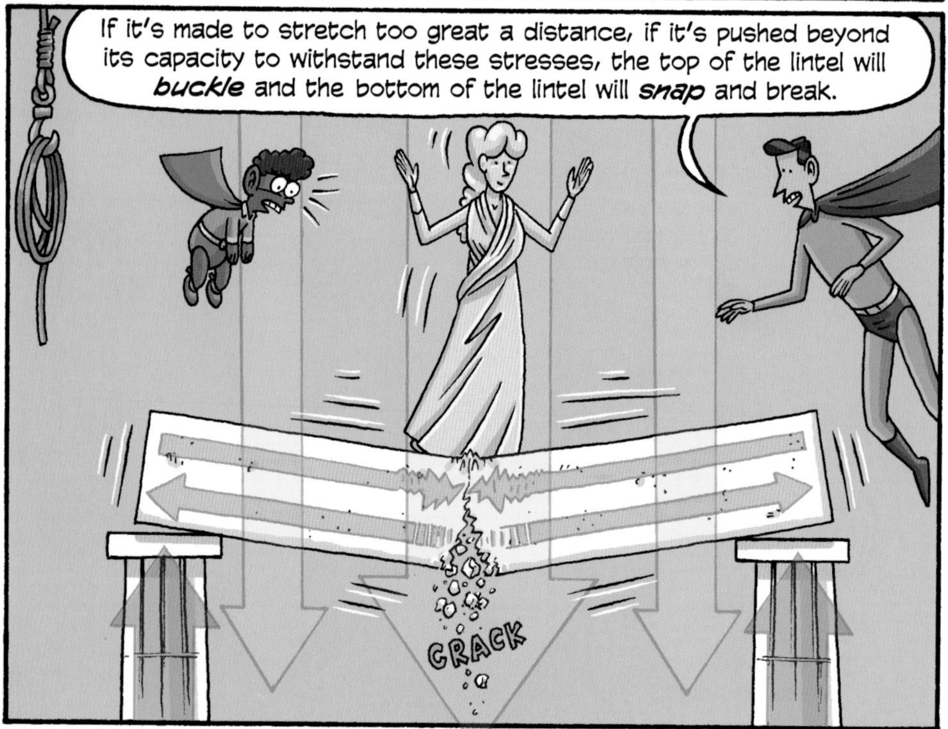
If it's made to stretch too great a distance, if it's pushed beyond its capacity to withstand these stresses, the top of the lintel will ***buckle*** and the bottom of the lintel will ***snap*** and break.
CRACK

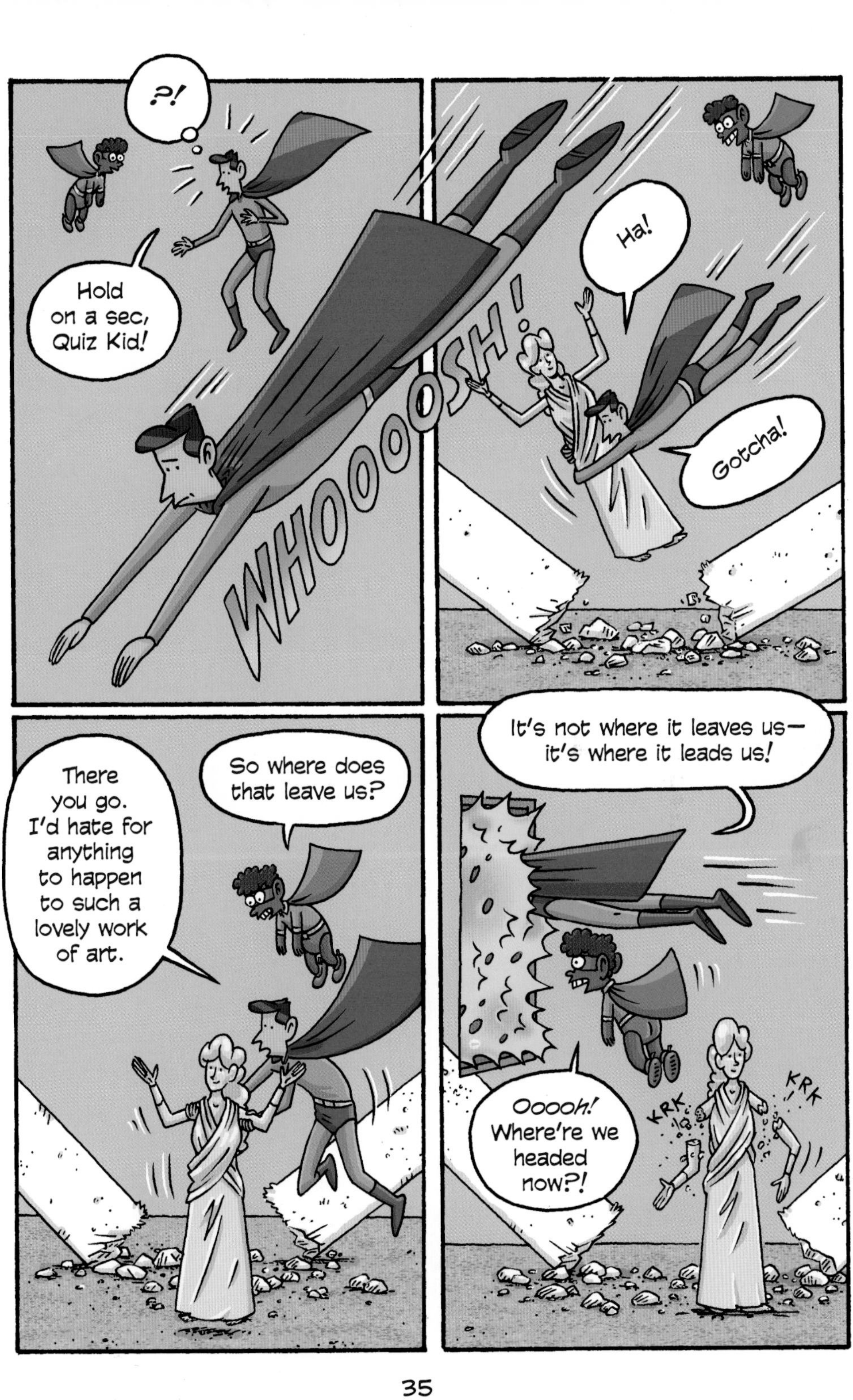
?!
Hold on a sec, Quiz Kid!
WHOOOOSH!
Ha!
Gotcha!
There you go. I'd hate for anything to happen to such a lovely work of art.
So where does that leave us?
It's not where it leaves us—it's where it leads us!
Ooooh! Where're we headed now?!
KRK
KRK

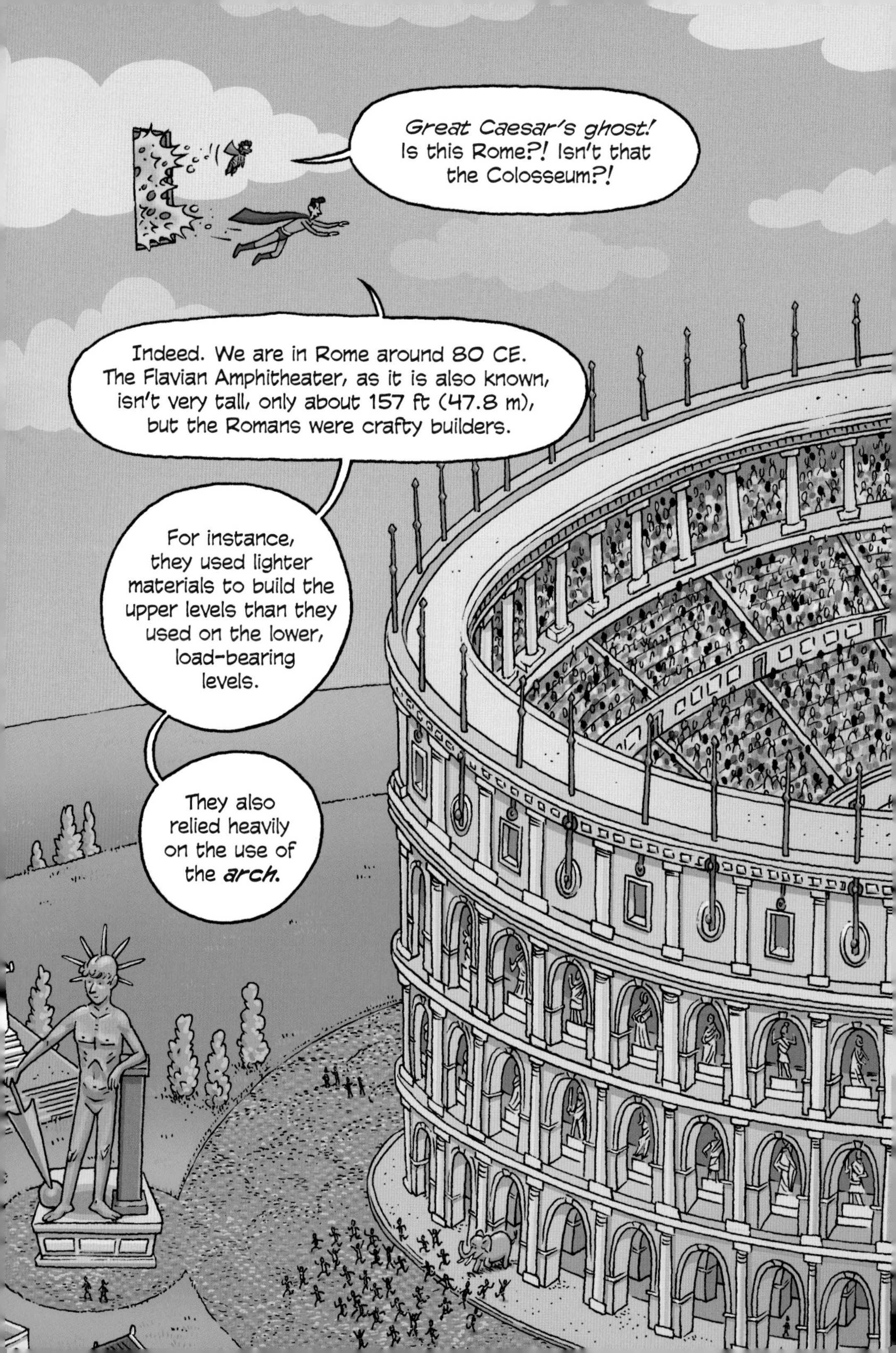
Great Caesar's ghost! Is this Rome?! Isn't that the Colosseum?!
Indeed. We are in Rome around 80 CE. The Flavian Amphitheater, as it is also known, isn't very tall, only about 157 ft (47.8 m), but the Romans were crafty builders.
For instance, they used lighter materials to build the upper levels than they used on the lower, load-bearing levels.
They also relied heavily on the use of the ***arch.***

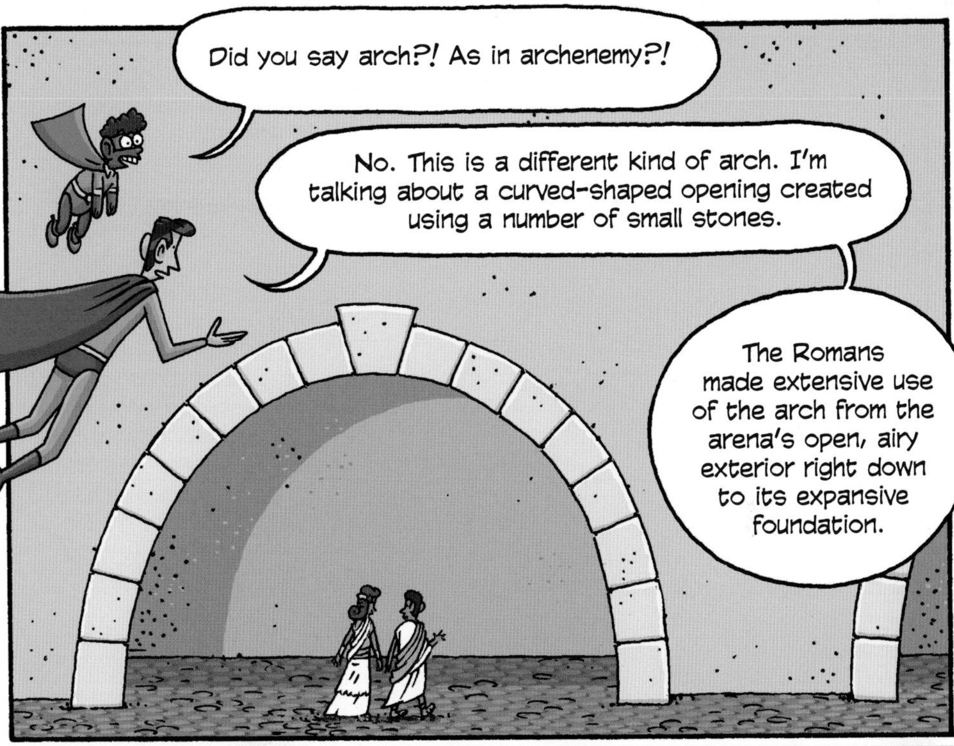
Did you say arch?! As in archenemy?!
No. This is a different kind of arch. I'm talking about a curved-shaped opening created using a number of small stones.
The Romans made extensive use of the arch from the arena's open, airy exterior right down to its expansive foundation.

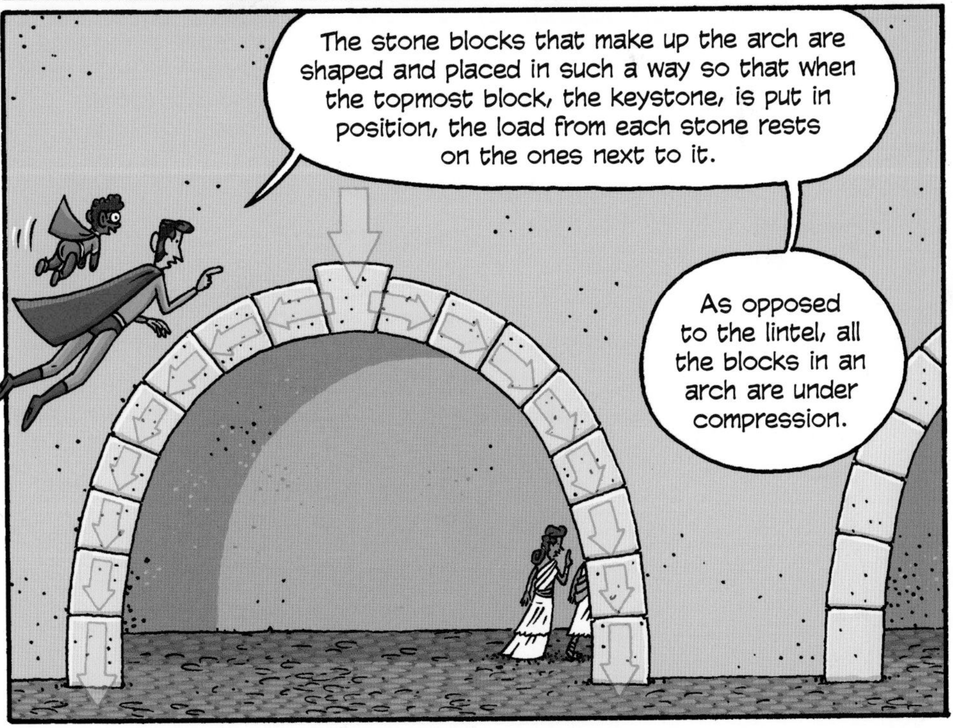
The stone blocks that make up the arch are shaped and placed in such a way so that when the topmost block, the keystone, is put in position, the load from each stone rests on the ones next to it.
As opposed to the lintel, all the blocks in an arch are under compression.

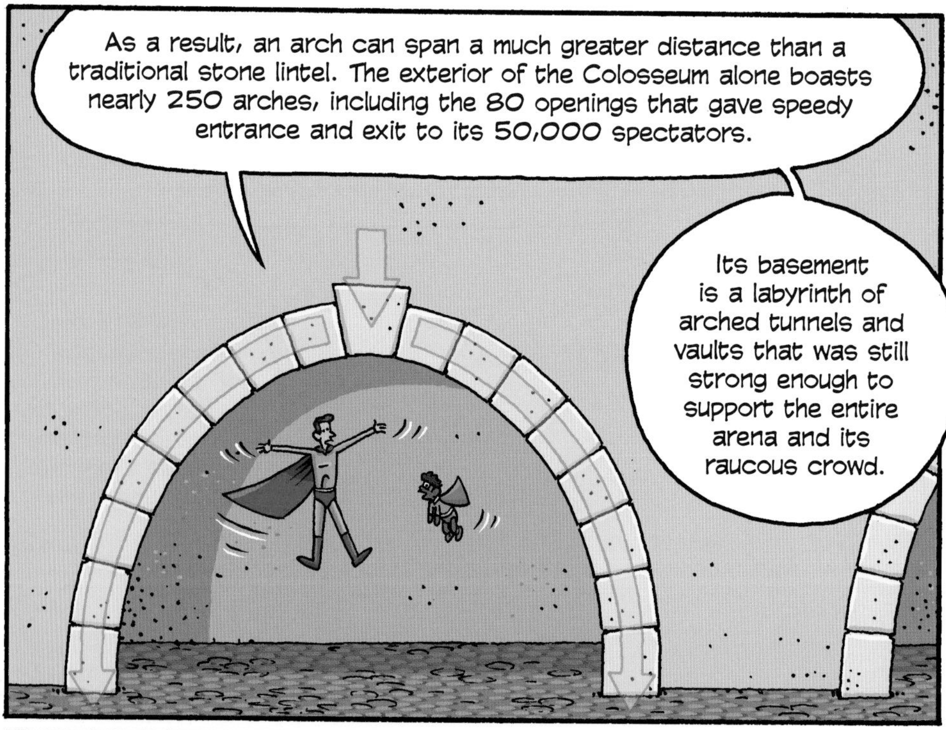
As a result, an arch can span a much greater distance than a traditional stone lintel. The exterior of the Colosseum alone boasts nearly 250 arches, including the 80 openings that gave speedy entrance and exit to its 50,000 spectators.
Its basement is a labyrinth of arched tunnels and vaults that was still strong enough to support the entire arena and its raucous crowd.

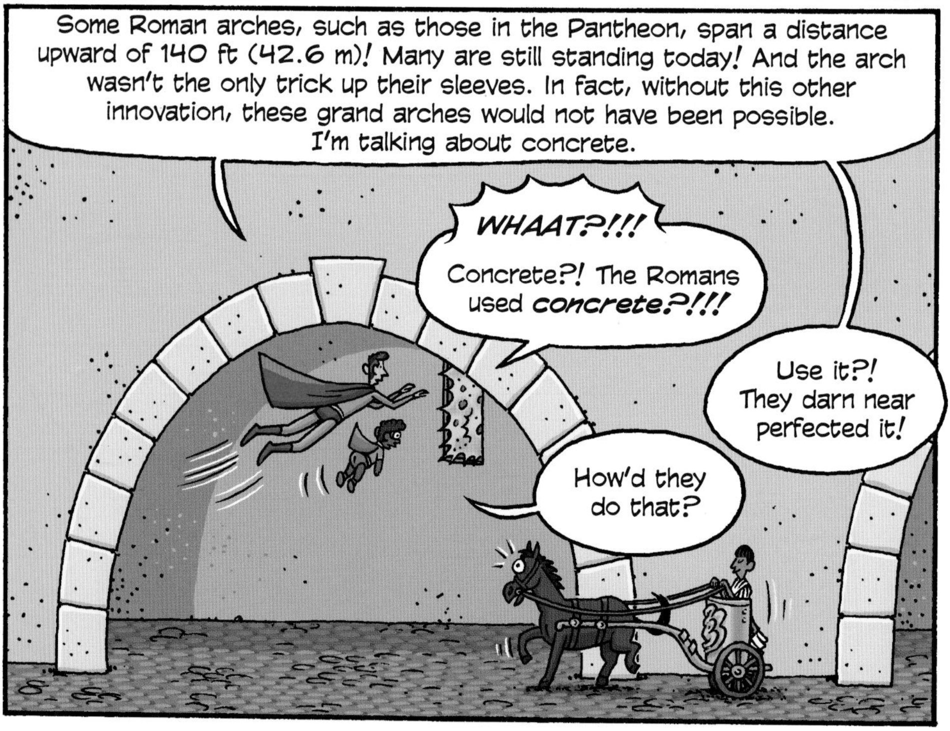
Some Roman arches, such as those in the Pantheon, span a distance upward of 140 ft (42.6 m)! Many are still standing today! And the arch wasn't the only trick up their sleeves. In fact, without this other innovation, these grand arches would not have been possible. I'm talking about concrete.
WHAAT?!!! Concrete?! The Romans used concrete?!!!
Use it?! They darn near perfected it!
How'd they do that?

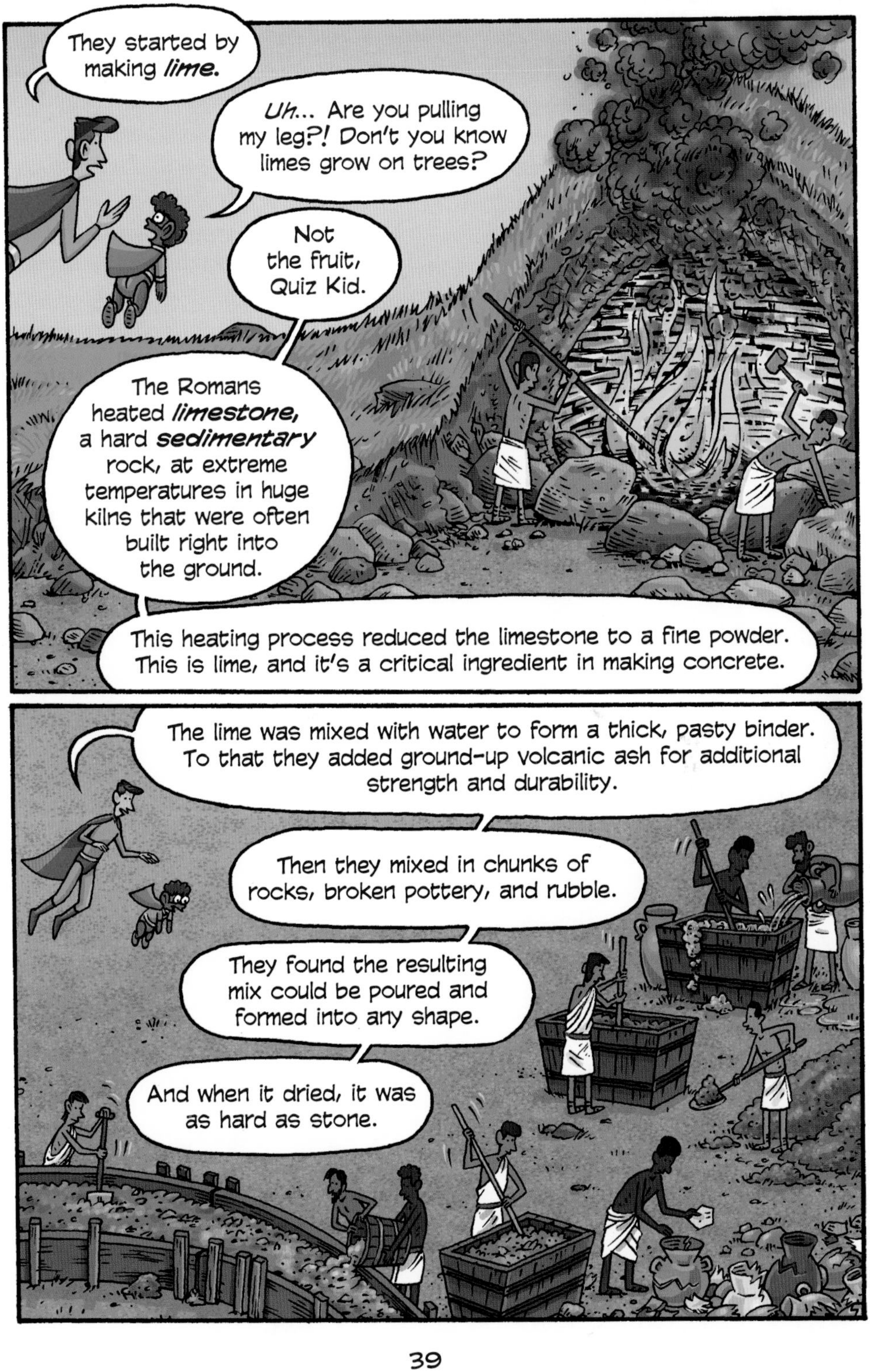

They started by making *lime.*
Uh... Are you pulling my leg?! Don't you know limes grow on trees?
Not the fruit, Quiz Kid.
The Romans heated ***limestone,*** a hard ***sedimentary*** rock, at extreme temperatures in huge kilns that were often built right into the ground.
This heating process reduced the limestone to a fine powder. This is lime, and it's a critical ingredient in making concrete.
The lime was mixed with water to form a thick, pasty binder. To that they added ground-up volcanic ash for additional strength and durability.
Then they mixed in chunks of rocks, broken pottery, and rubble.
They found the resulting mix could be poured and formed into any shape.
And when it dried, it was as hard as stone.

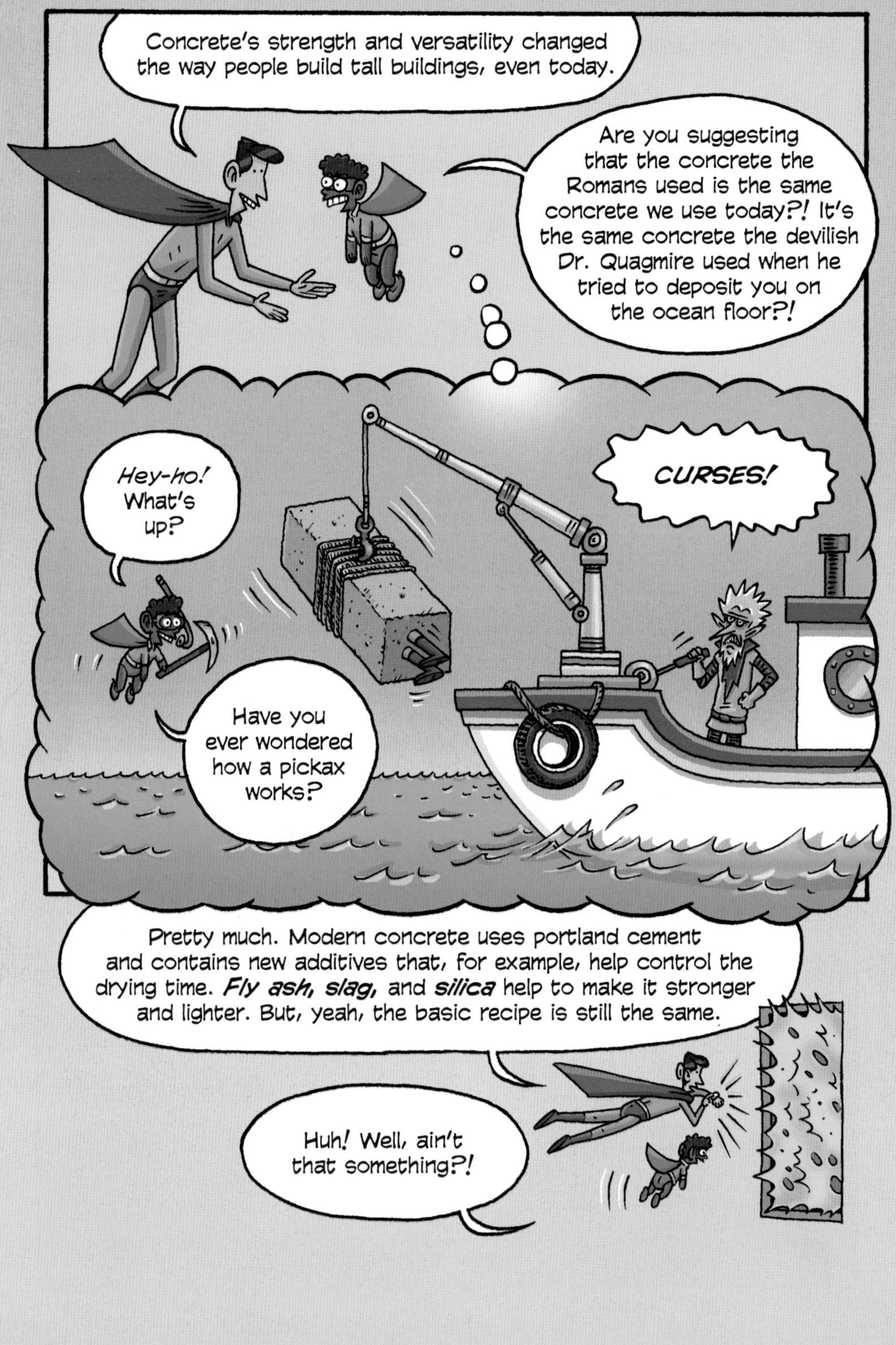
Concrete's strength and versatility changed the way people build tall buildings, even today.
Are you suggesting that the concrete the Romans used is the same concrete we use today?! It's the same concrete the devilish Dr. Quagmire used when he tried to deposit you on the ocean floor?!
Hey-ho! What's up?
CURSES!
Have you ever wondered how a pickax works?
Pretty much. Modern concrete uses portland cement and contains new additives that, for example, help control the drying time. *Fly ash, slag,* and *silica* help to make it stronger and lighter. But, yeah, the basic recipe is still the same.
Huh! Well, ain't that something?!

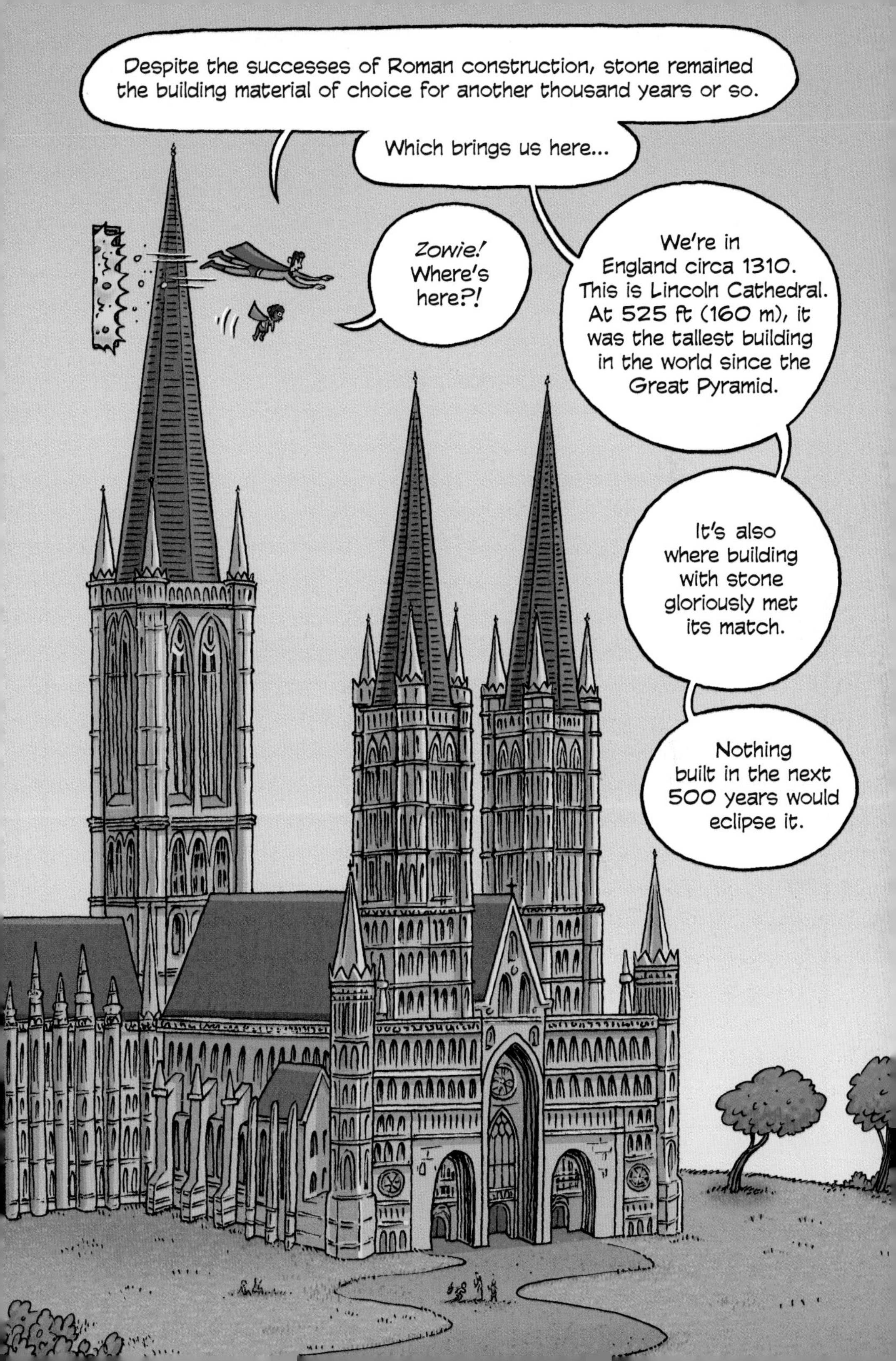
Despite the successes of Roman construction, stone remained the building material of choice for another thousand years or so.
Which brings us here...
Zowie! Where's here?!
We're in England circa 1310. This is Lincoln Cathedral. At 525 ft (160 m), it was the tallest building in the world since the Great Pyramid.
It's also where building with stone gloriously met its match.
Nothing built in the next 500 years would eclipse it.

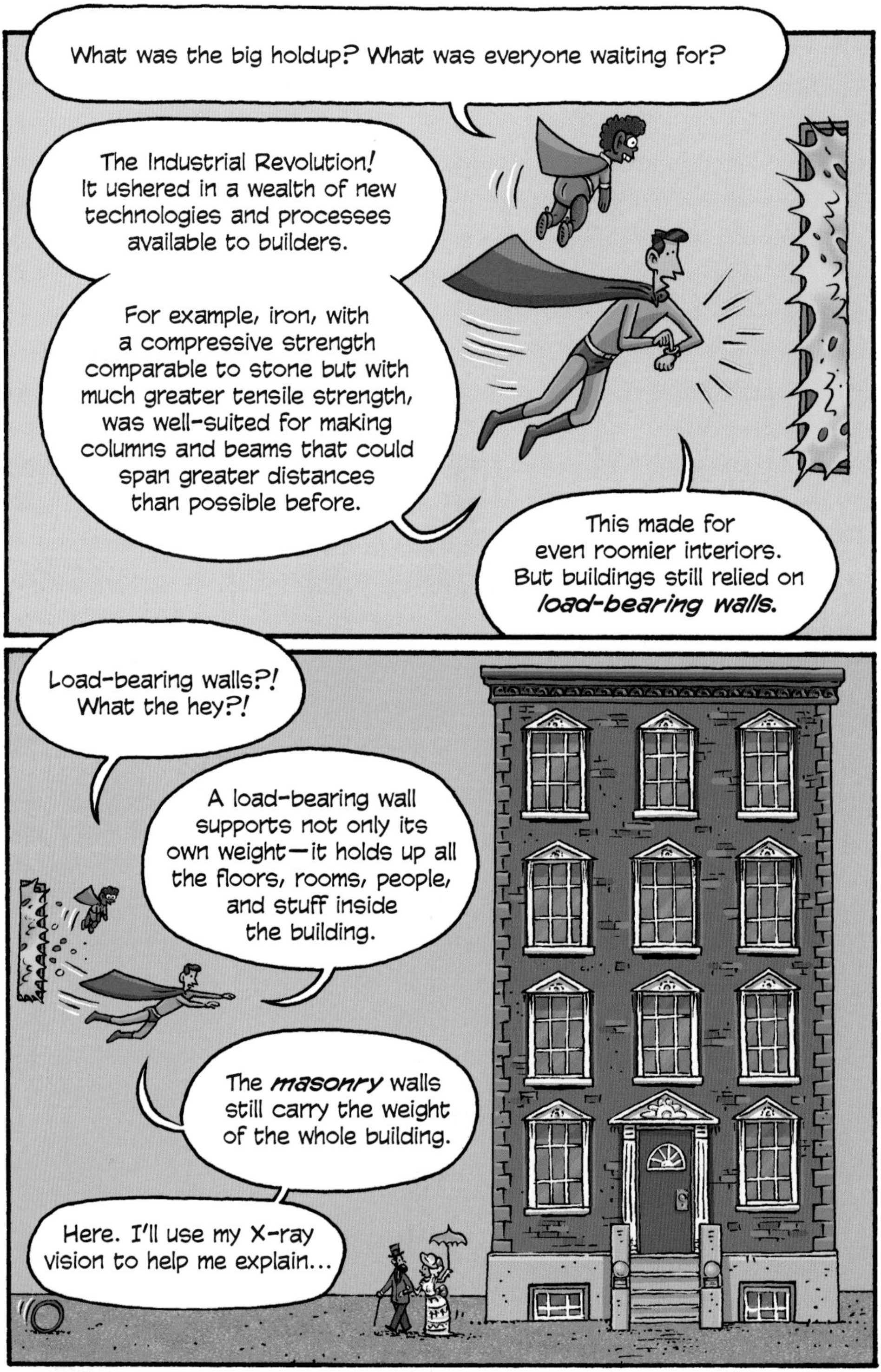
What was the big holdup? What was everyone waiting for?
The Industrial Revolution! It ushered in a wealth of new technologies and processes available to builders.
For example, iron, with a compressive strength comparable to stone but with much greater tensile strength, was well-suited for making columns and beams that could span greater distances than possible before.
This made for even roomier interiors. But buildings still relied on *load-bearing walls.*
Load-bearing walls?! What the hey?!
A load-bearing wall supports not only its own weight—it holds up all the floors, rooms, people, and stuff inside the building.
The *masonry* walls still carry the weight of the whole building.
Here. I'll use my X-ray vision to help me explain...

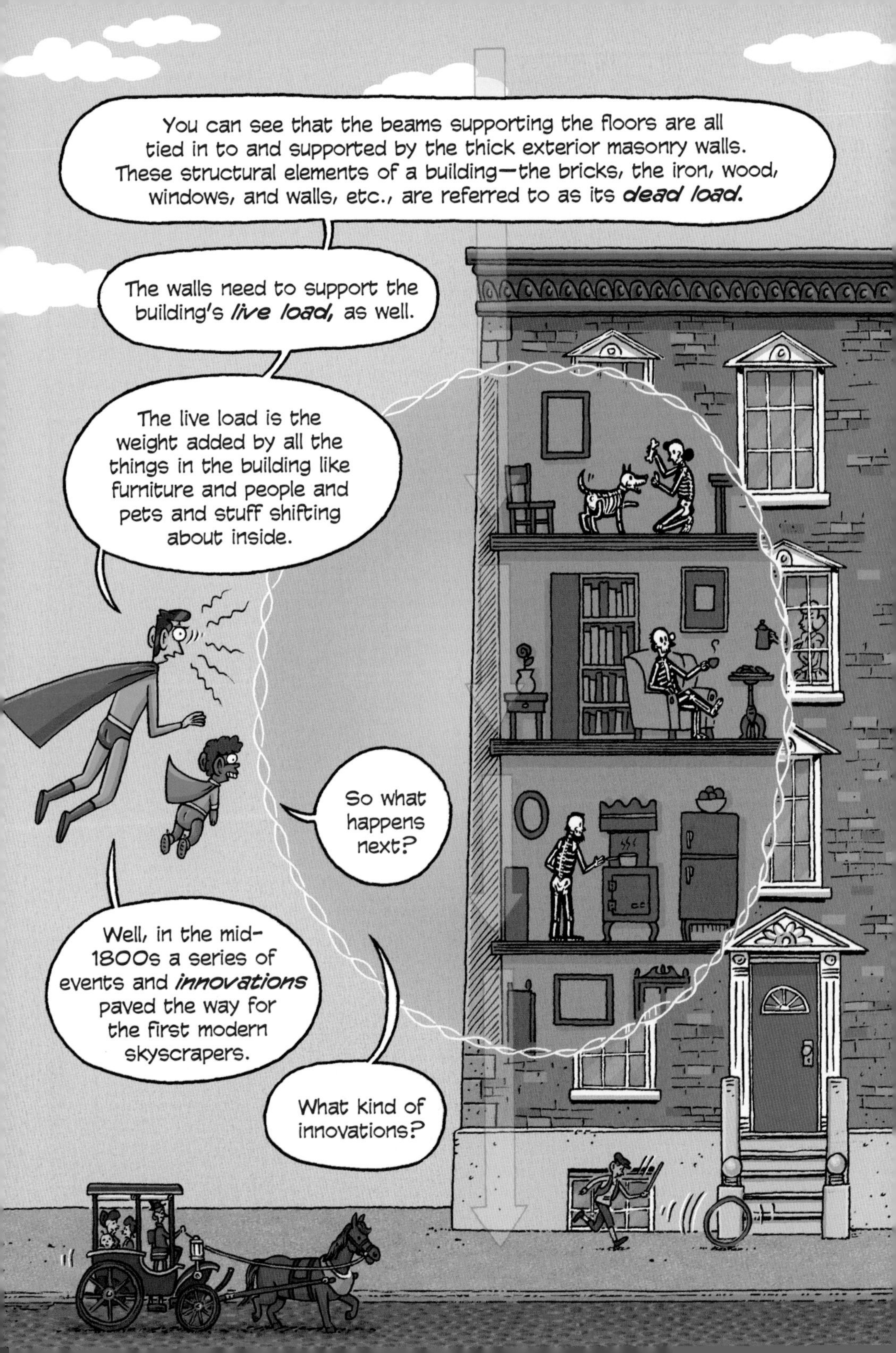
You can see that the beams supporting the floors are all tied in to and supported by the thick exterior masonry walls. These structural elements of a building—the bricks, the iron, wood, windows, and walls, etc., are referred to as its *dead load.*
The walls need to support the building's *live load,* as well.
The live load is the weight added by all the things in the building like furniture and people and pets and stuff shifting about inside.
So what happens next?
Well, in the mid-1800s a series of events and *innovations* paved the way for the first modern skyscrapers.
What kind of innovations?

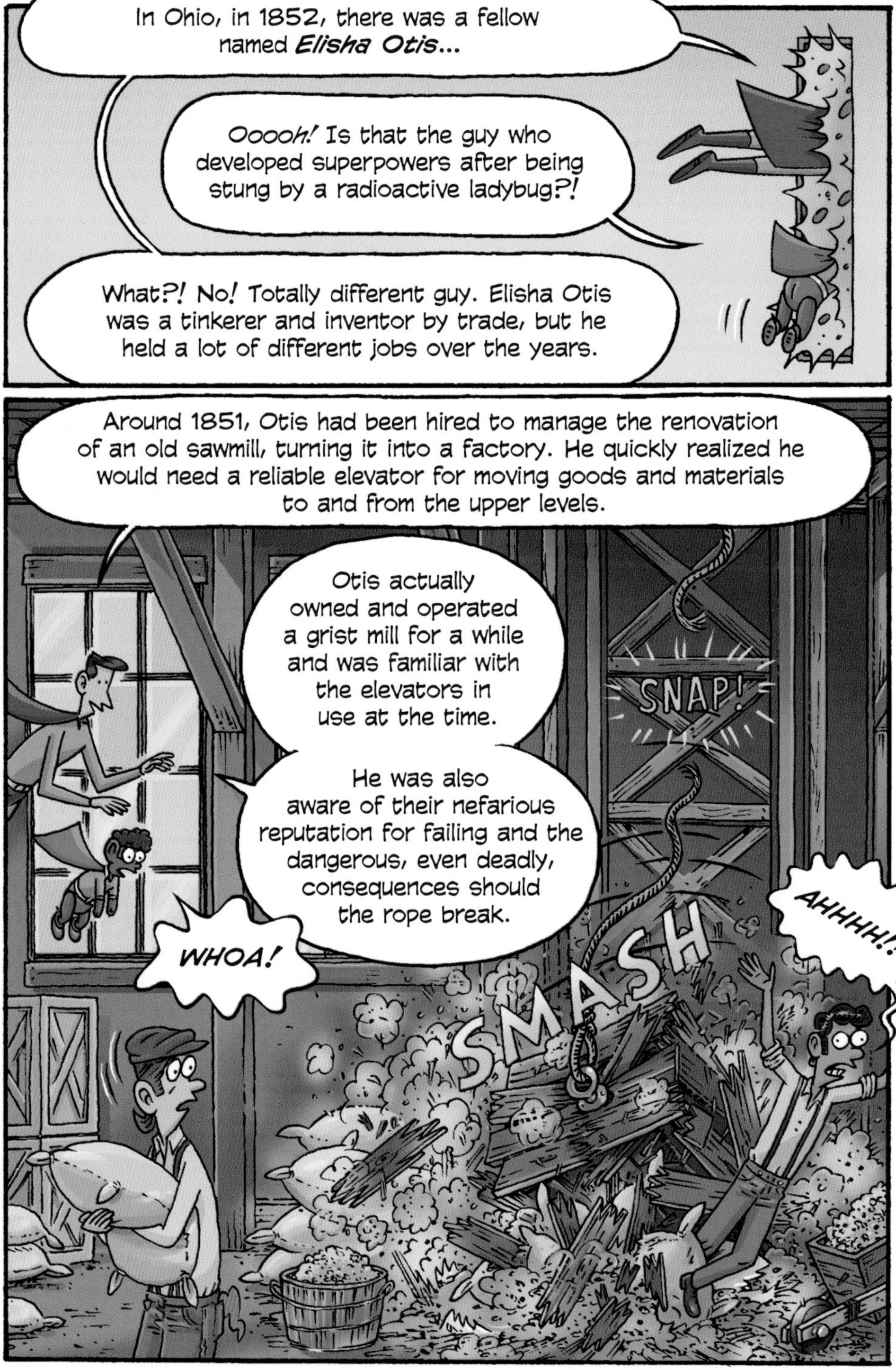
In Ohio, in 1852, there was a fellow named *Elisha Otis*...
Ooooh! Is that the guy who developed superpowers after being stung by a radioactive ladybug?!
What?! No! Totally different guy. Elisha Otis was a tinkerer and inventor by trade, but he held a lot of different jobs over the years.
Around 1851, Otis had been hired to manage the renovation of an old sawmill, turning it into a factory. He quickly realized he would need a reliable elevator for moving goods and materials to and from the upper levels.
Otis actually owned and operated a grist mill for a while and was familiar with the elevators in use at the time.
He was also aware of their nefarious reputation for failing and the dangerous, even deadly, consequences should the rope break.
SNAP!
WHOA!
SMASH
AHHHH!!!

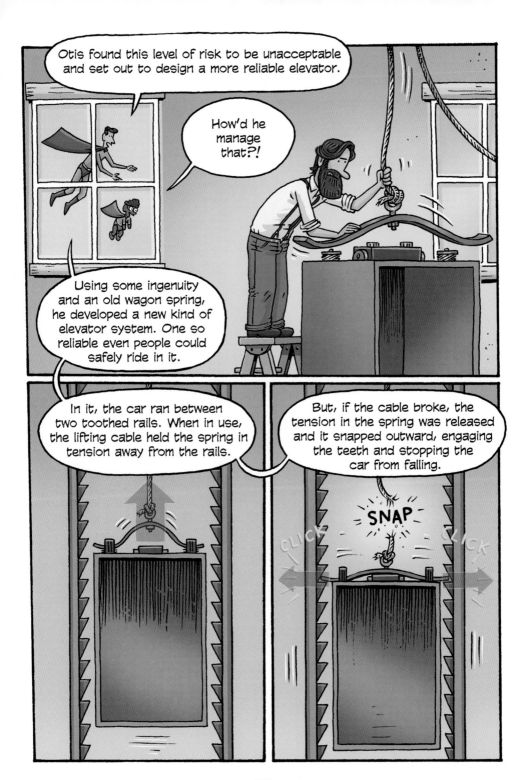

Otis found this level of risk to be unacceptable and set out to design a more reliable elevator.

How'd he manage that?!

Using some ingenuity and an old wagon spring, he developed a new kind of elevator system. One so reliable even people could safely ride in it.

In it, the car ran between two toothed rails. When in use, the lifting cable held the spring in tension away from the rails.

But, if the cable broke, the tension in the spring was released and it snapped outward, engaging the teeth and stopping the car from falling.

SNAP

CLICK

CLICK

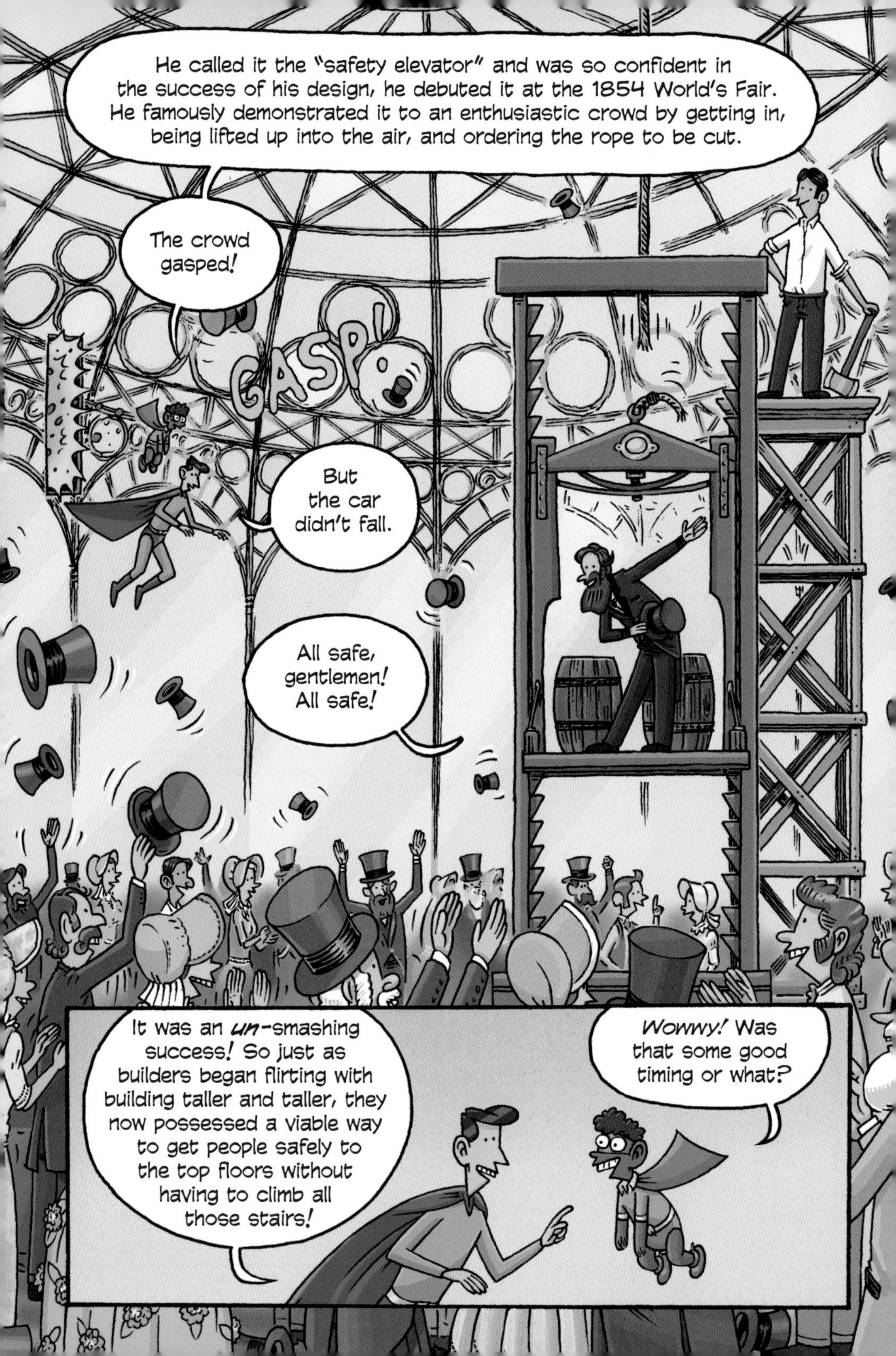
He called it the "safety elevator" and was so confident in the success of his design, he debuted it at the 1854 World's Fair. He famously demonstrated it to an enthusiastic crowd by getting in, being lifted up into the air, and ordering the rope to be cut.
The crowd gasped!
GASP!
But the car didn't fall.
All safe, gentlemen! All safe!
It was an *un*-smashing success! So just as builders began flirting with building taller and taller, they now possessed a viable way to get people safely to the top floors without having to climb all those stairs!
Wowwy! Was that some good timing or what?

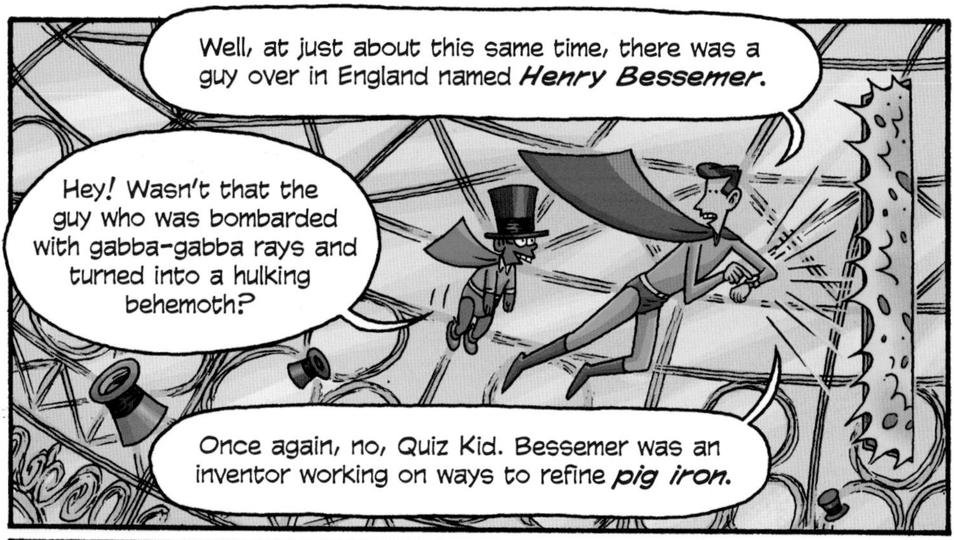
Well, at just about this same time, there was a guy over in England named *Henry Bessemer*.
Hey! Wasn't that the guy who was bombarded with gabba-gabba rays and turned into a hulking behemoth?
Once again, no, Quiz Kid. Bessemer was an inventor working on ways to refine *pig iron*.

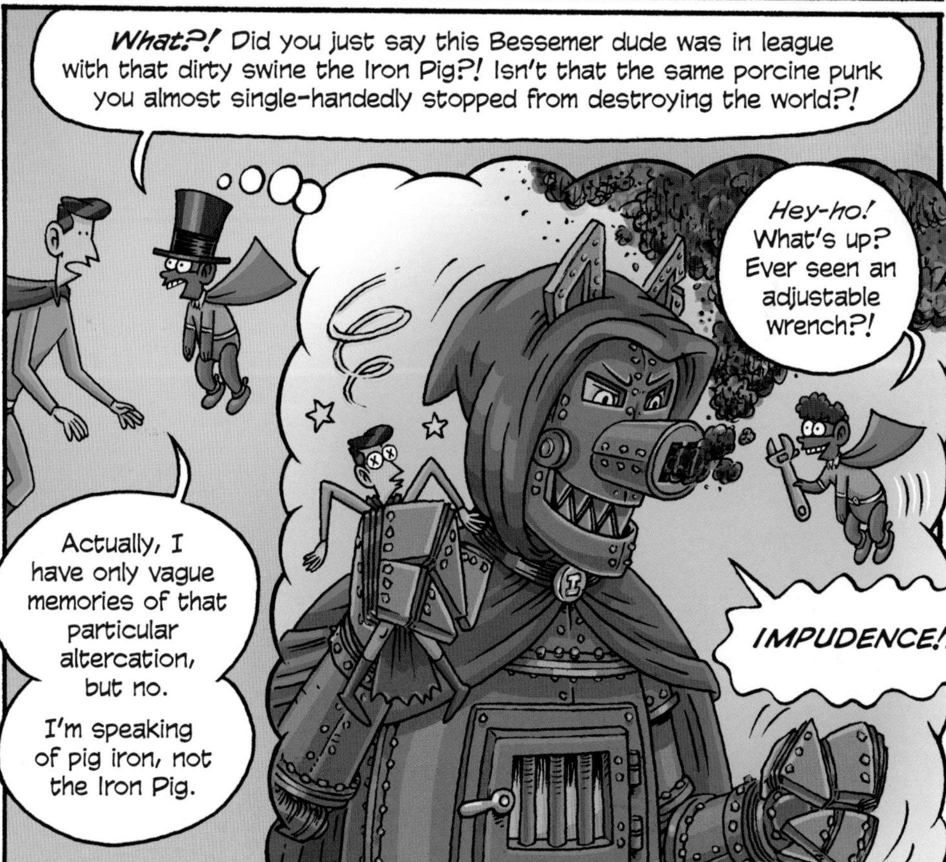
What?! Did you just say this Bessemer dude was in league with that dirty swine the Iron Pig?! Isn't that the same porcine punk you almost single-handedly stopped from destroying the world?!
Hey-ho! What's up? Ever seen an adjustable wrench?!
IMPUDENCE!!!
Actually, I have only vague memories of that particular altercation, but no.
I'm speaking of pig iron, not the Iron Pig.

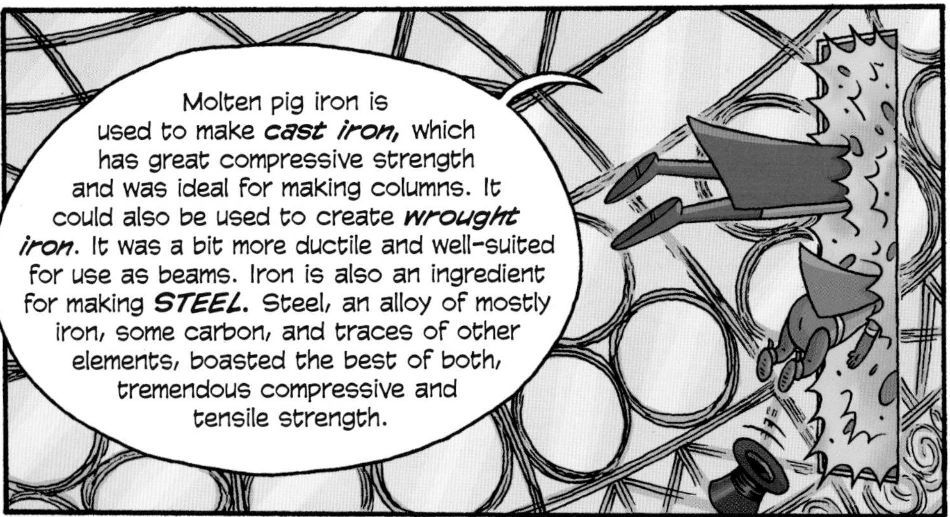
Molten pig iron is used to make *cast iron,* which has great compressive strength and was ideal for making columns. It could also be used to create *wrought iron*. It was a bit more ductile and well-suited for use as beams. Iron is also an ingredient for making ***STEEL.*** Steel, an alloy of mostly iron, some carbon, and traces of other elements, boasted the best of both, tremendous compressive and tensile strength.

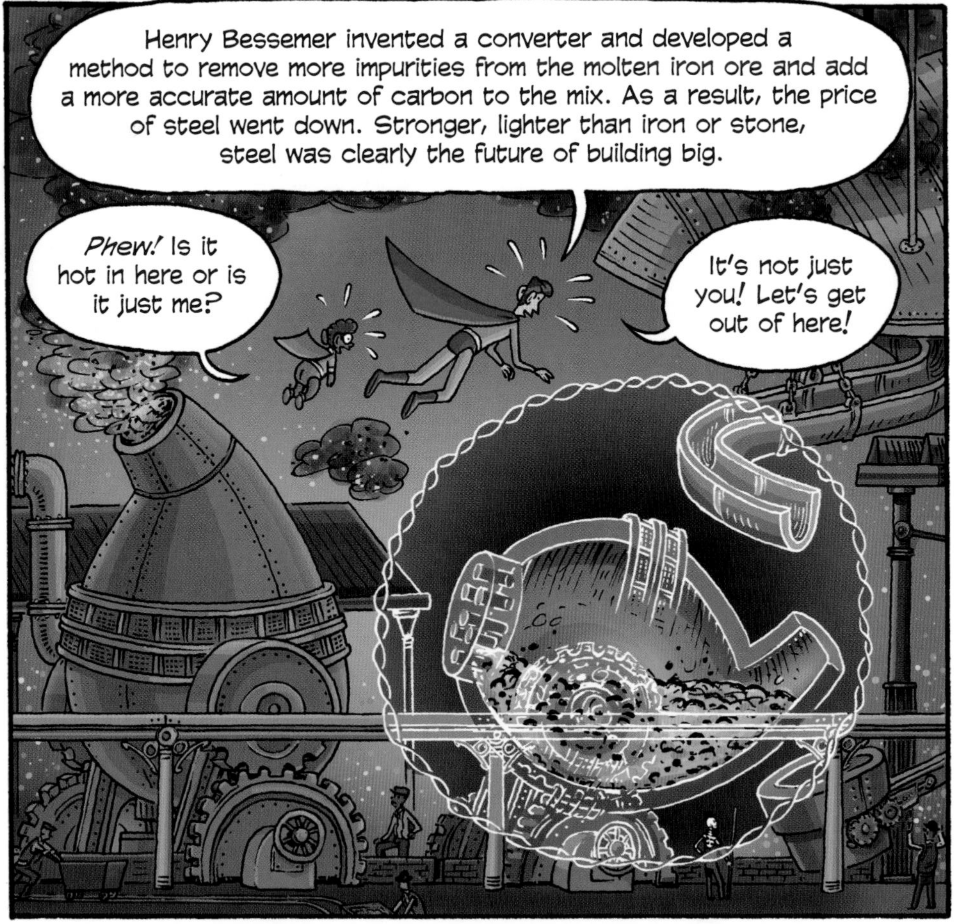
Henry Bessemer invented a converter and developed a method to remove more impurities from the molten iron ore and add a more accurate amount of carbon to the mix. As a result, the price of steel went down. Stronger, lighter than iron or stone, steel was clearly the future of building big.
Phew! Is it hot in here or is it just me?
It's not just you! Let's get out of here!

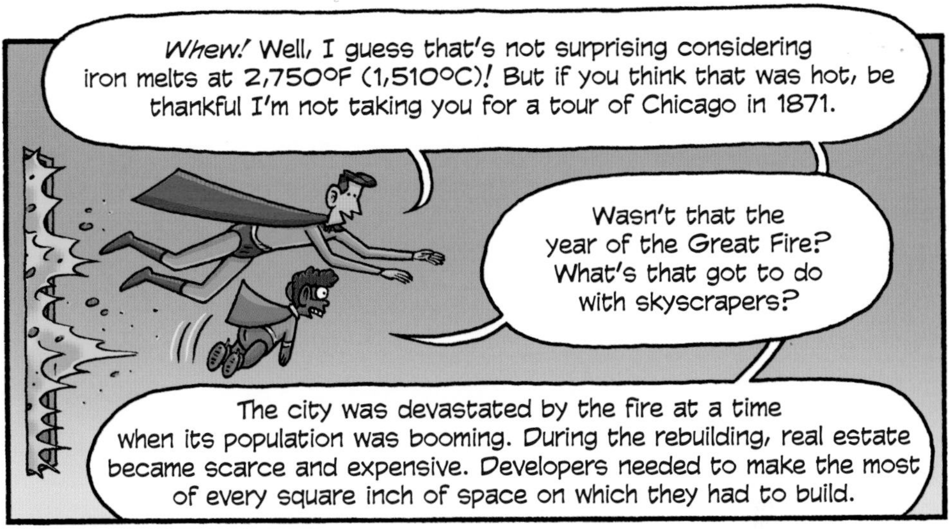
Whew! Well, I guess that's not surprising considering iron melts at 2,750°F (1,510°C)! But if you think that was hot, be thankful I'm not taking you for a tour of Chicago in 1871.
Wasn't that the year of the Great Fire? What's that got to do with skyscrapers?
The city was devastated by the fire at a time when its population was booming. During the rebuilding, real estate became scarce and expensive. Developers needed to make the most of every square inch of space on which they had to build.

There was only one way to go and that was ***up!*** So in 1884, armed with ample knowledge, sturdy materials, and the proper motivation, designer ***William Le Baron Jenney*** took a newly developing approach to building and pushed it to the forefront of construction, the Home Insurance Building.

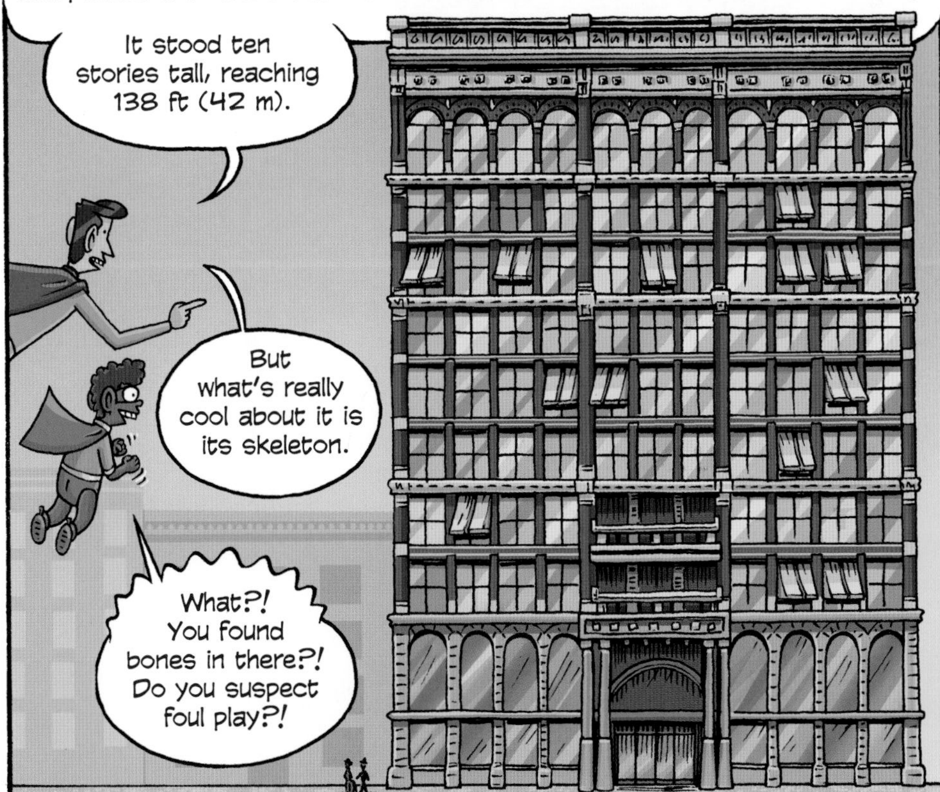
It stood ten stories tall, reaching 138 ft (42 m).
But what's really cool about it is its skeleton.
What?! You found bones in there?! Do you suspect foul play?!

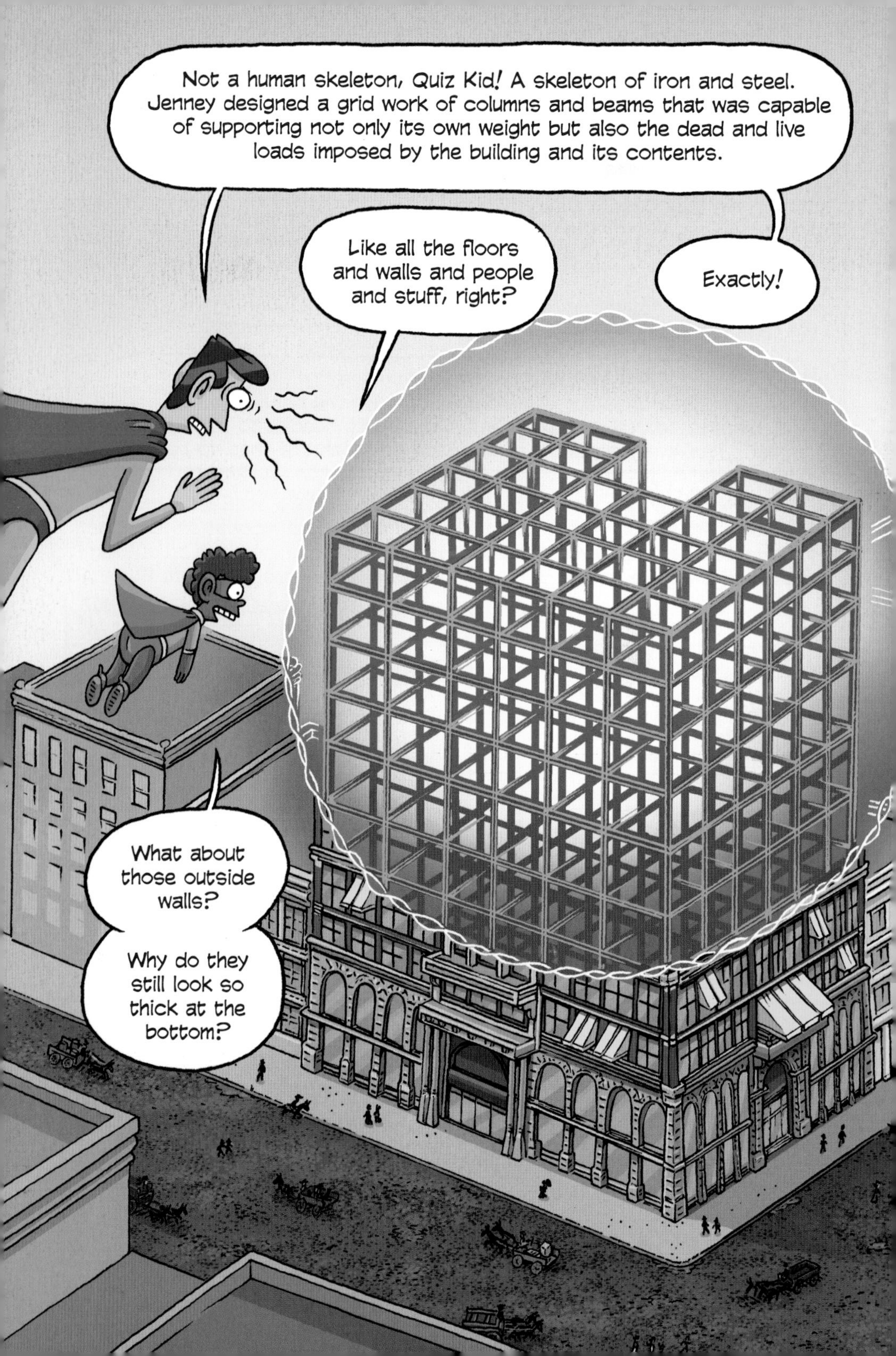
Not a human skeleton, Quiz Kid! A skeleton of iron and steel. Jenney designed a grid work of columns and beams that was capable of supporting not only its own weight but also the dead and live loads imposed by the building and its contents.
Like all the floors and walls and people and stuff, right?
Exactly!
What about those outside walls?
Why do they still look so thick at the bottom?

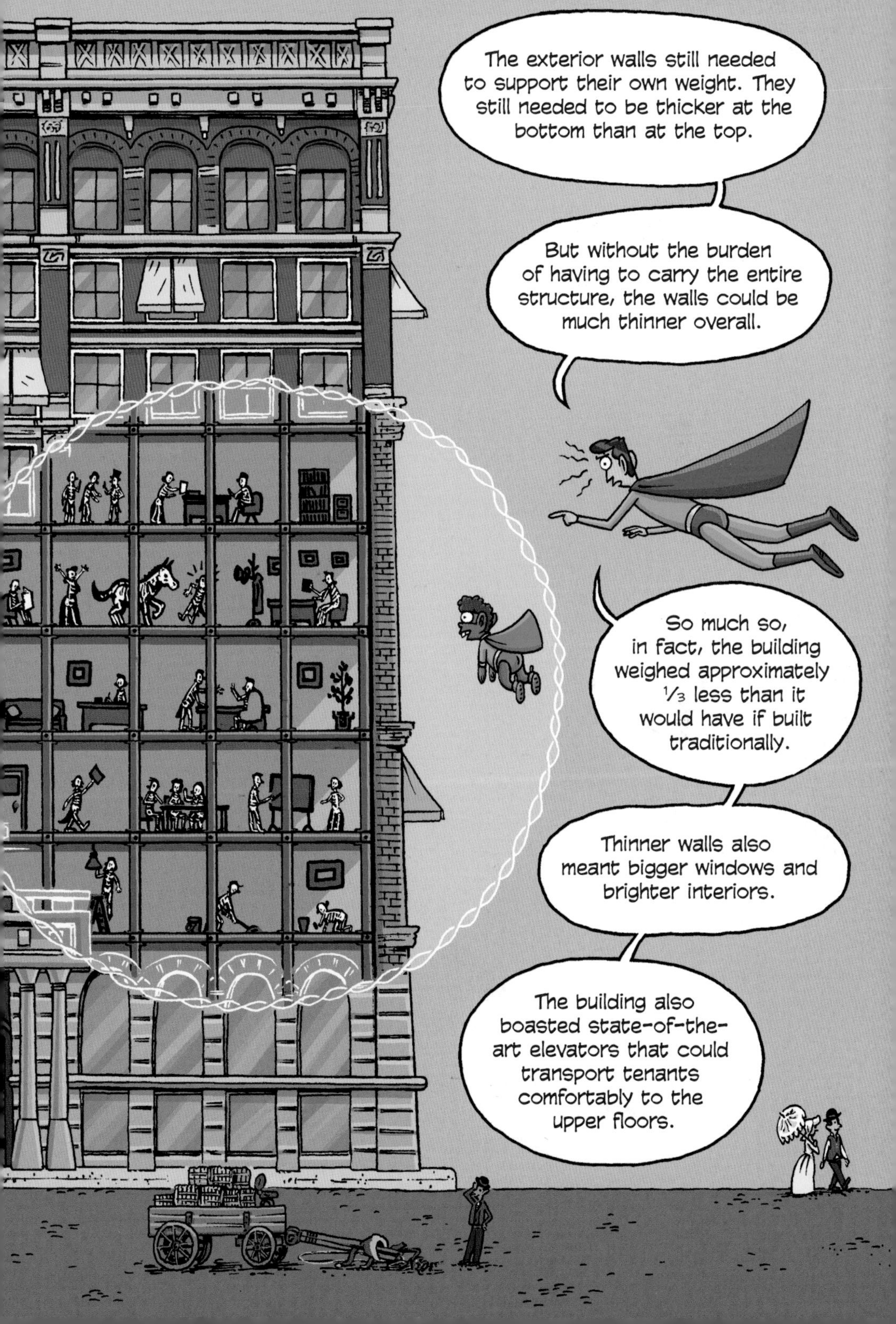
The exterior walls still needed to support their own weight. They still needed to be thicker at the bottom than at the top.
But without the burden of having to carry the entire structure, the walls could be much thinner overall.
So much so, in fact, the building weighed approximately 1/3 less than it would have if built traditionally.
Thinner walls also meant bigger windows and brighter interiors.
The building also boasted state-of-the-art elevators that could transport tenants comfortably to the upper floors.

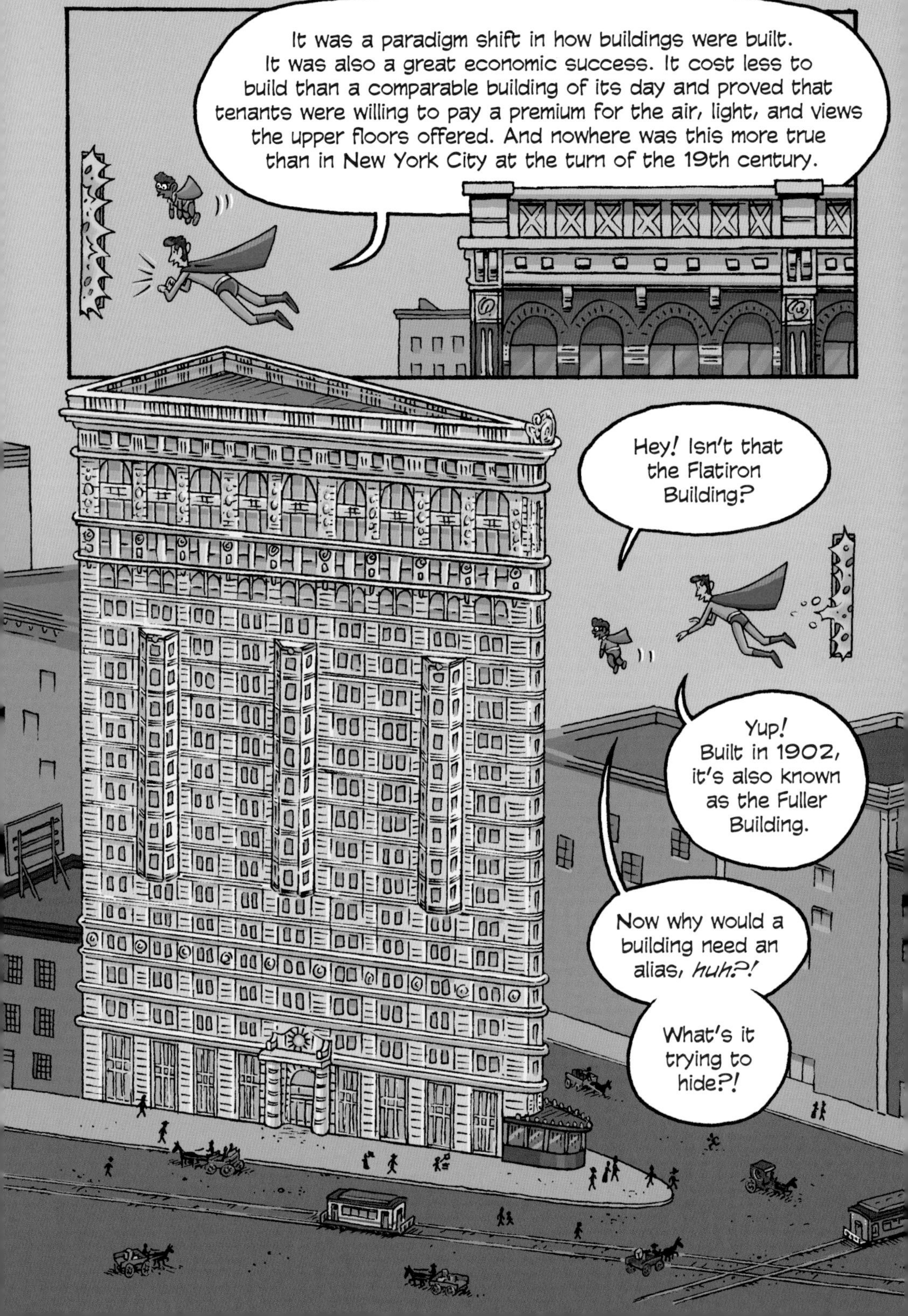
It was a paradigm shift in how buildings were built. It was also a great economic success. It cost less to build than a comparable building of its day and proved that tenants were willing to pay a premium for the air, light, and views the upper floors offered. And nowhere was this more true than in New York City at the turn of the 19th century.
Hey! Isn't that the Flatiron Building?
Yup! Built in 1902, it's also known as the Fuller Building.
Now why would a building need an alias, *huh?!*
What's it trying to hide?!

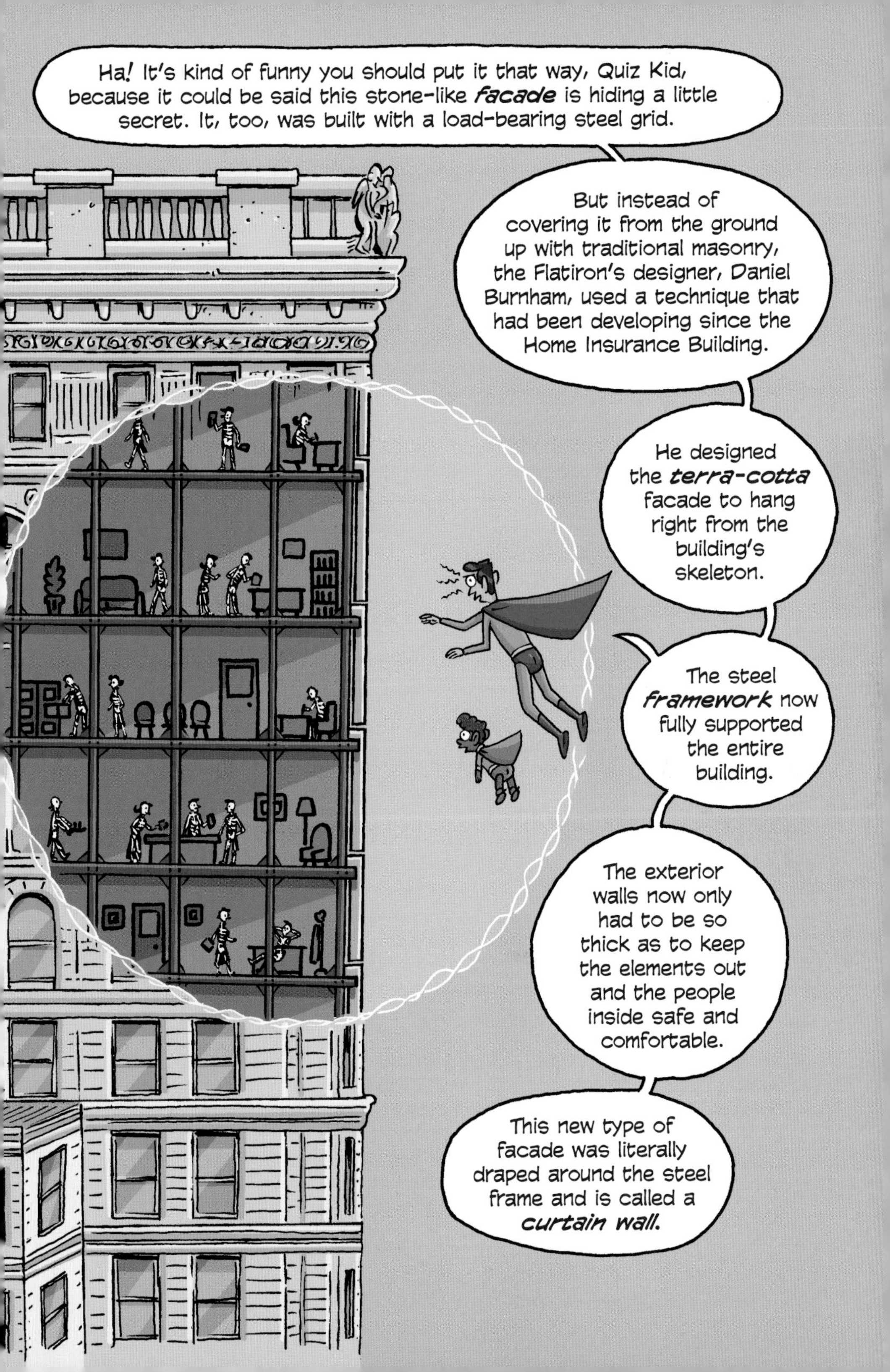
Ha! It's kind of funny you should put it that way, Quiz Kid, because it could be said this stone-like *facade* is hiding a little secret. It, too, was built with a load-bearing steel grid.
But instead of covering it from the ground up with traditional masonry, the Flatiron's designer, Daniel Burnham, used a technique that had been developing since the Home Insurance Building.
He designed the *terra-cotta* facade to hang right from the building's skeleton.
The steel *framework* now fully supported the entire building.
The exterior walls now only had to be so thick as to keep the elements out and the people inside safe and comfortable.
This new type of facade was literally draped around the steel frame and is called a *curtain wall.*

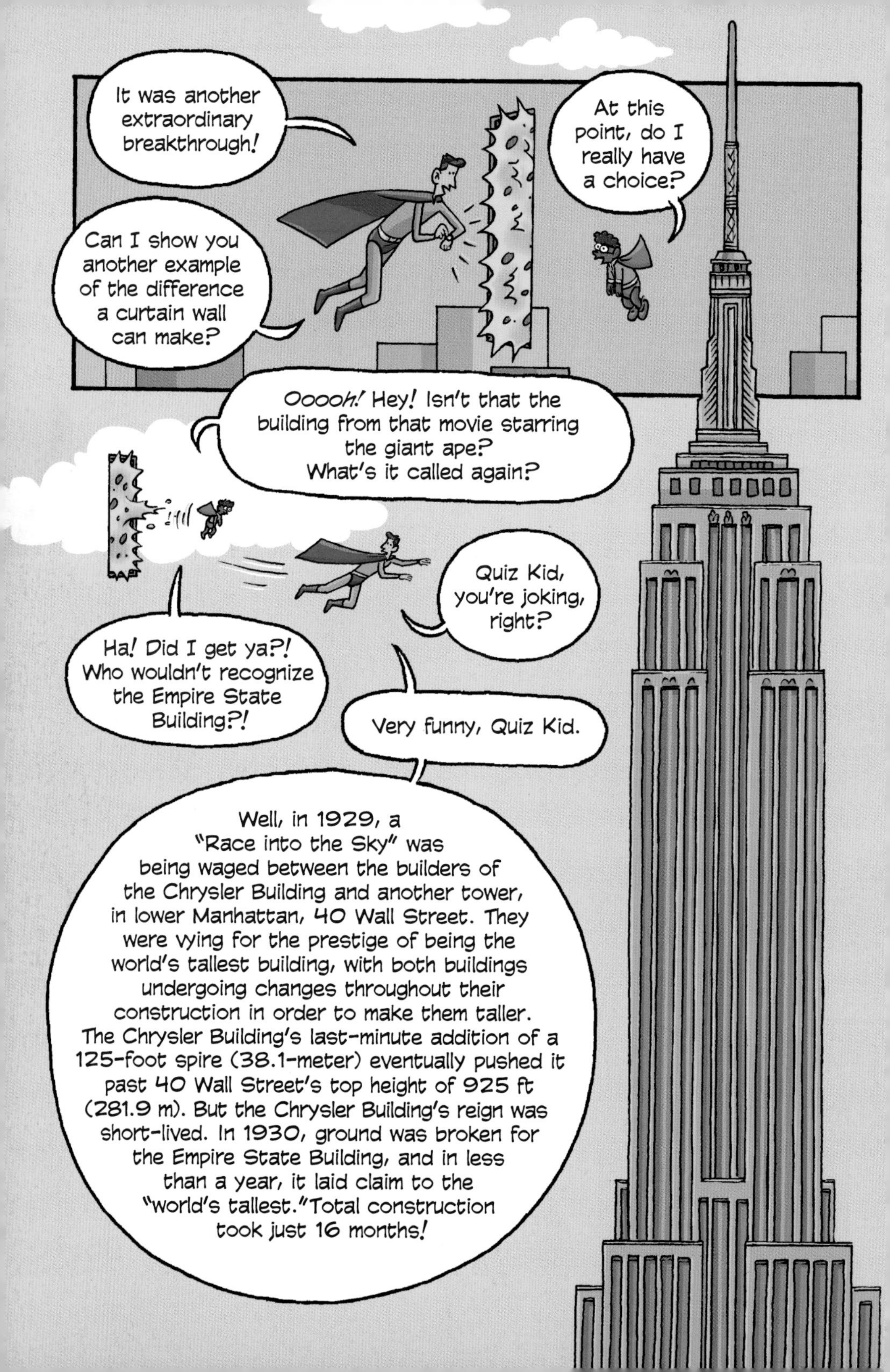
It was another extraordinary breakthrough!
At this point, do I really have a choice?
Can I show you another example of the difference a curtain wall can make?
Ooooh! Hey! Isn't that the building from that movie starring the giant ape? What's it called again?
Quiz Kid, you're joking, right?
Ha! Did I get ya?! Who wouldn't recognize the Empire State Building?!
Very funny, Quiz Kid.
Well, in 1929, a "Race into the Sky" was being waged between the builders of the Chrysler Building and another tower, in lower Manhattan, 40 Wall Street. They were vying for the prestige of being the world's tallest building, with both buildings undergoing changes throughout their construction in order to make them taller. The Chrysler Building's last-minute addition of a 125-foot spire (38.1-meter) eventually pushed it past 40 Wall Street's top height of 925 ft (281.9 m). But the Chrysler Building's reign was short-lived. In 1930, ground was broken for the Empire State Building, and in less than a year, it laid claim to the "world's tallest." Total construction took just 16 months!

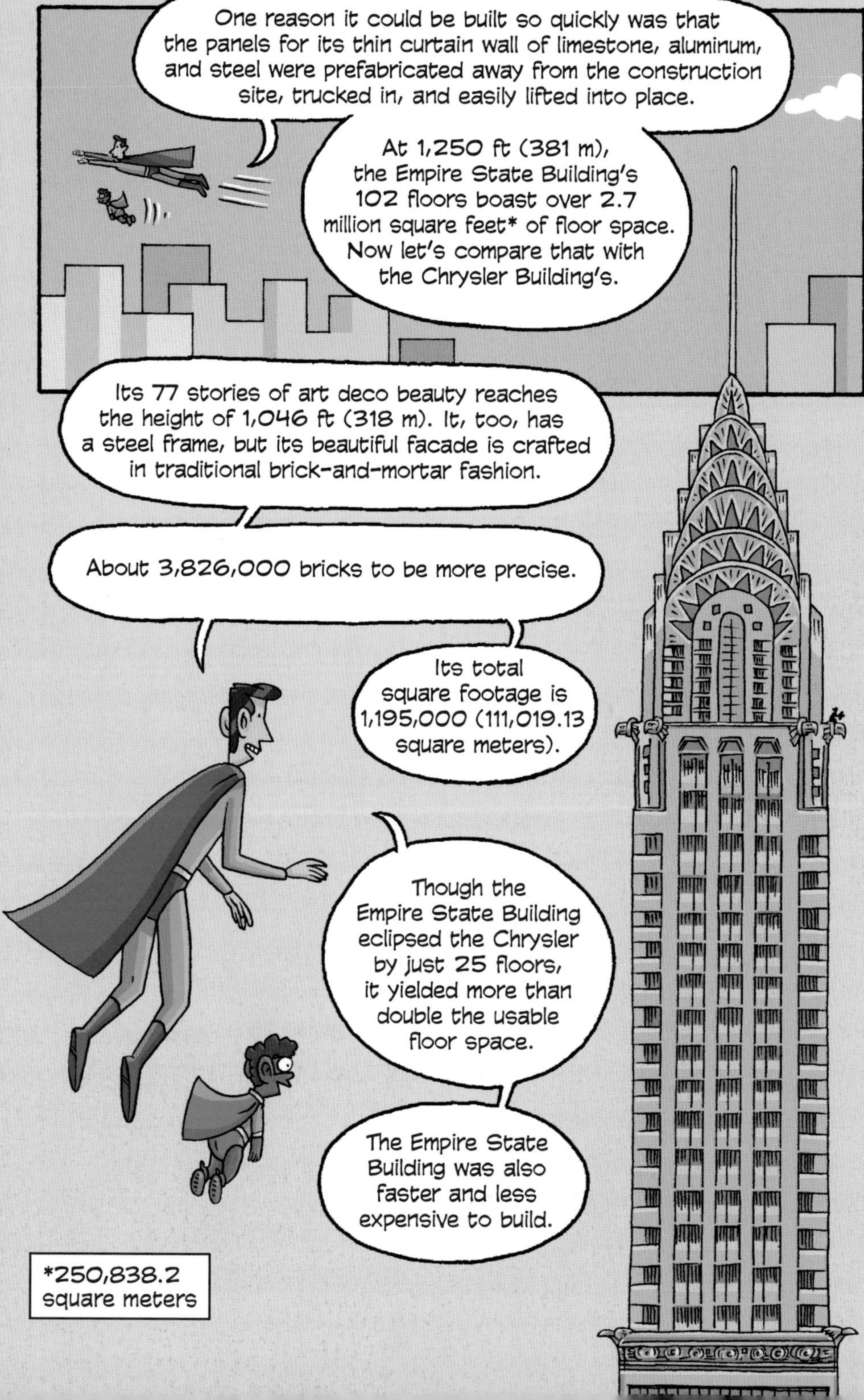
One reason it could be built so quickly was that the panels for its thin curtain wall of limestone, aluminum, and steel were prefabricated away from the construction site, trucked in, and easily lifted into place.
At 1,250 ft (381 m), the Empire State Building's 102 floors boast over 2.7 million square feet* of floor space. Now let's compare that with the Chrysler Building's.
Its 77 stories of art deco beauty reaches the height of 1,046 ft (318 m). It, too, has a steel frame, but its beautiful facade is crafted in traditional brick-and-mortar fashion.
About 3,826,000 bricks to be more precise.
Its total square footage is 1,195,000 (111,019.13 square meters).
Though the Empire State Building eclipsed the Chrysler by just 25 floors, it yielded more than double the usable floor space.
The Empire State Building was also faster and less expensive to build.
*250,838.2 square meters

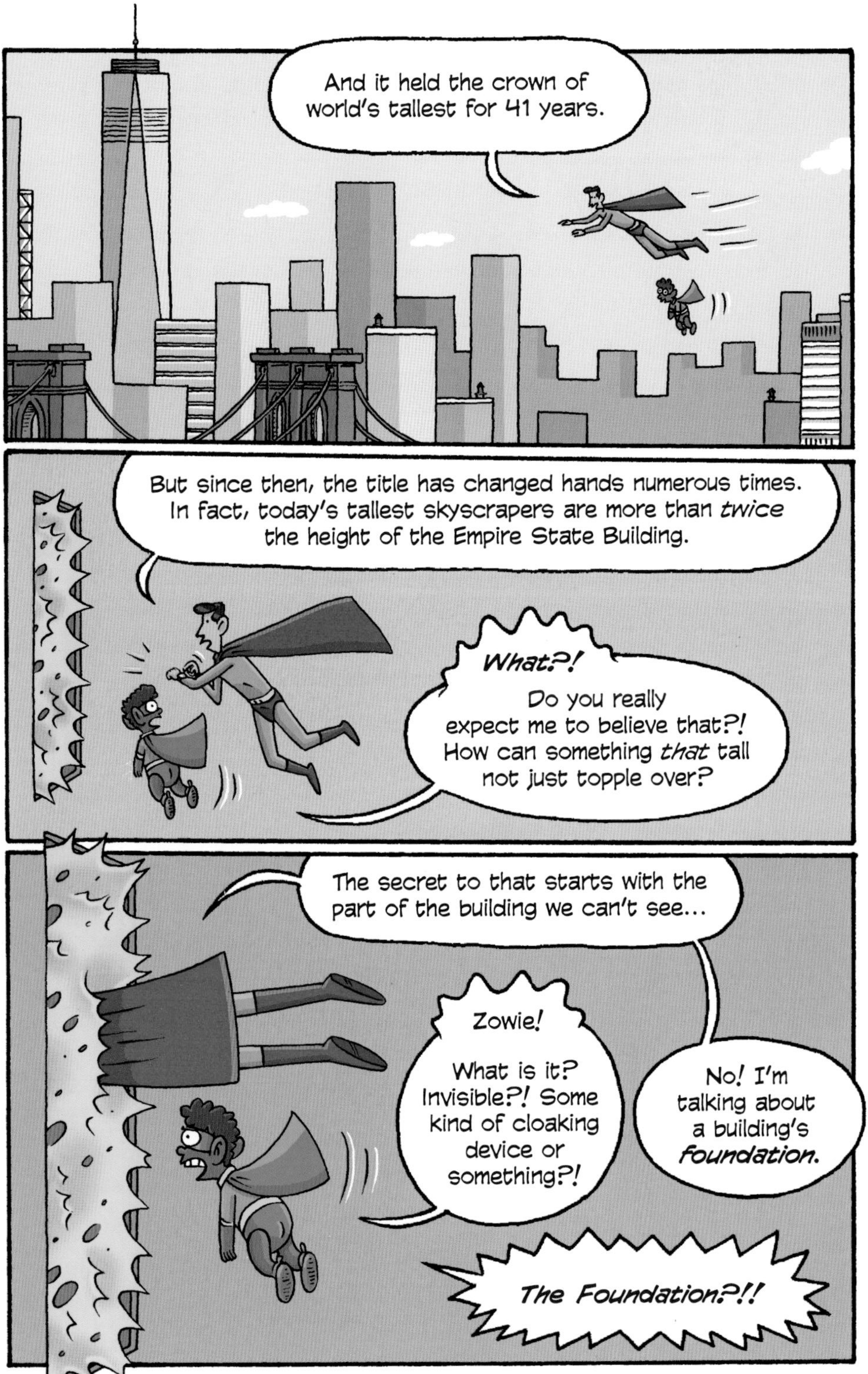

And it held the crown of world's tallest for 41 years.
But since then, the title has changed hands numerous times. In fact, today's tallest skyscrapers are more than *twice* the height of the Empire State Building.
What?!
Do you really expect me to believe that?! How can something *that* tall not just topple over?
The secret to that starts with the part of the building we can't see...
Zowie!
What is it? Invisible?! Some kind of cloaking device or something?!
No! I'm talking about a building's ***foundation.***
The Foundation?!!

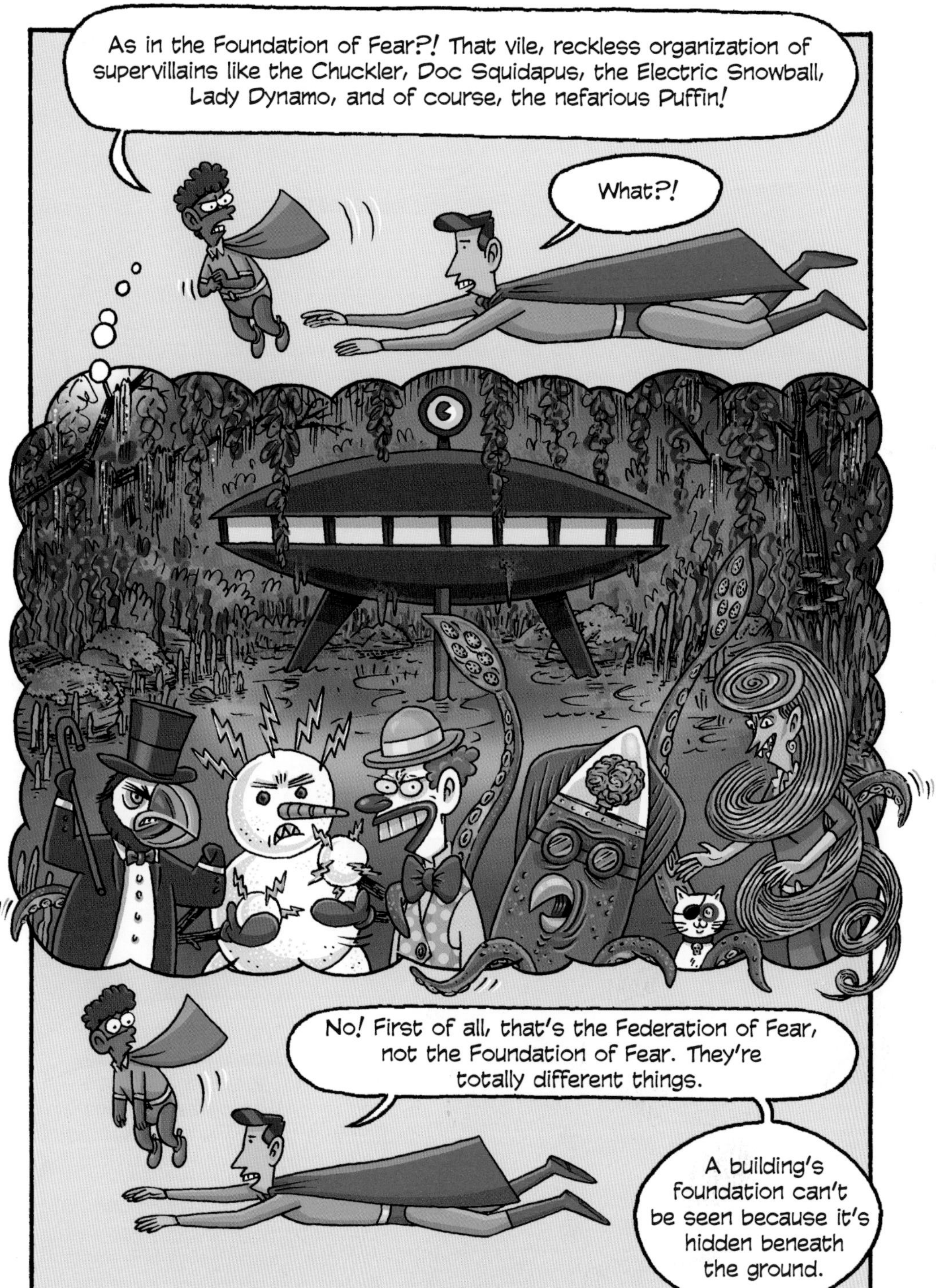
As in the Foundation of Fear?! That vile, reckless organization of supervillains like the Chuckler, Doc Squidapus, the Electric Snowball, Lady Dynamo, and of course, the nefarious Puffin!
What?!
No! First of all, that's the Federation of Fear, not the Foundation of Fear. They're totally different things.
A building's foundation can't be seen because it's hidden beneath the ground.

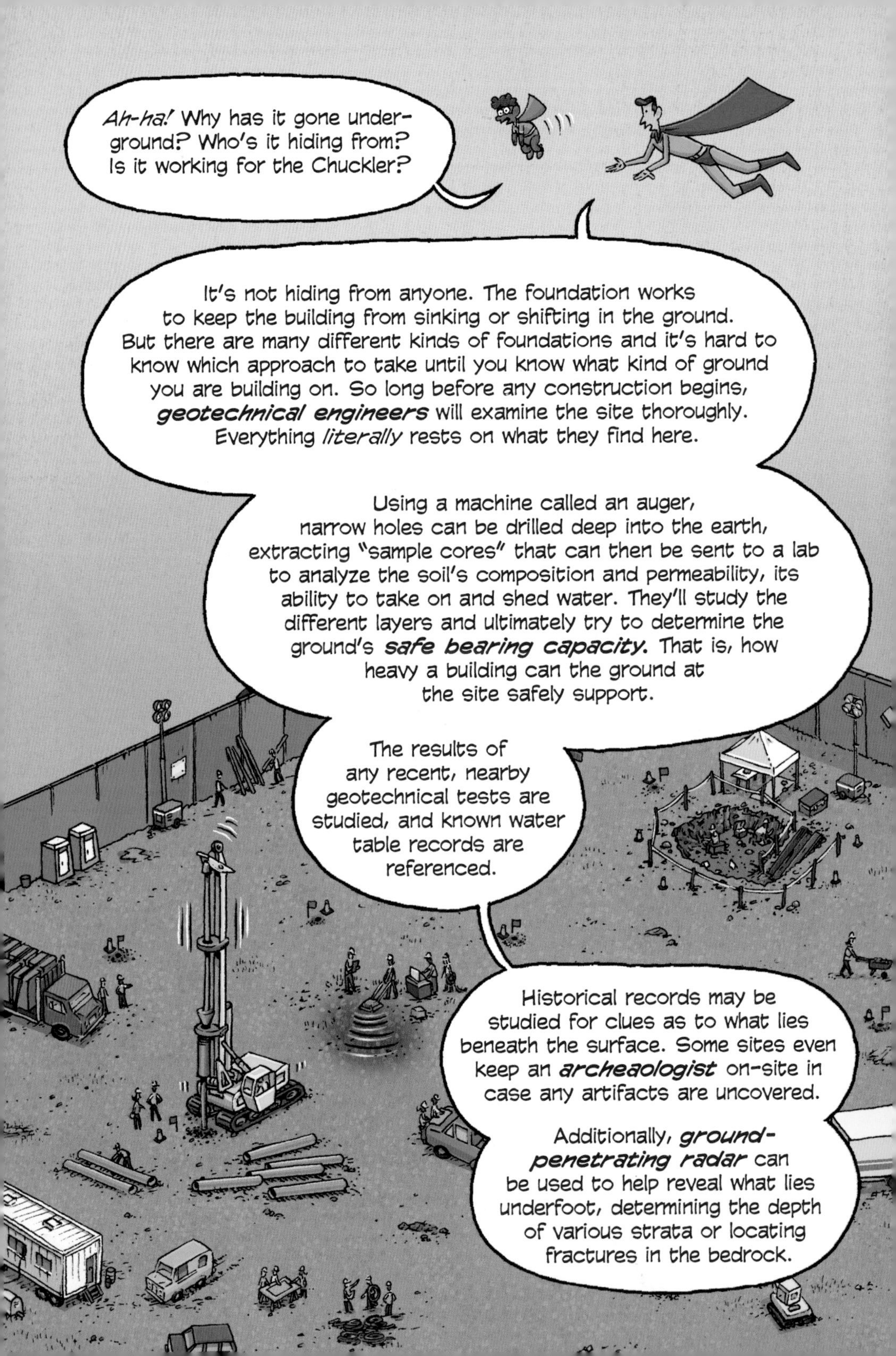

Ah-ha! Why has it gone underground? Who's it hiding from? Is it working for the Chuckler?
It's not hiding from anyone. The foundation works to keep the building from sinking or shifting in the ground. But there are many different kinds of foundations and it's hard to know which approach to take until you know what kind of ground you are building on. So long before any construction begins, ***geotechnical engineers*** will examine the site thoroughly. Everything *literally* rests on what they find here.
Using a machine called an auger, narrow holes can be drilled deep into the earth, extracting "sample cores" that can then be sent to a lab to analyze the soil's composition and permeability, its ability to take on and shed water. They'll study the different layers and ultimately try to determine the ground's ***safe bearing capacity.*** That is, how heavy a building can the ground at the site safely support.
The results of any recent, nearby geotechnical tests are studied, and known water table records are referenced.
Historical records may be studied for clues as to what lies beneath the surface. Some sites even keep an ***archeaologist*** on-site in case any artifacts are uncovered.
Additionally, ***ground-penetrating radar*** can be used to help reveal what lies underfoot, determining the depth of various strata or locating fractures in the bedrock.

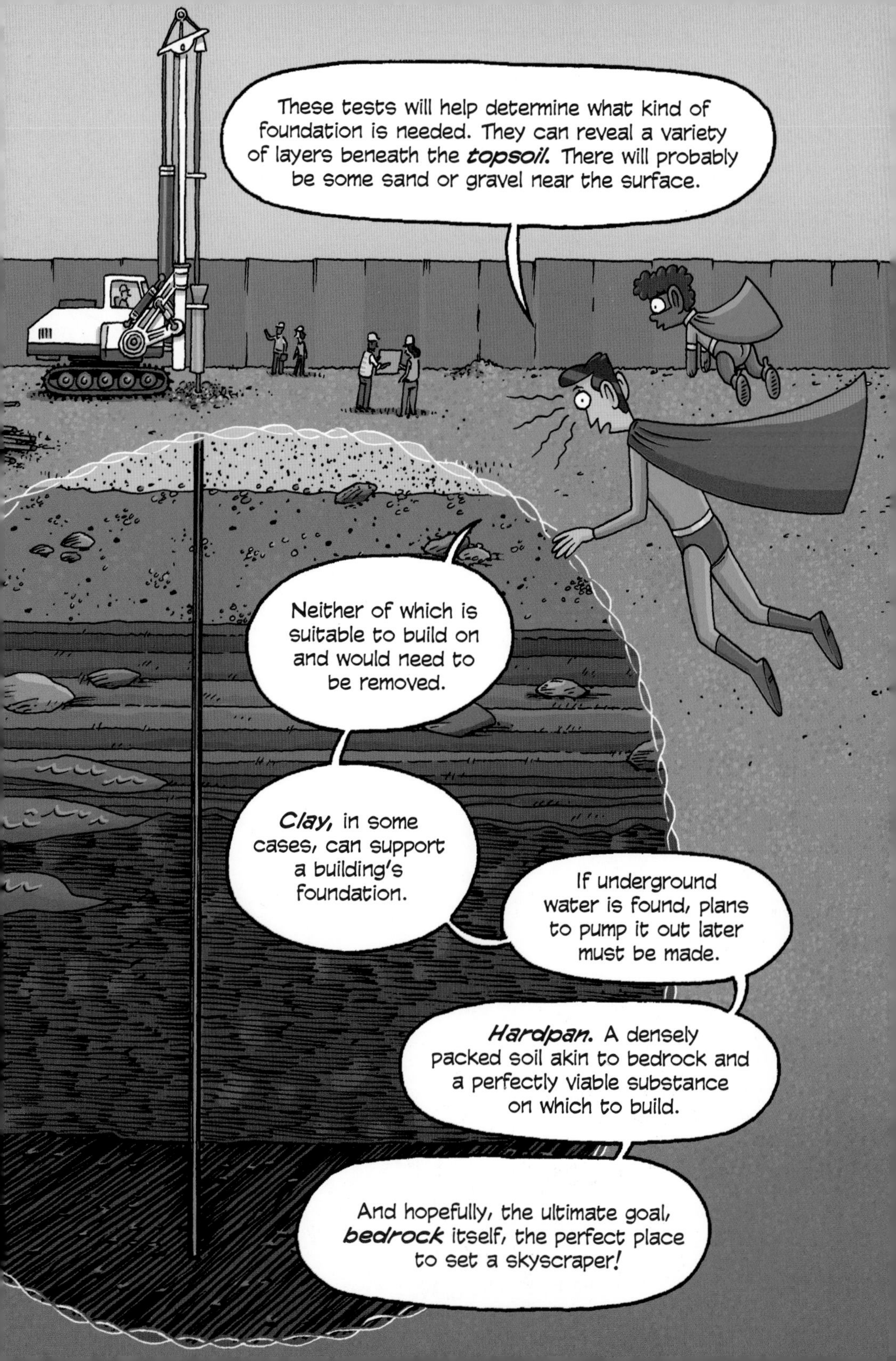
These tests will help determine what kind of foundation is needed. They can reveal a variety of layers beneath the *topsoil.* There will probably be some sand or gravel near the surface.
Neither of which is suitable to build on and would need to be removed.
Clay, in some cases, can support a building's foundation.
If underground water is found, plans to pump it out later must be made.
Hardpan. A densely packed soil akin to bedrock and a perfectly viable substance on which to build.
And hopefully, the ultimate goal, *bedrock* itself, the perfect place to set a skyscraper!

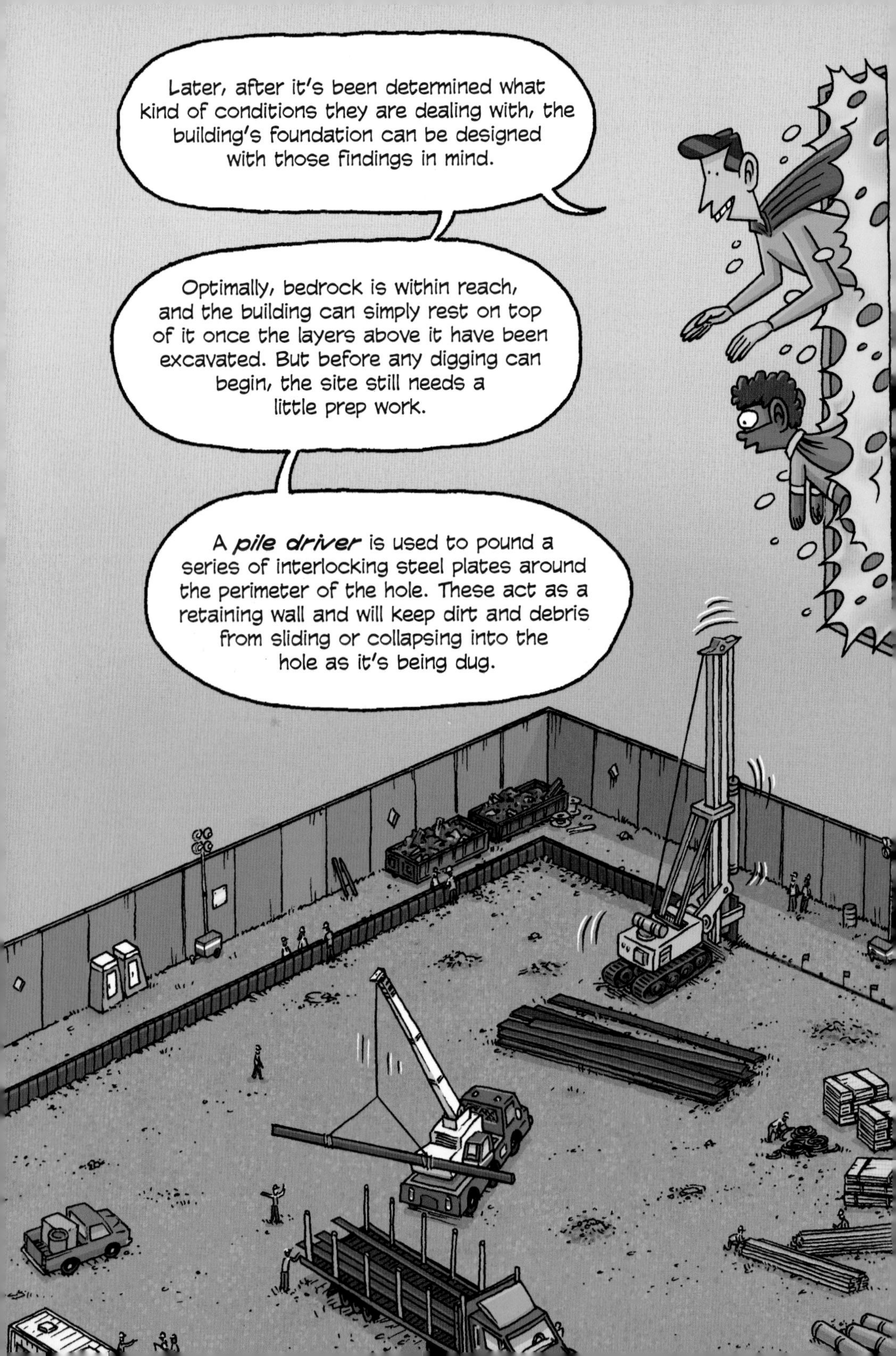
Later, after it's been determined what kind of conditions they are dealing with, the building's foundation can be designed with those findings in mind.
Optimally, bedrock is within reach, and the building can simply rest on top of it once the layers above it have been excavated. But before any digging can begin, the site still needs a little prep work.
A *pile driver* is used to pound a series of interlocking steel plates around the perimeter of the hole. These act as a retaining wall and will keep dirt and debris from sliding or collapsing into the hole as it's being dug.

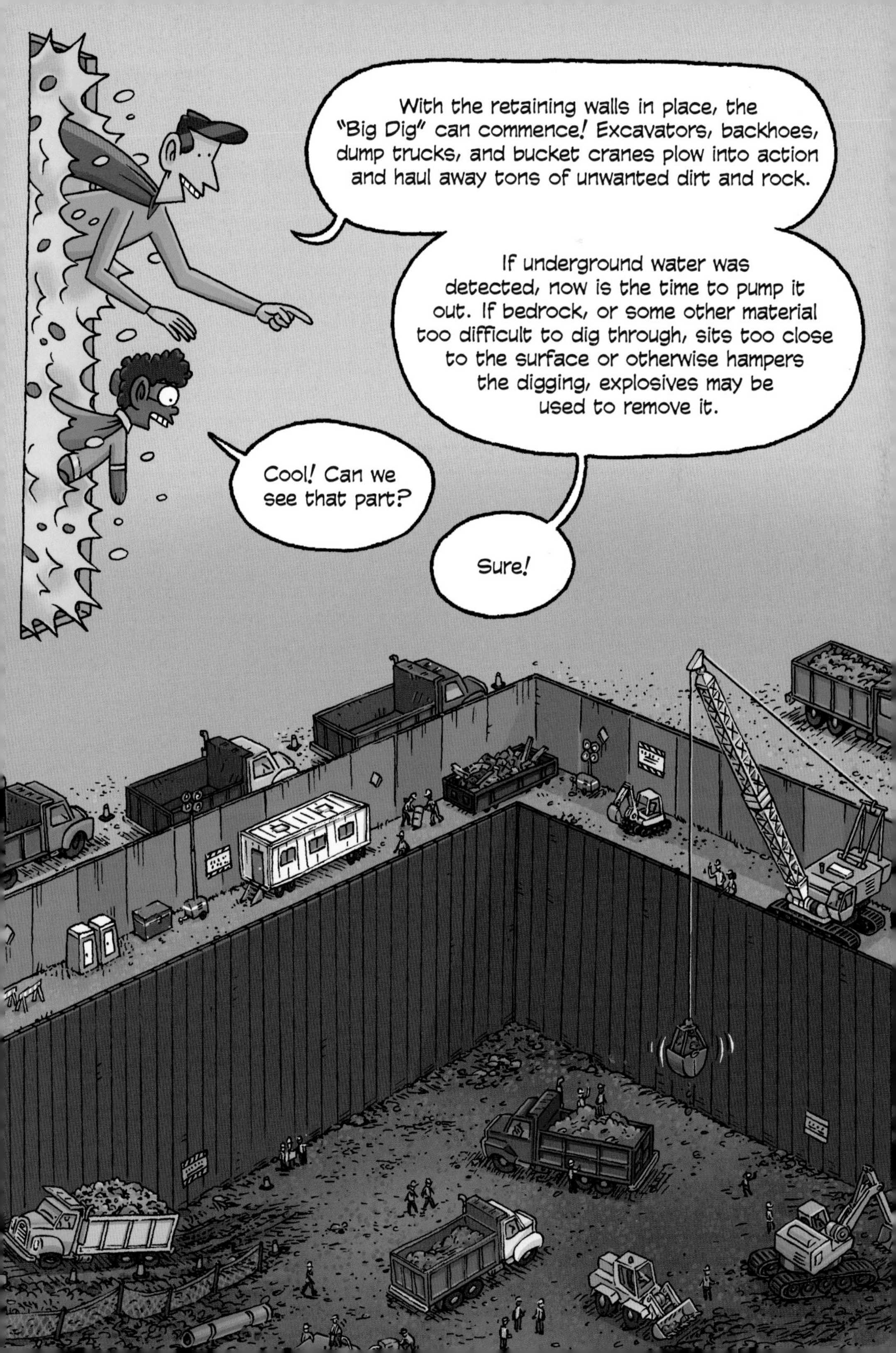
With the retaining walls in place, the "Big Dig" can commence! Excavators, backhoes, dump trucks, and bucket cranes plow into action and haul away tons of unwanted dirt and rock.
If underground water was detected, now is the time to pump it out. If bedrock, or some other material too difficult to dig through, sits too close to the surface or otherwise hampers the digging, explosives may be used to remove it.
Cool! Can we see that part?
Sure!

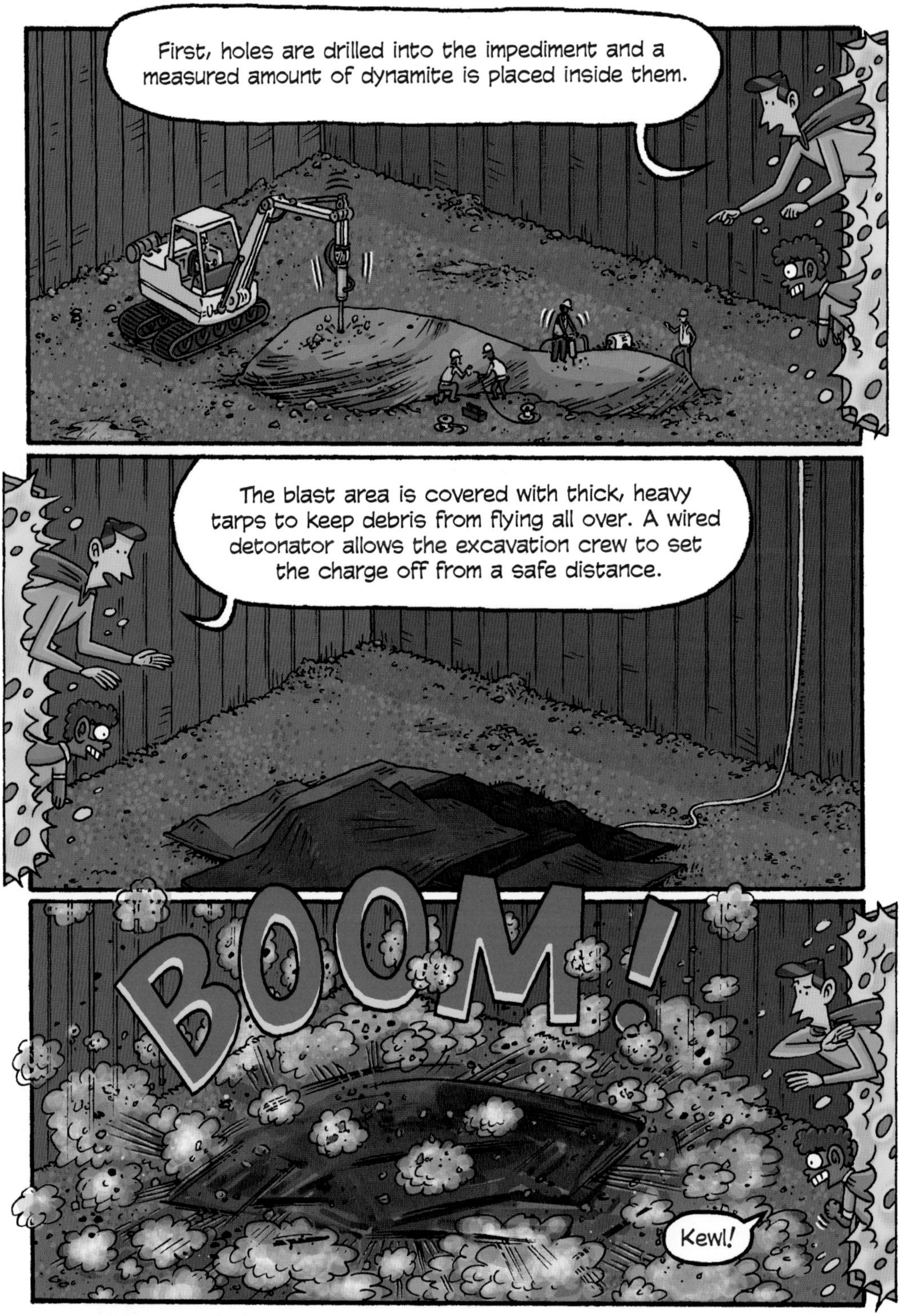
First, holes are drilled into the impediment and a measured amount of dynamite is placed inside them.
The blast area is covered with thick, heavy tarps to keep debris from flying all over. A wired detonator allows the excavation crew to set the charge off from a safe distance.
BOOM!
Kewl!

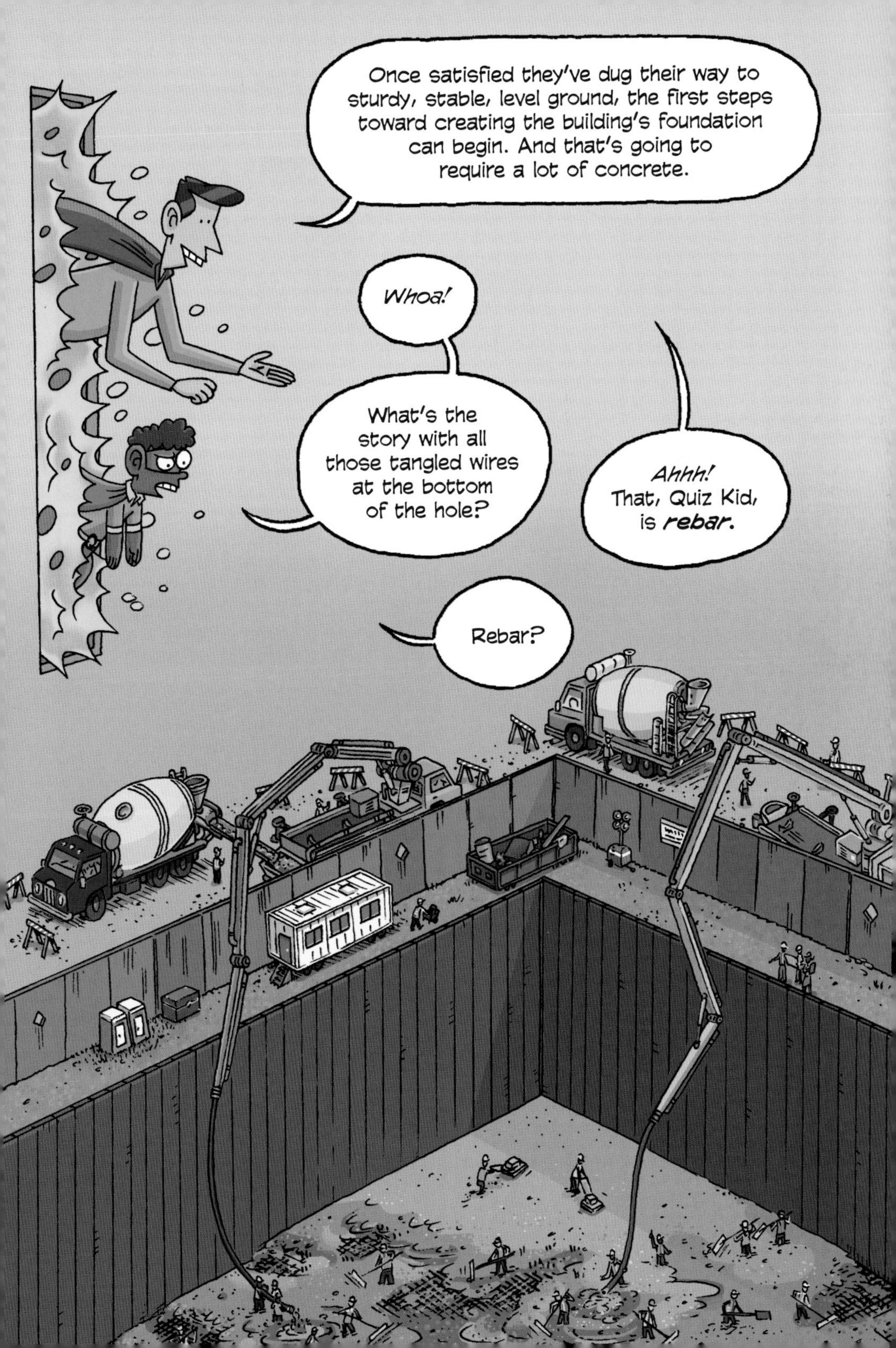
Once satisfied they've dug their way to sturdy, stable, level ground, the first steps toward creating the building's foundation can begin. And that's going to require a lot of concrete.
Whoa!
What's the story with all those tangled wires at the bottom of the hole?
Ahhh! That, Quiz Kid, is ***rebar***.
Rebar?

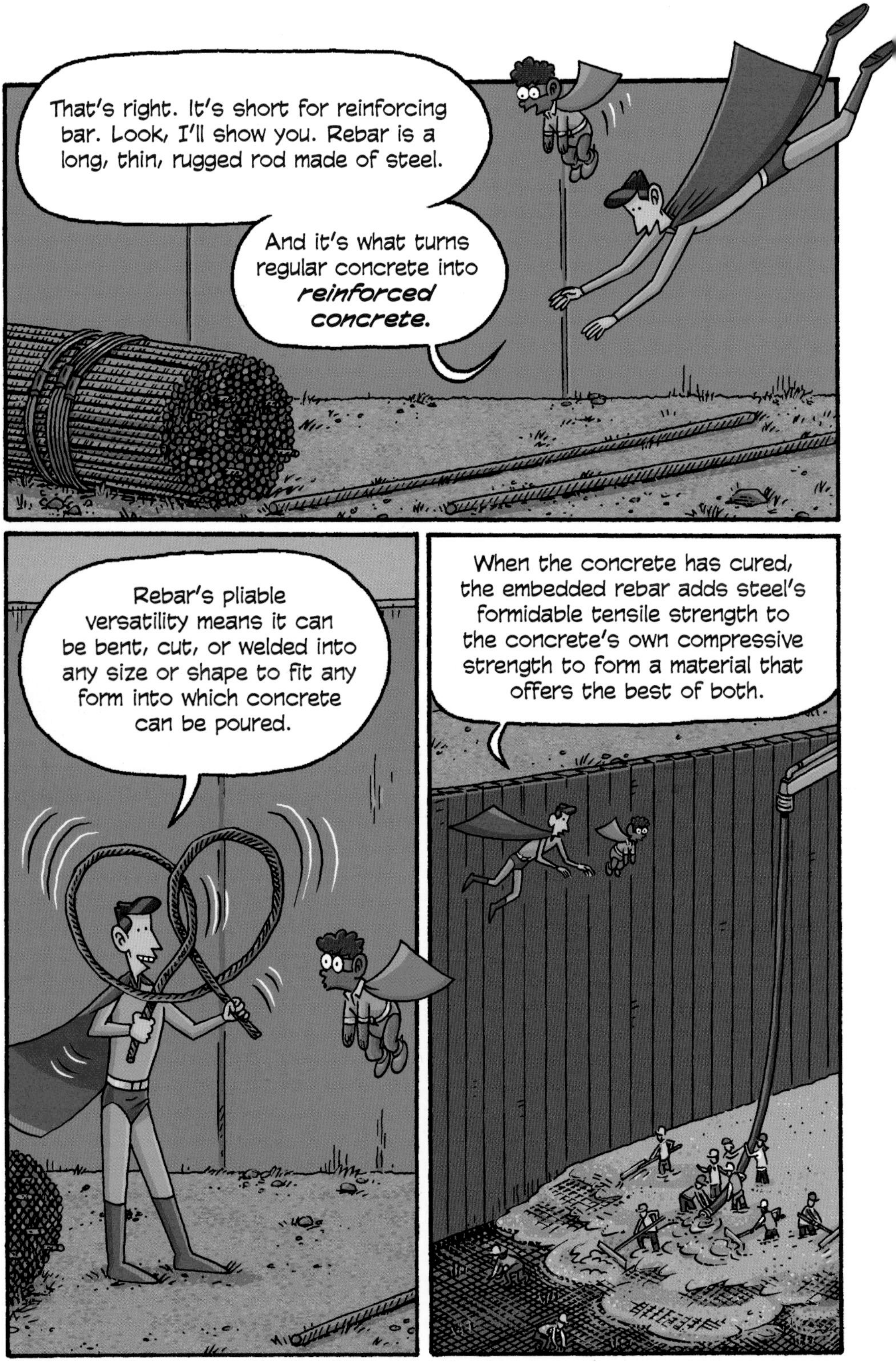
That's right. It's short for reinforcing bar. Look, I'll show you. Rebar is a long, thin, rugged rod made of steel.
And it's what turns regular concrete into *reinforced concrete.*
Rebar's pliable versatility means it can be bent, cut, or welded into any size or shape to fit any form into which concrete can be poured.
When the concrete has cured, the embedded rebar adds steel's formidable tensile strength to the concrete's own compressive strength to form a material that offers the best of both.

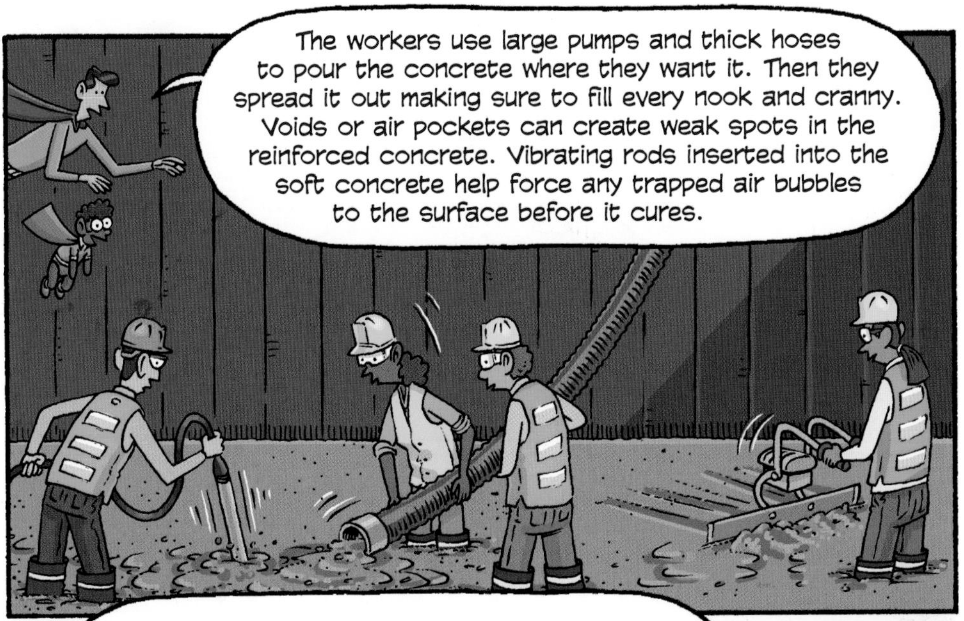
The workers use large pumps and thick hoses to pour the concrete where they want it. Then they spread it out making sure to fill every nook and cranny. Voids or air pockets can create weak spots in the reinforced concrete. Vibrating rods inserted into the soft concrete help force any trapped air bubbles to the surface before it cures.

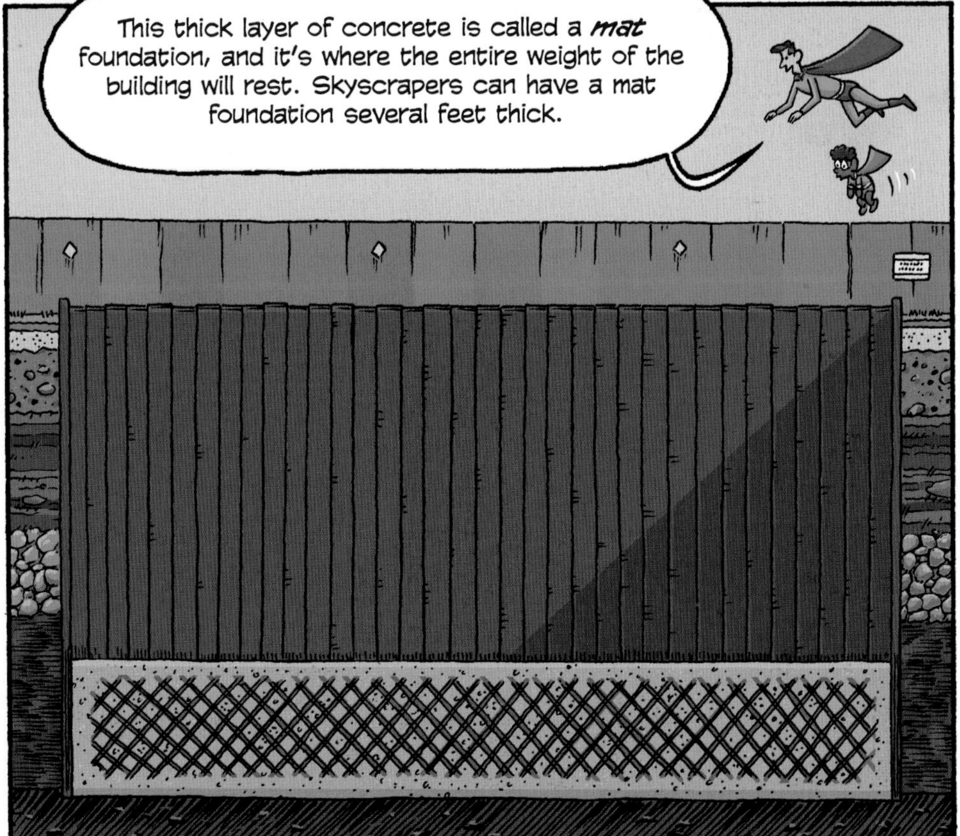
This thick layer of concrete is called a *mat* foundation, and it's where the entire weight of the building will rest. Skyscrapers can have a mat foundation several feet thick.

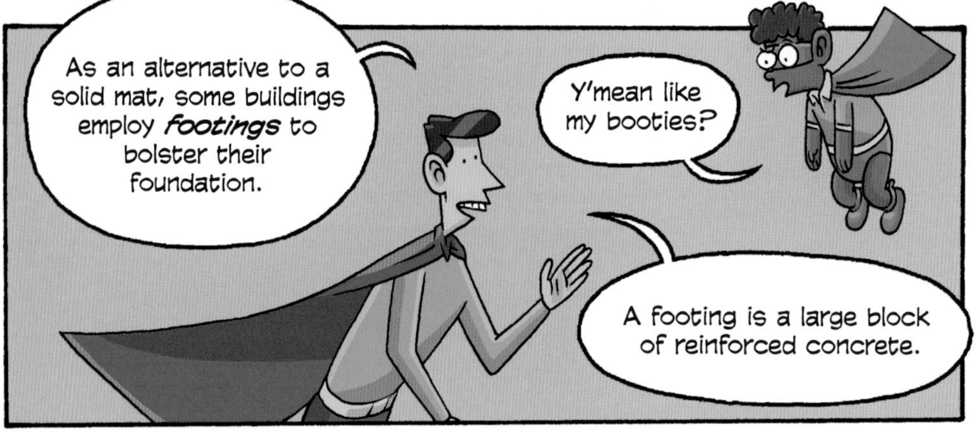
As an alternative to a solid mat, some buildings employ *footings* to bolster their foundation.
Y'mean like my booties?
A footing is a large block of reinforced concrete.

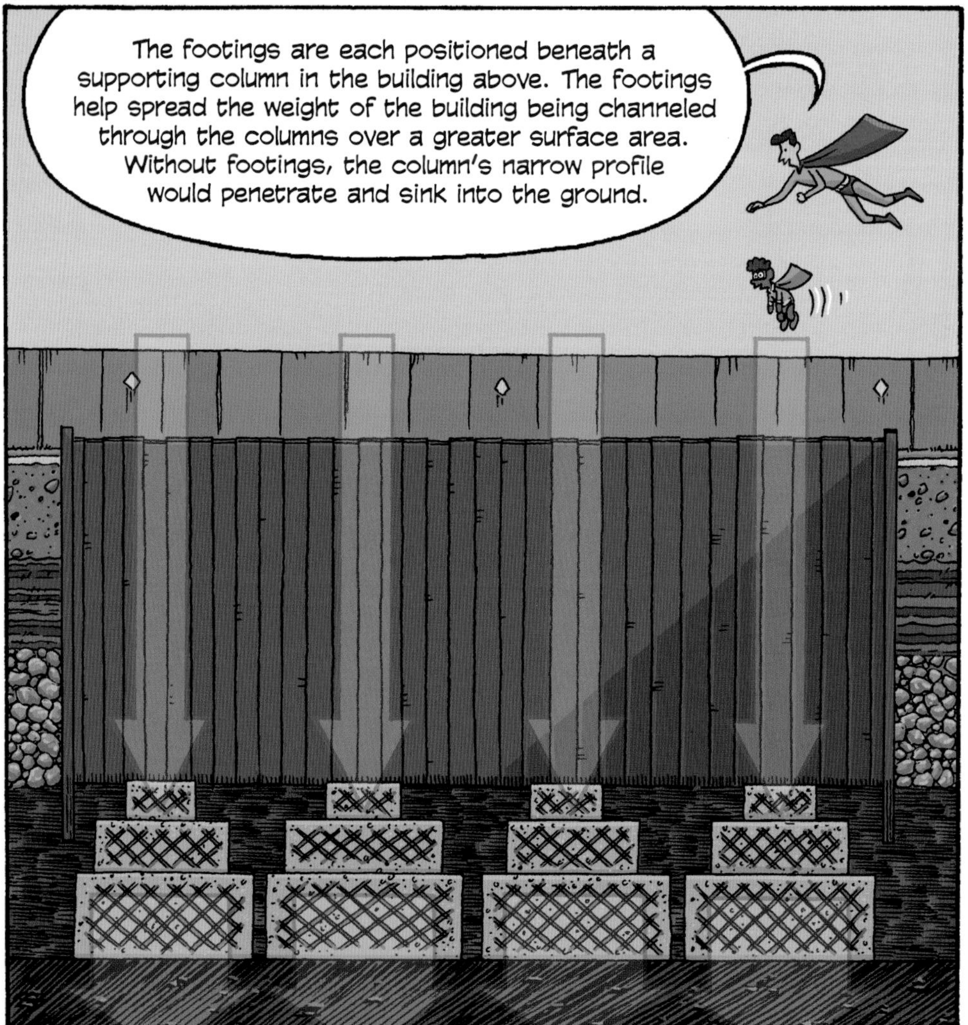
The footings are each positioned beneath a supporting column in the building above. The footings help spread the weight of the building being channeled through the columns over a greater surface area. Without footings, the column's narrow profile would penetrate and sink into the ground.

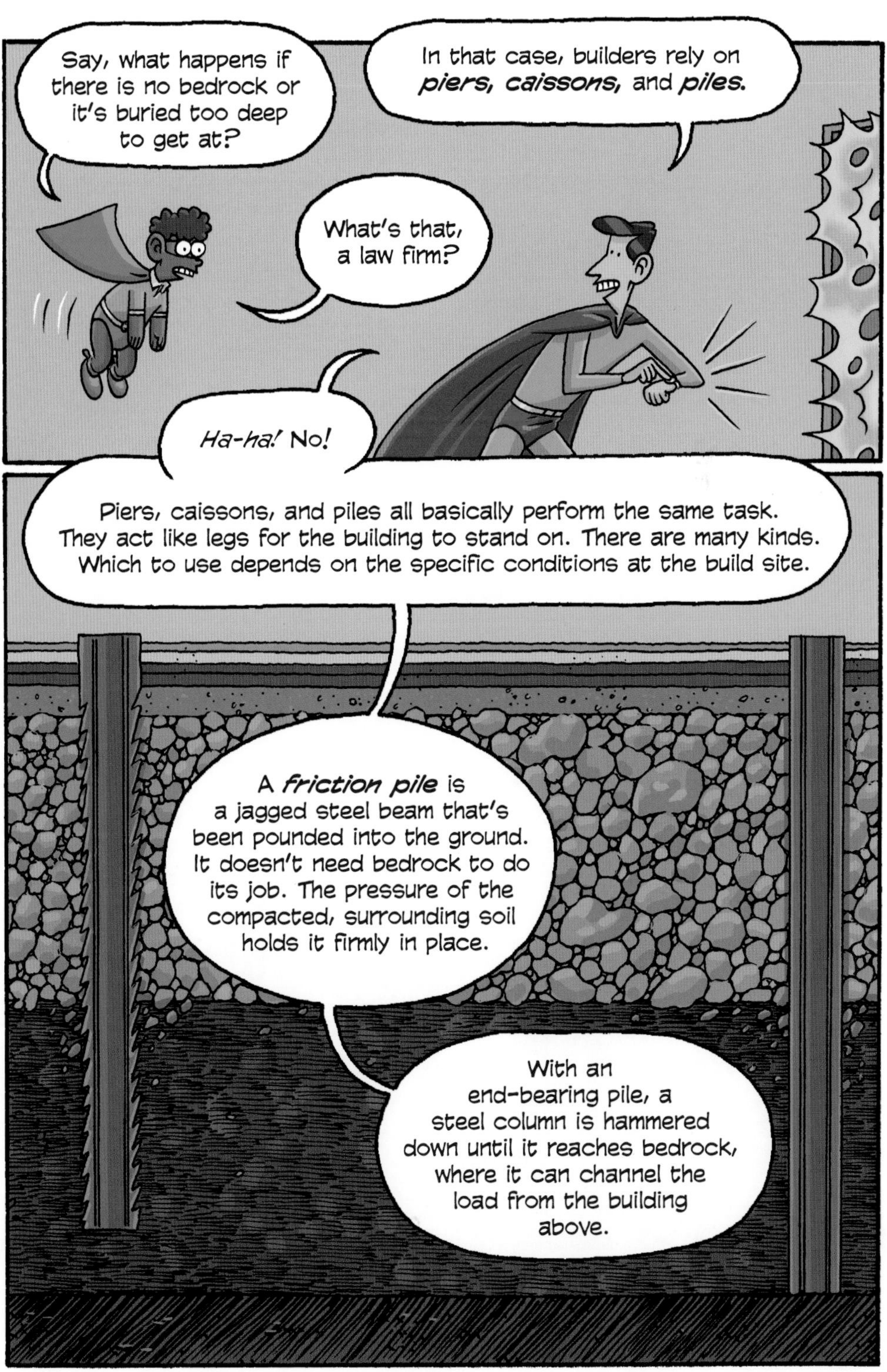
Say, what happens if there is no bedrock or it's buried too deep to get at?
In that case, builders rely on *piers, caissons,* and *piles.*
What's that, a law firm?
Ha-ha! No!
Piers, caissons, and piles all basically perform the same task. They act like legs for the building to stand on. There are many kinds. Which to use depends on the specific conditions at the build site.
A *friction pile* is a jagged steel beam that's been pounded into the ground. It doesn't need bedrock to do its job. The pressure of the compacted, surrounding soil holds it firmly in place.
With an end-bearing pile, a steel column is hammered down until it reaches bedrock, where it can channel the load from the building above.

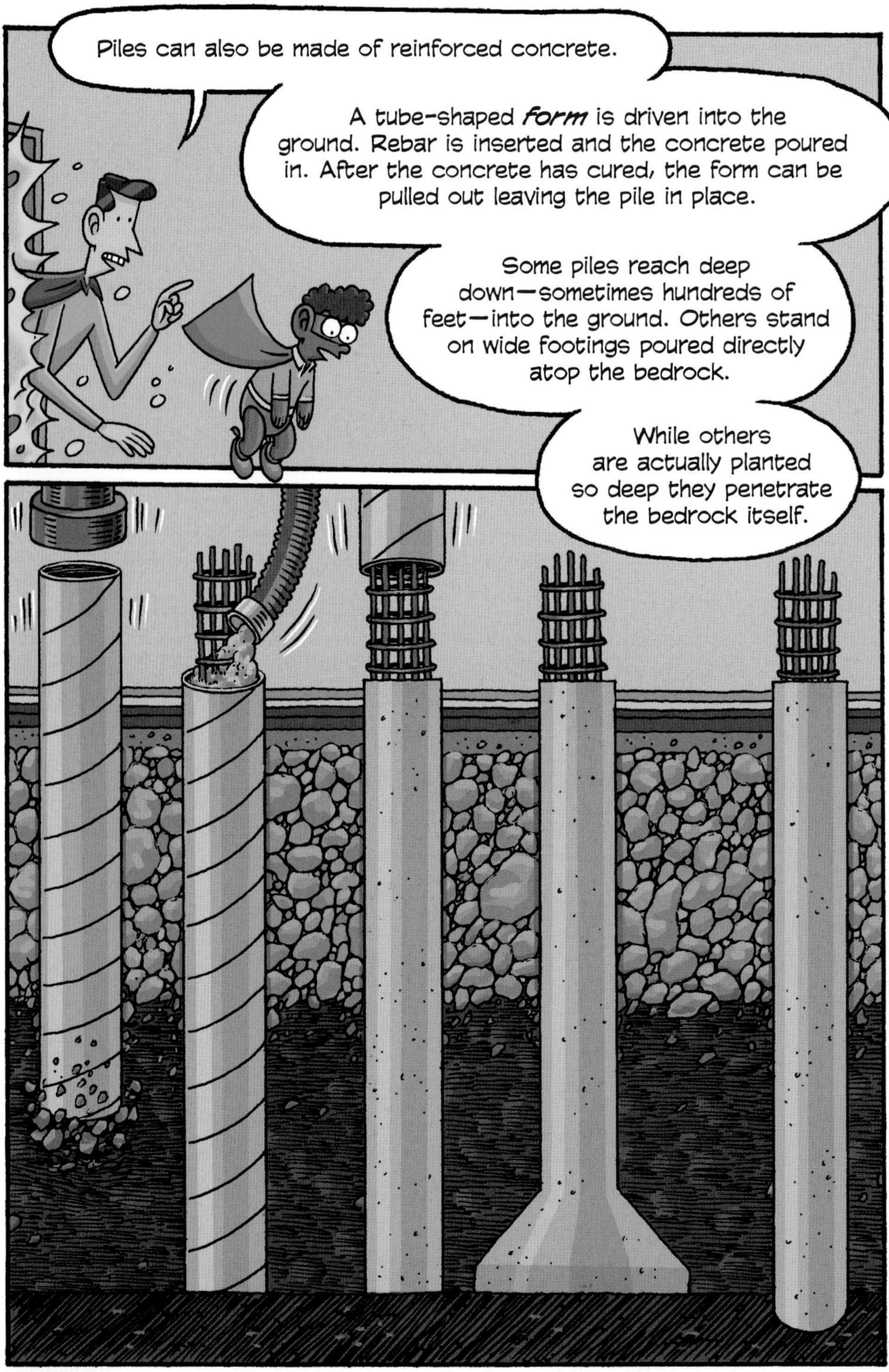
Piles can also be made of reinforced concrete.
A tube-shaped *form* is driven into the ground. Rebar is inserted and the concrete poured in. After the concrete has cured, the form can be pulled out leaving the pile in place.
Some piles reach deep down—sometimes hundreds of feet—into the ground. Others stand on wide footings poured directly atop the bedrock.
While others are actually planted so deep they penetrate the bedrock itself.

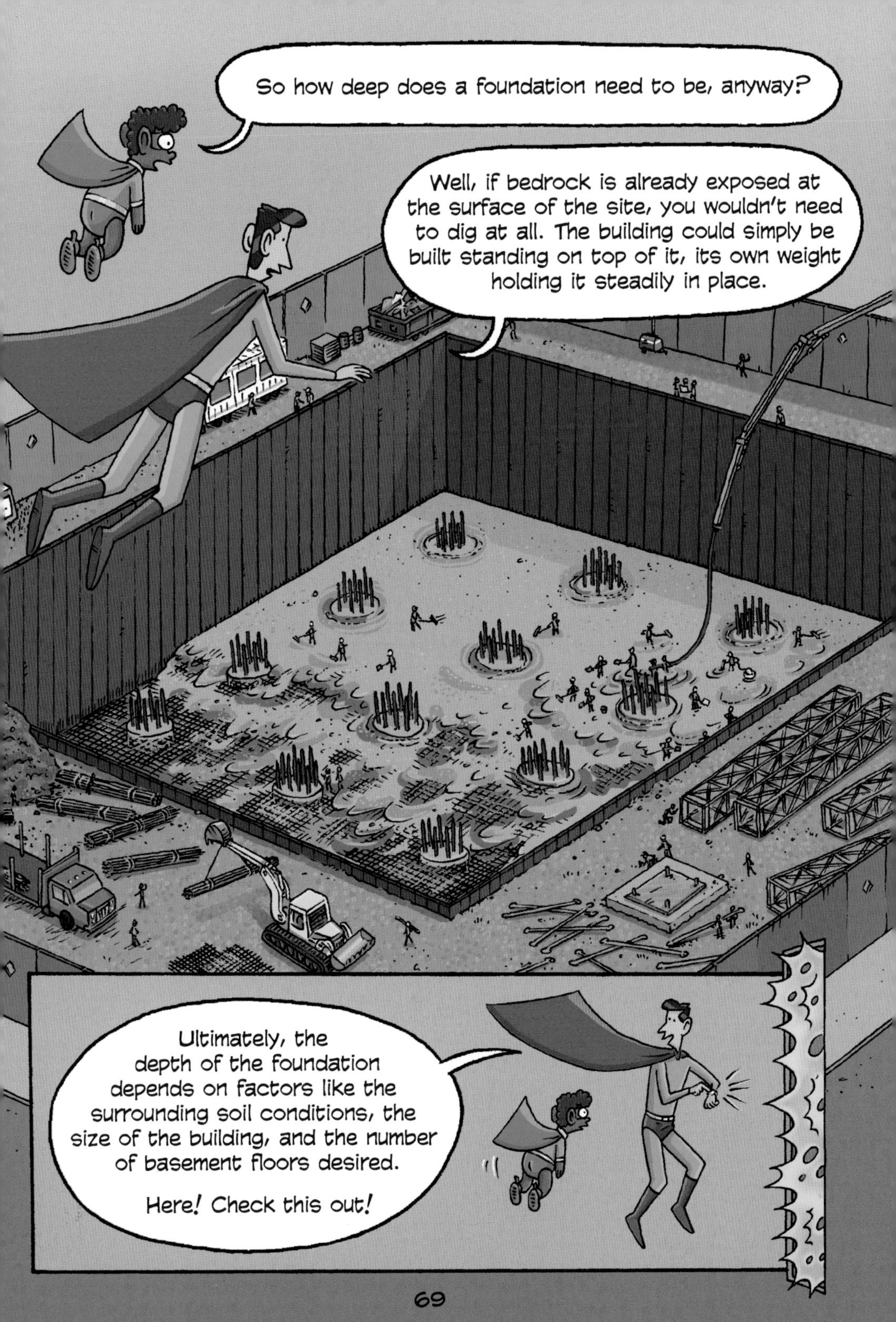
So how deep does a foundation need to be, anyway?
Well, if bedrock is already exposed at the surface of the site, you wouldn't need to dig at all. The building could simply be built standing on top of it, its own weight holding it steadily in place.
Ultimately, the depth of the foundation depends on factors like the surrounding soil conditions, the size of the building, and the number of basement floors desired.
Here! Check this out!

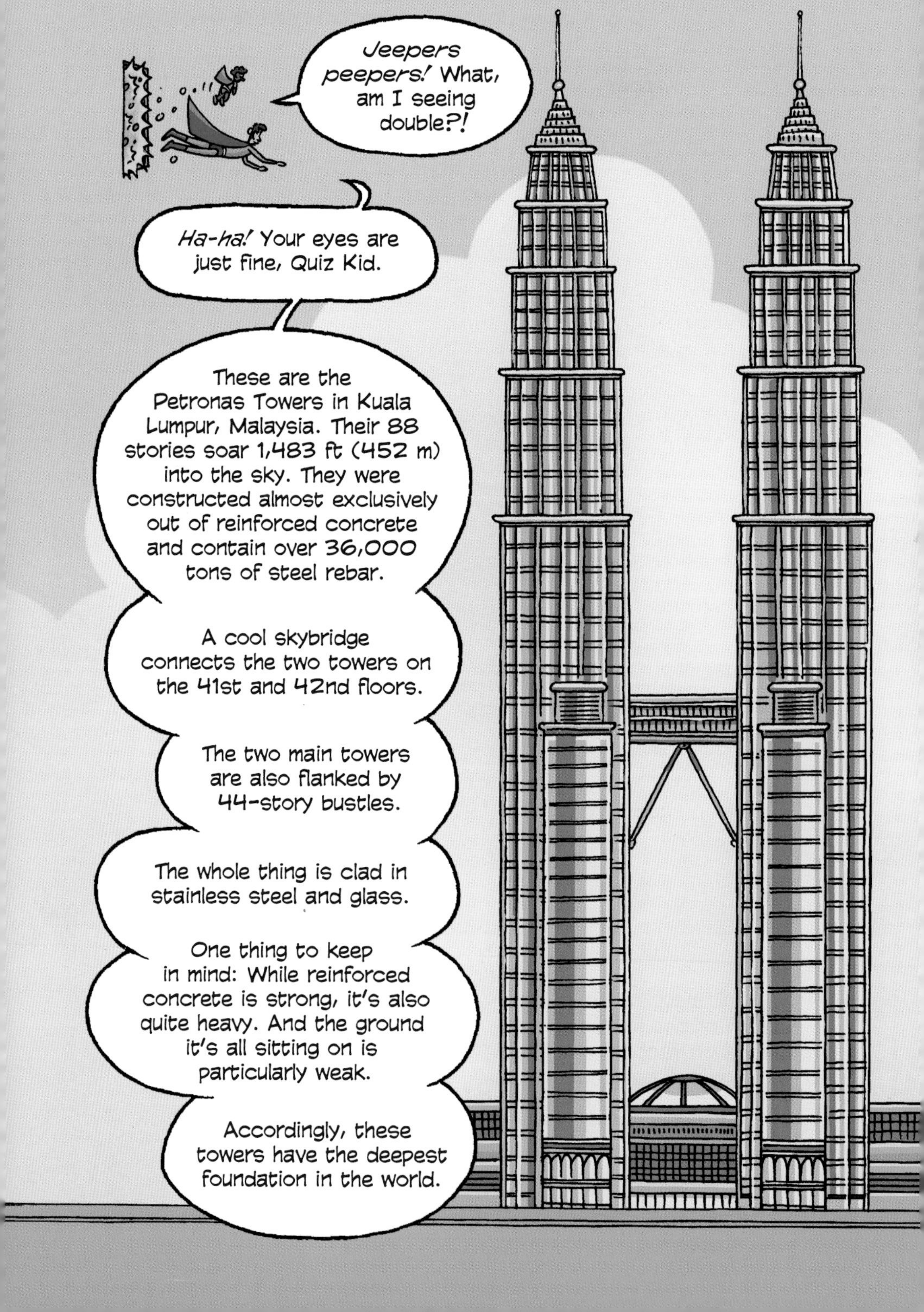
Jeepers peepers! What, am I seeing double?!
Ha-ha! Your eyes are just fine, Quiz Kid.
These are the Petronas Towers in Kuala Lumpur, Malaysia. Their 88 stories soar 1,483 ft (452 m) into the sky. They were constructed almost exclusively out of reinforced concrete and contain over 36,000 tons of steel rebar.
A cool skybridge connects the two towers on the 41st and 42nd floors.
The two main towers are also flanked by 44-story bustles.
The whole thing is clad in stainless steel and glass.
One thing to keep in mind: While reinforced concrete is strong, it's also quite heavy. And the ground it's all sitting on is particularly weak.
Accordingly, these towers have the deepest foundation in the world.

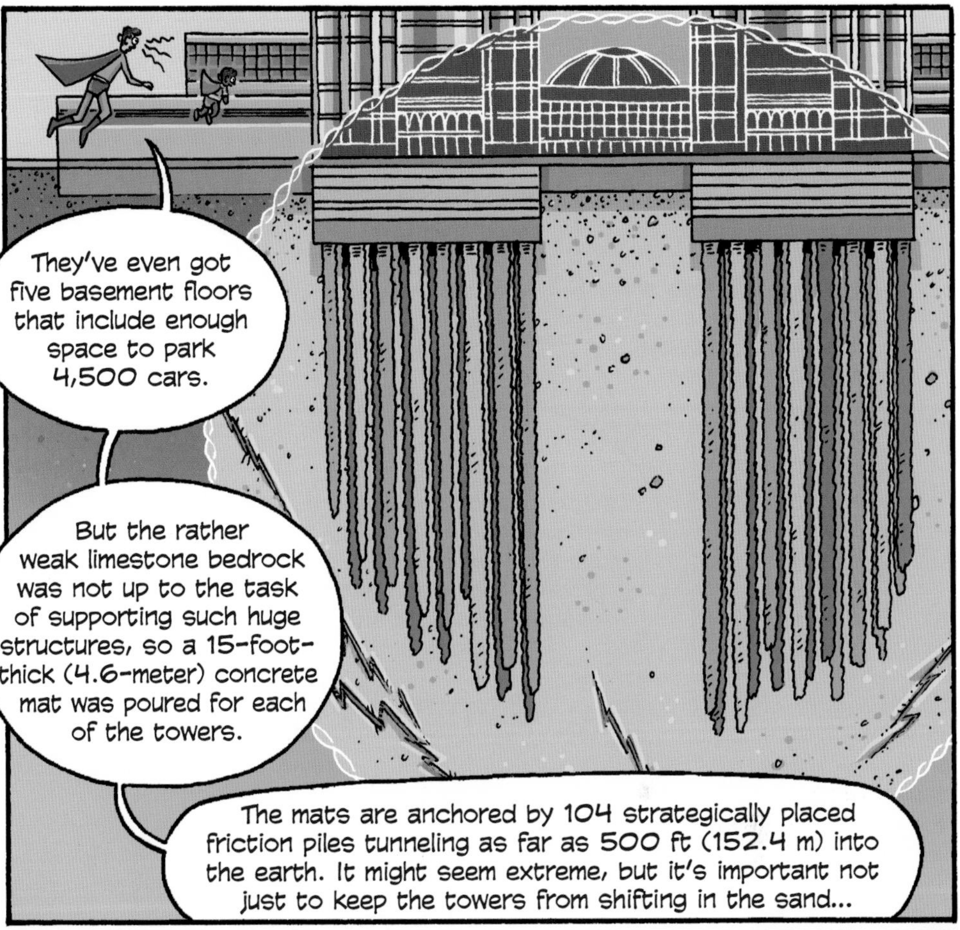
They've even got five basement floors that include enough space to park 4,500 cars.
But the rather weak limestone bedrock was not up to the task of supporting such huge structures, so a 15-foot-thick (4.6-meter) concrete mat was poured for each of the towers.
The mats are anchored by 104 strategically placed friction piles tunneling as far as 500 ft (152.4 m) into the earth. It might seem extreme, but it's important not just to keep the towers from shifting in the sand...

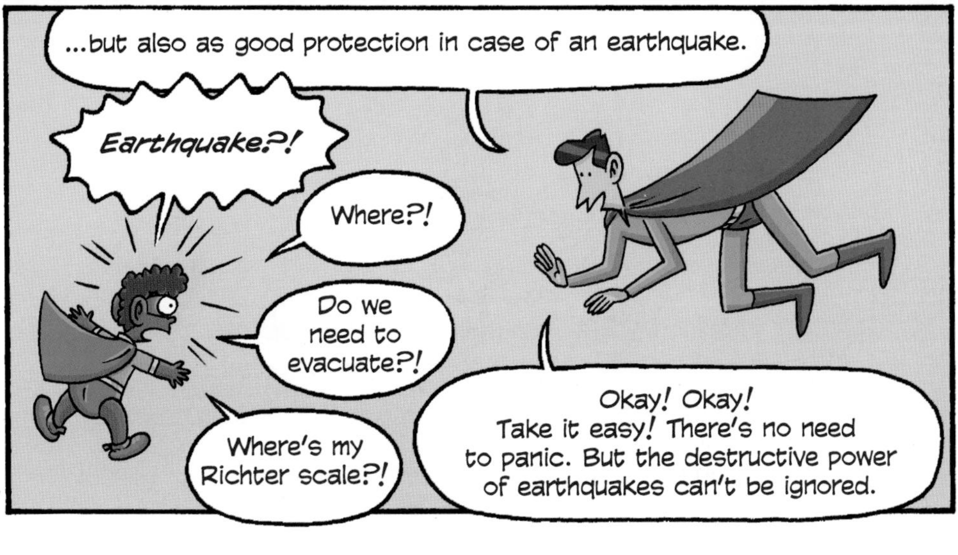
...but also as good protection in case of an earthquake.
Earthquake?!
Where?!
Do we need to evacuate?!
Where's my Richter scale?!
Okay! Okay! Take it easy! There's no need to panic. But the destructive power of earthquakes can't be ignored.

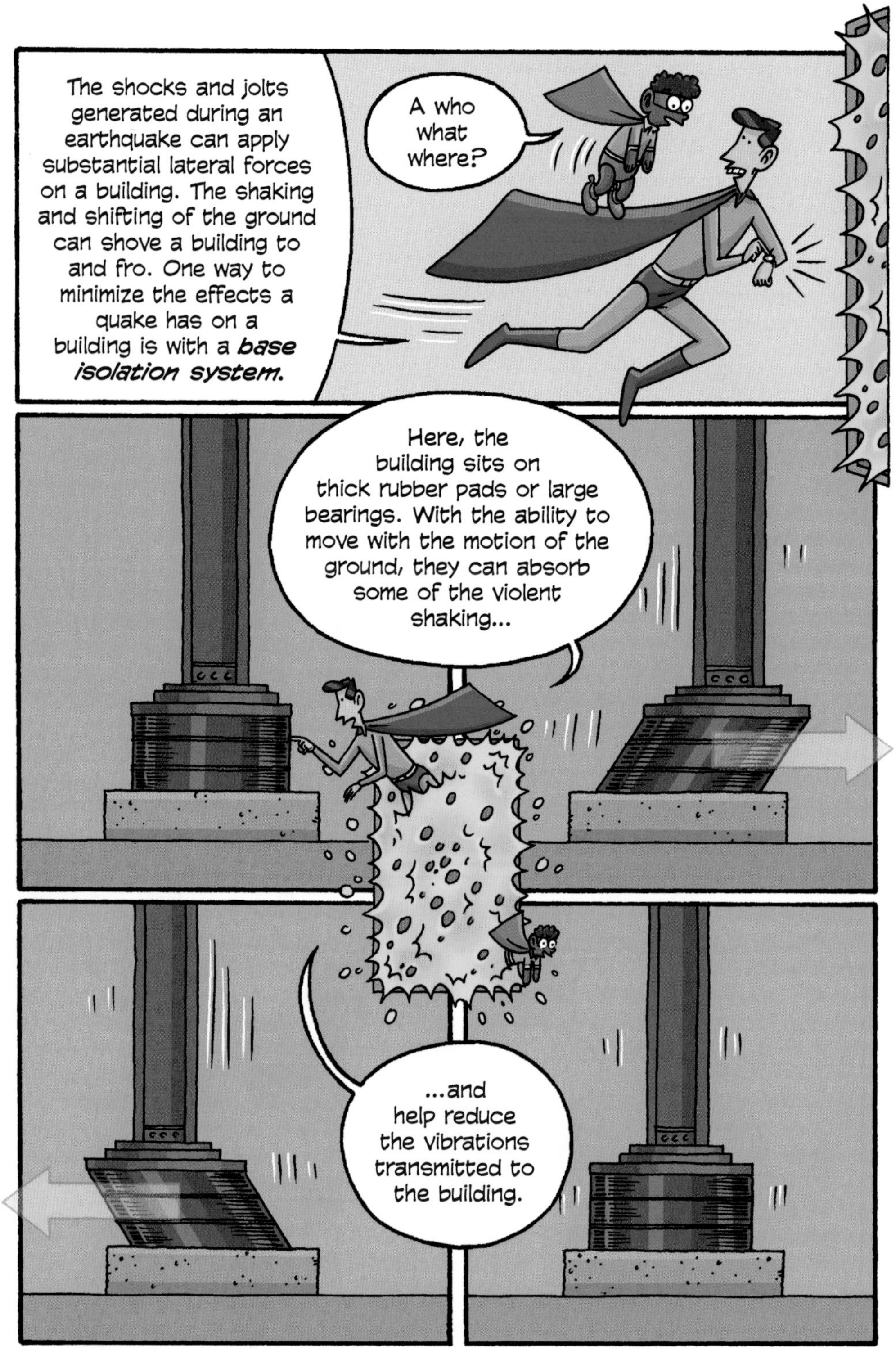
The shocks and jolts generated during an earthquake can apply substantial lateral forces on a building. The shaking and shifting of the ground can shove a building to and fro. One way to minimize the effects a quake has on a building is with a ***base isolation system.***
A who what where?
Here, the building sits on thick rubber pads or large bearings. With the ability to move with the motion of the ground, they can absorb some of the violent shaking...
...and help reduce the vibrations transmitted to the building.

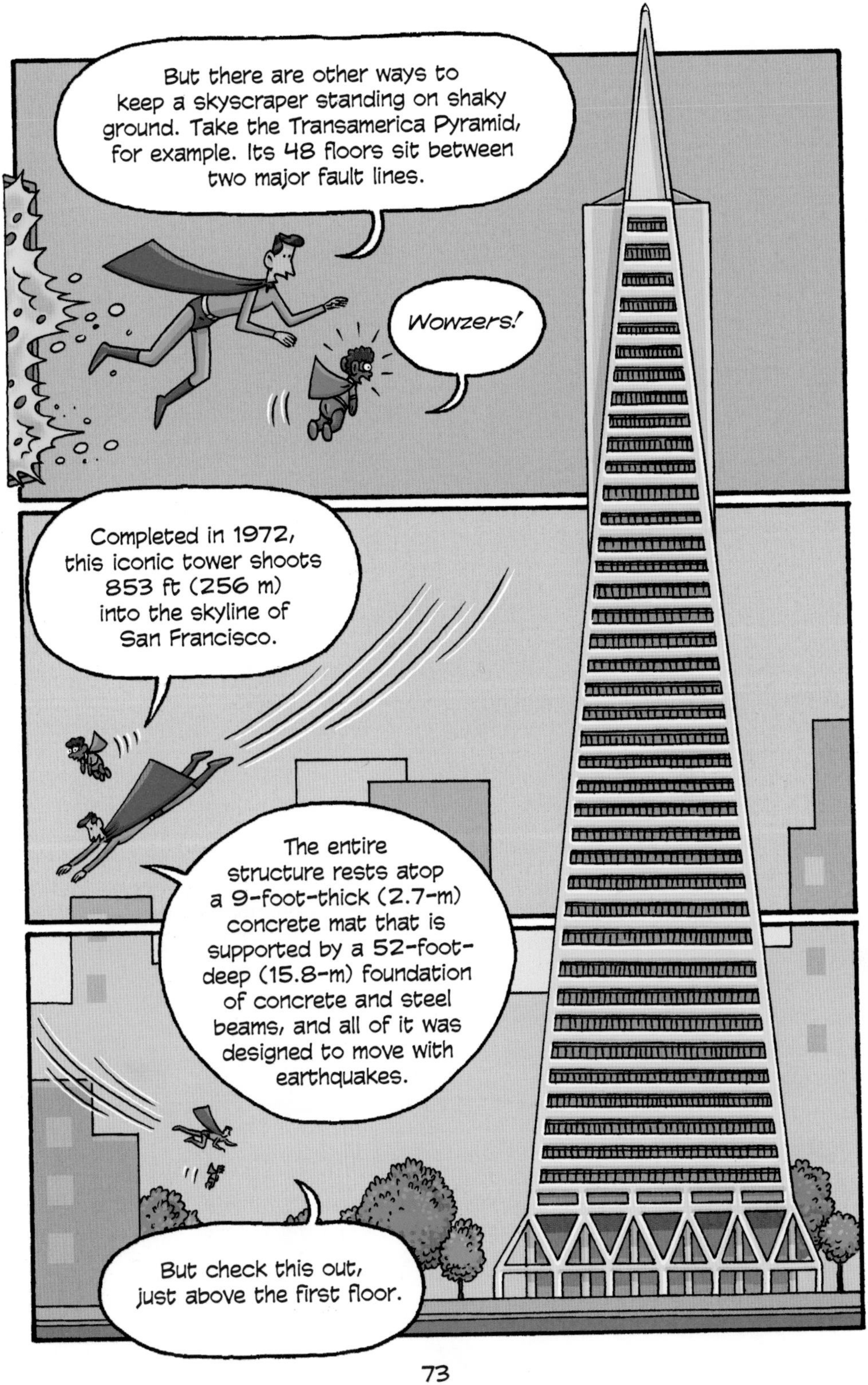

But there are other ways to keep a skyscraper standing on shaky ground. Take the Transamerica Pyramid, for example. Its 48 floors sit between two major fault lines.
Wowzers!
Completed in 1972, this iconic tower shoots 853 ft (256 m) into the skyline of San Francisco.
The entire structure rests atop a 9-foot-thick (2.7-m) concrete mat that is supported by a 52-foot-deep (15.8-m) foundation of concrete and steel beams, and all of it was designed to move with earthquakes.
But check this out, just above the first floor.

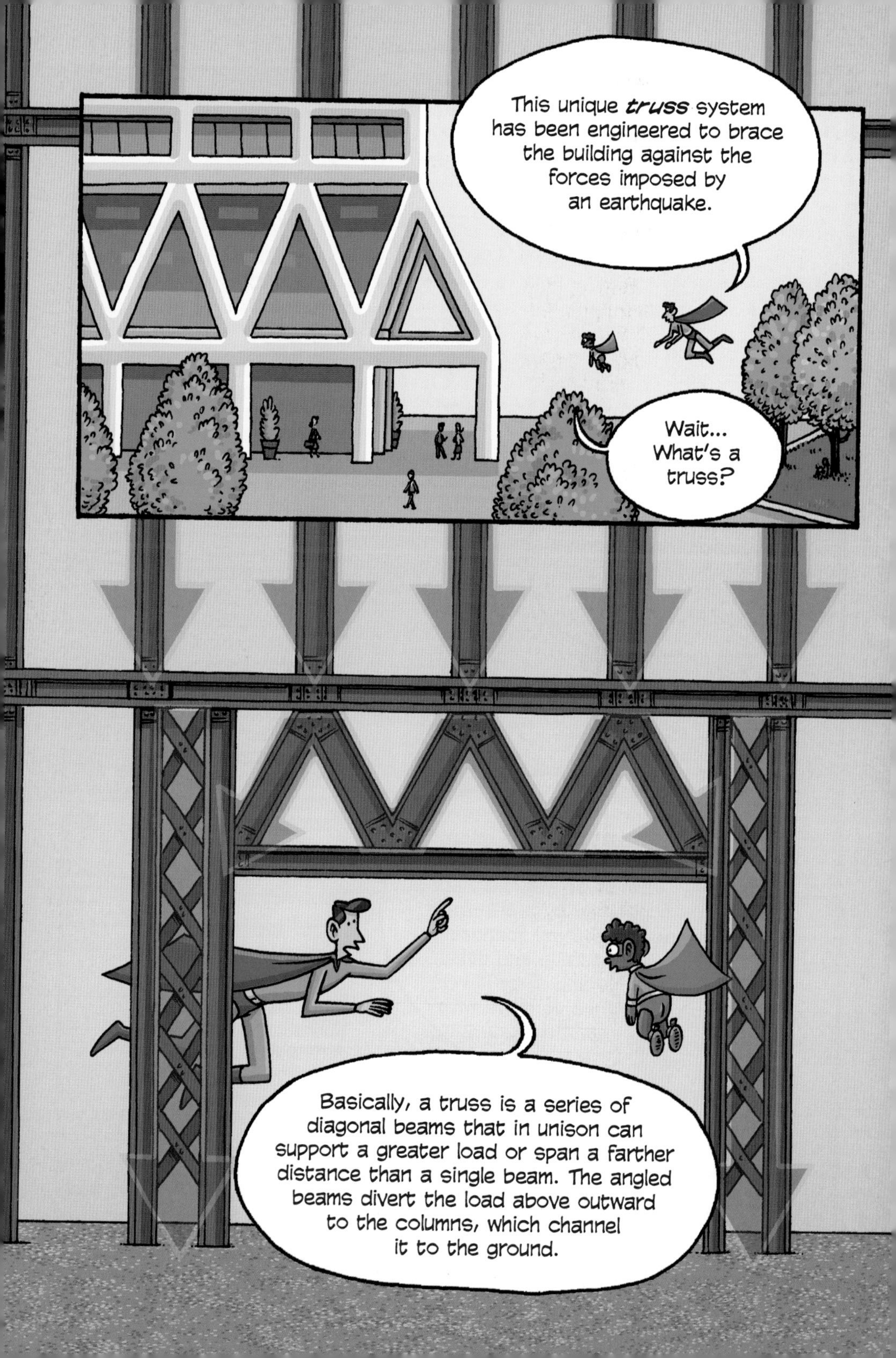
This unique truss system has been engineered to brace the building against the forces imposed by an earthquake.
Wait... What's a truss?
Basically, a truss is a series of diagonal beams that in unison can support a greater load or span a farther distance than a single beam. The angled beams divert the load above outward to the columns, which channel it to the ground.

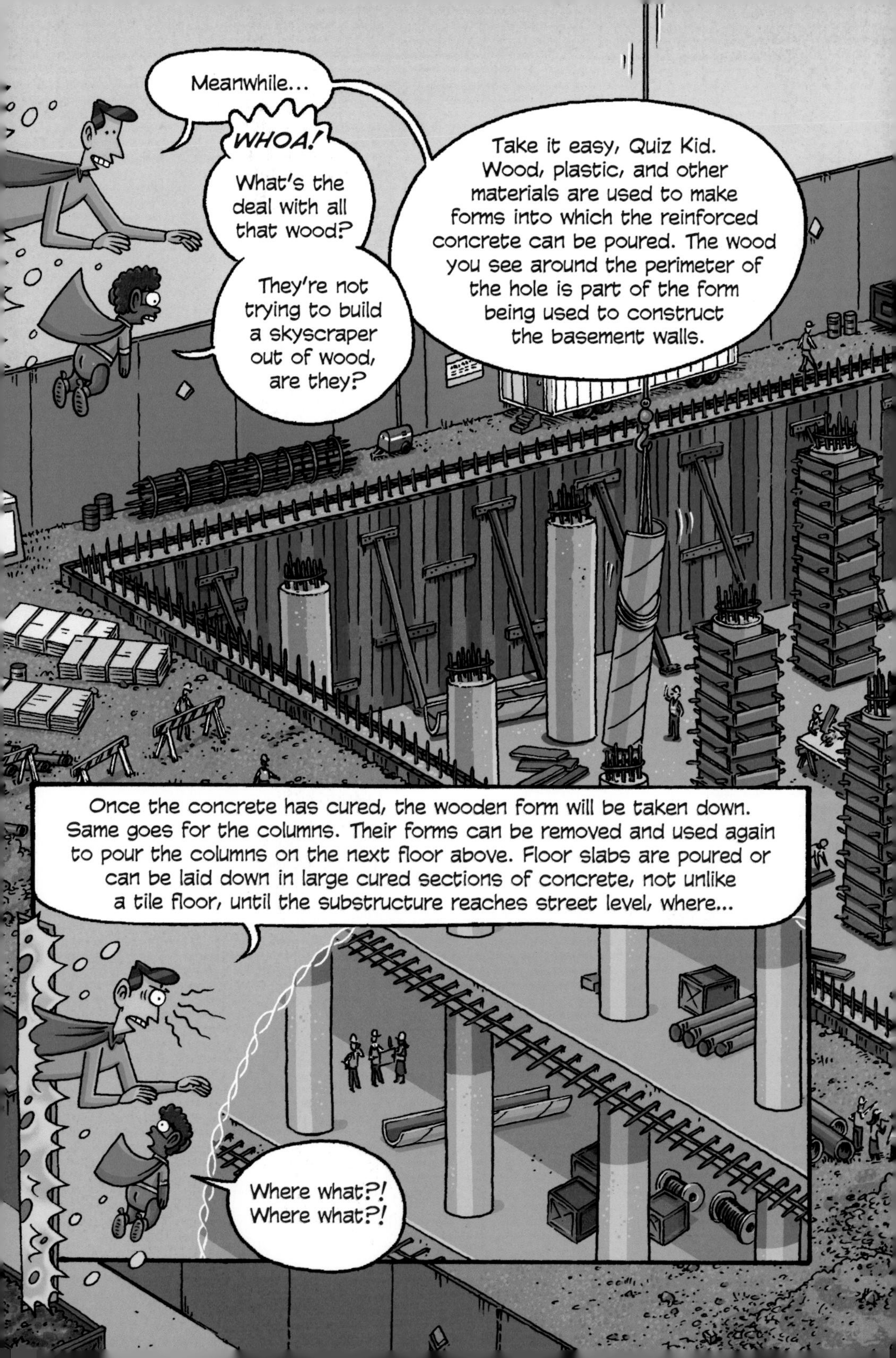
Meanwhile...
WHOA!
What's the deal with all that wood?
They're not trying to build a skyscraper out of wood, are they?
Take it easy, Quiz Kid. Wood, plastic, and other materials are used to make forms into which the reinforced concrete can be poured. The wood you see around the perimeter of the hole is part of the form being used to construct the basement walls.
Once the concrete has cured, the wooden form will be taken down. Same goes for the columns. Their forms can be removed and used again to pour the columns on the next floor above. Floor slabs are poured or can be laid down in large cured sections of concrete, not unlike a tile floor, until the substructure reaches street level, where...
Where what?! Where what?!

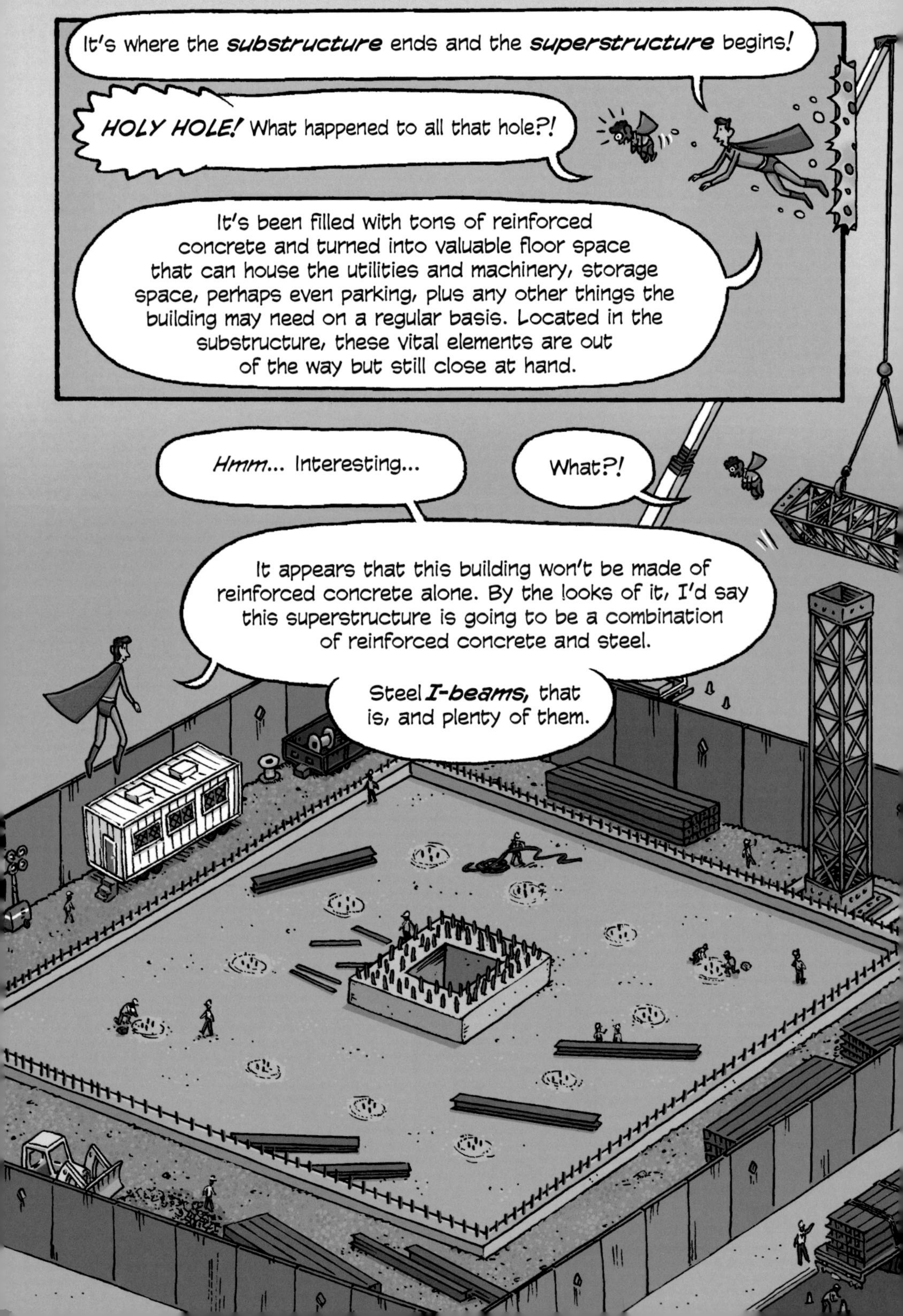

It's where the *substructure* ends and the *superstructure* begins!
HOLY HOLE! What happened to all that hole?!
It's been filled with tons of reinforced concrete and turned into valuable floor space that can house the utilities and machinery, storage space, perhaps even parking, plus any other things the building may need on a regular basis. Located in the substructure, these vital elements are out of the way but still close at hand.
Hmm... Interesting...
What?!
It appears that this building won't be made of reinforced concrete alone. By the looks of it, I'd say this superstructure is going to be a combination of reinforced concrete and steel.
Steel *I-beams,* that is, and plenty of them.

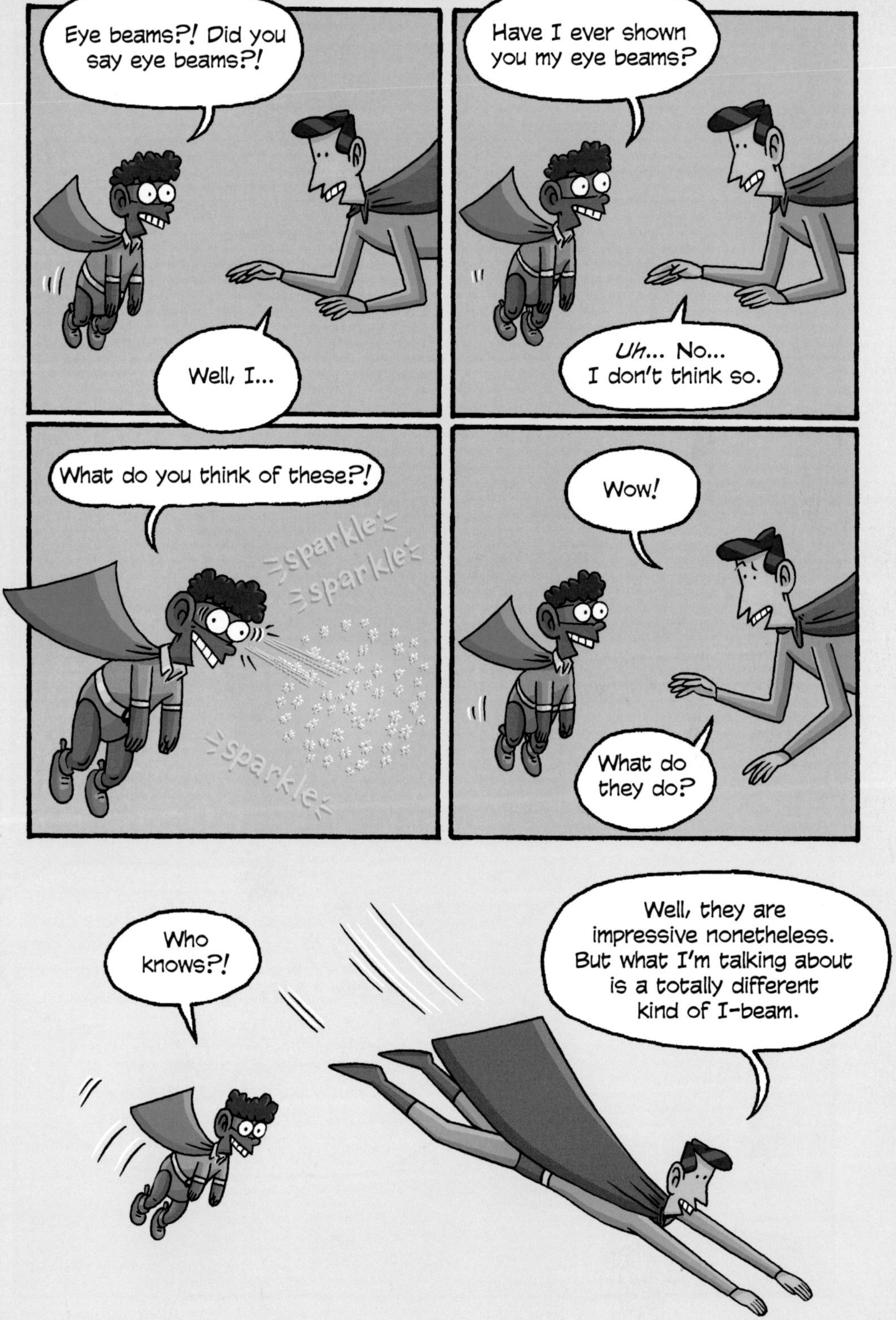
Eye beams?! Did you say eye beams?!
Well, I...
Have I ever shown you my eye beams?
Uh... No... I don't think so.
What do you think of these?!
sparkle
sparkle
sparkle
Wow!
What do they do?
Who knows?!
Well, they are impressive nonetheless. But what I'm talking about is a totally different kind of I-beam.

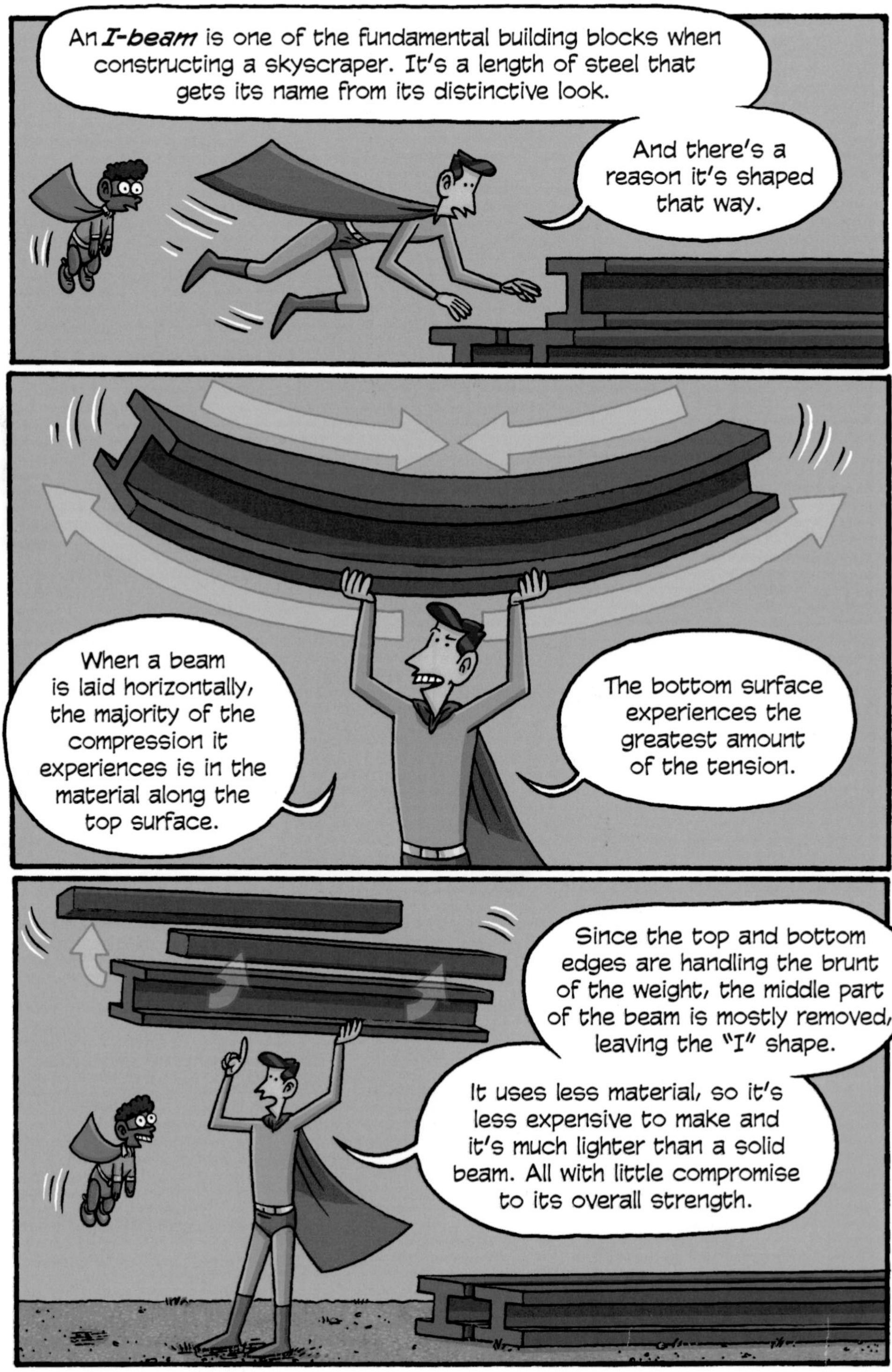
An *I-beam* is one of the fundamental building blocks when constructing a skyscraper. It's a length of steel that gets its name from its distinctive look.
And there's a reason it's shaped that way.
When a beam is laid horizontally, the majority of the compression it experiences is in the material along the top surface.
The bottom surface experiences the greatest amount of the tension.
Since the top and bottom edges are handling the brunt of the weight, the middle part of the beam is mostly removed, leaving the "I" shape.
It uses less material, so it's less expensive to make and it's much lighter than a solid beam. All with little compromise to its overall strength.

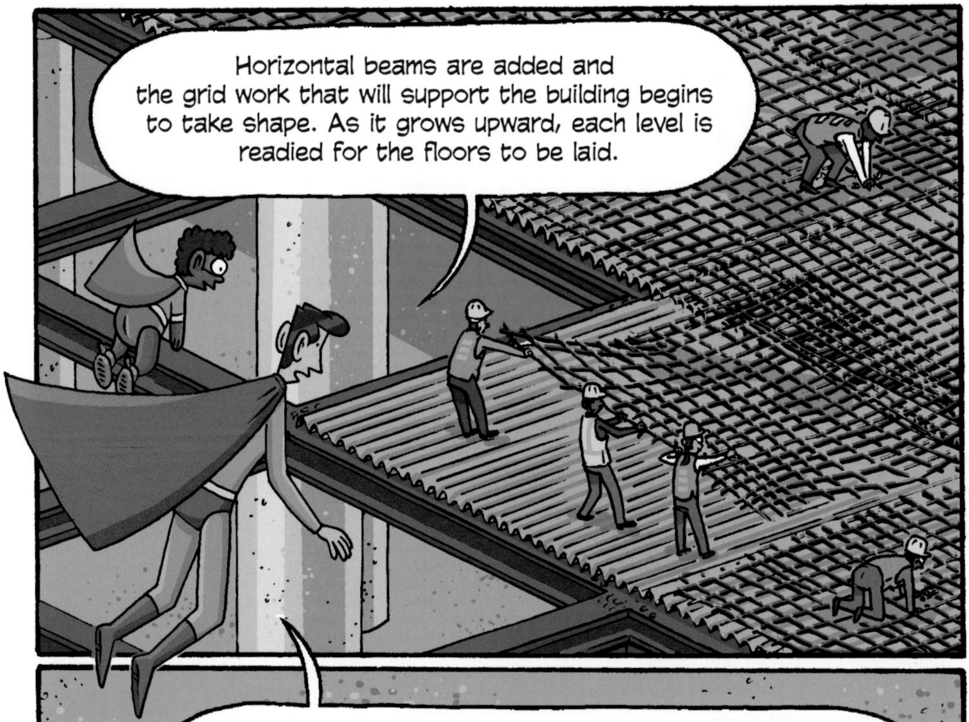
Horizontal beams are added and the grid work that will support the building begins to take shape. As it grows upward, each level is readied for the floors to be laid.

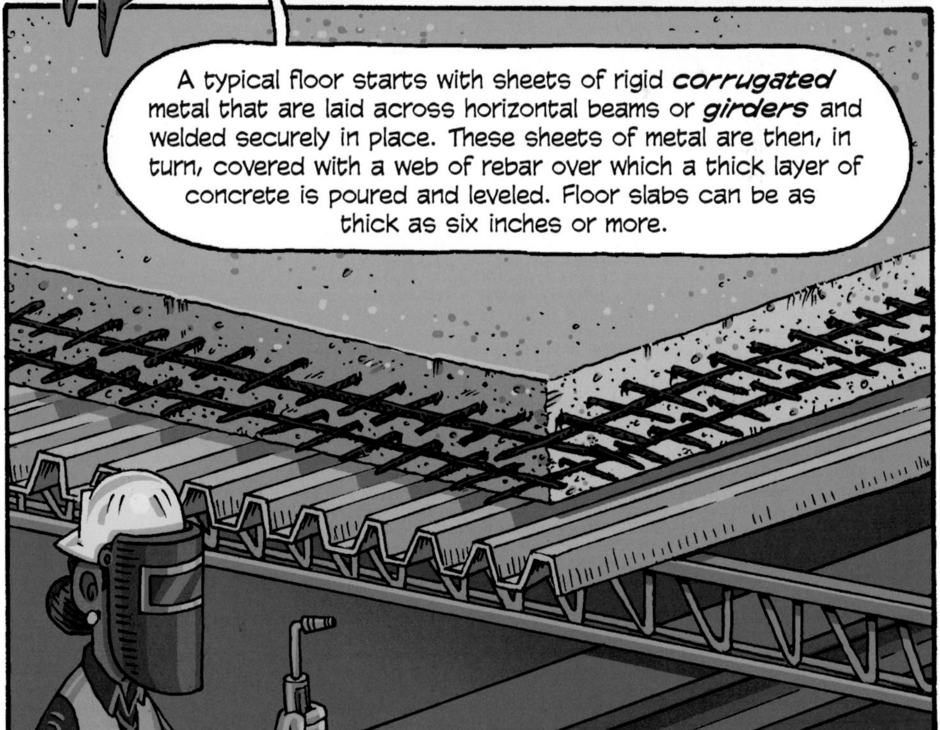
A typical floor starts with sheets of rigid *corrugated* metal that are laid across horizontal beams or *girders* and welded securely in place. These sheets of metal are then, in turn, covered with a web of rebar over which a thick layer of concrete is poured and leveled. Floor slabs can be as thick as six inches or more.

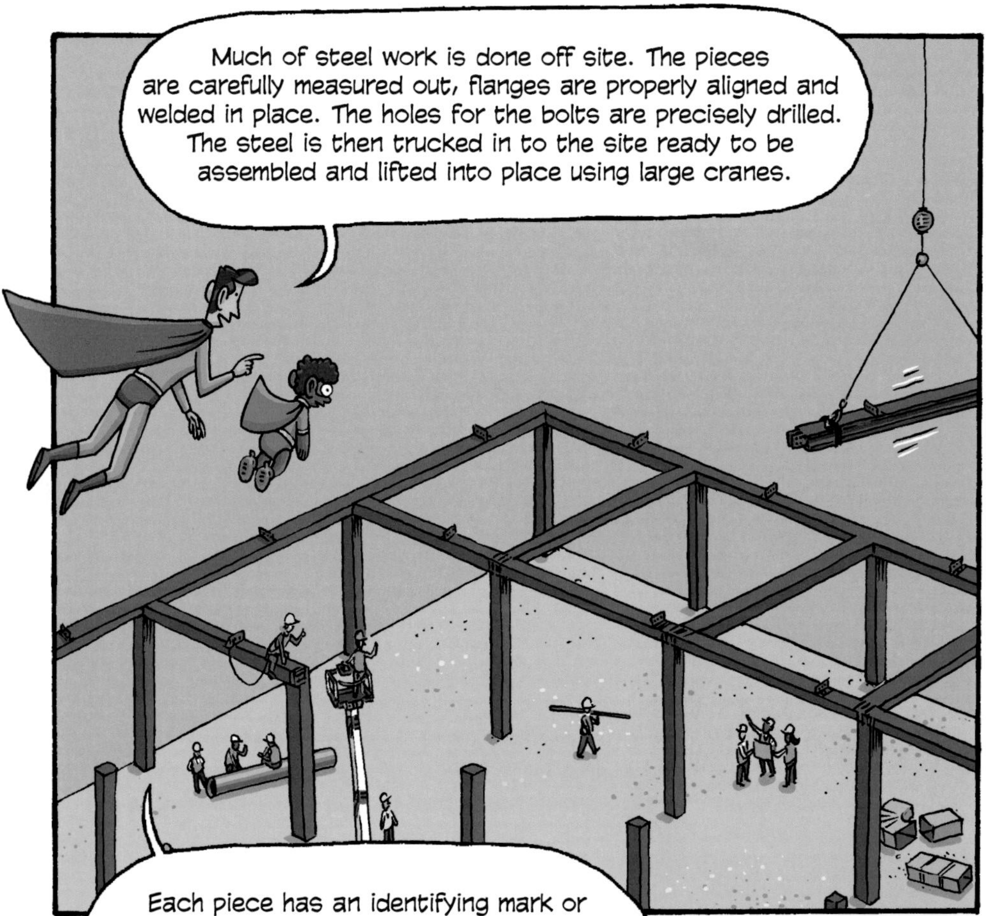
Much of steel work is done off site. The pieces are carefully measured out, flanges are properly aligned and welded in place. The holes for the bolts are precisely drilled. The steel is then trucked in to the site ready to be assembled and lifted into place using large cranes.

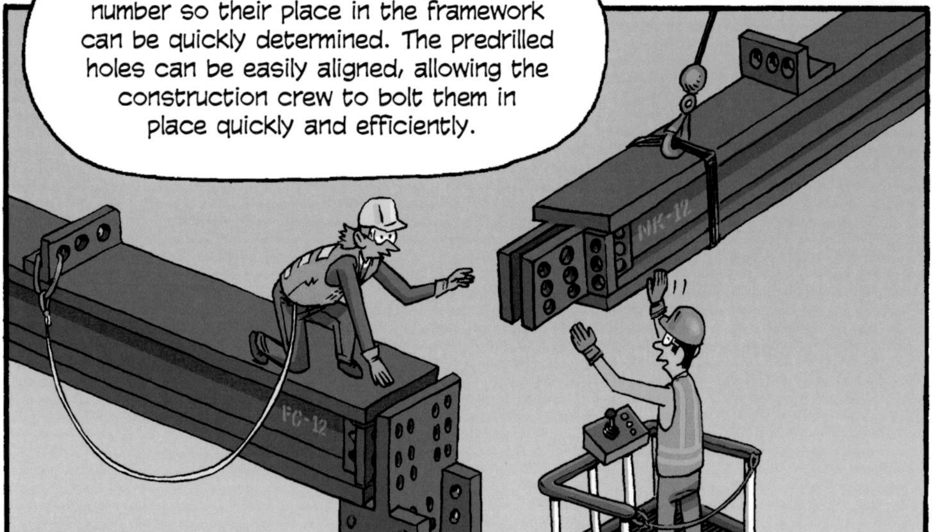
Each piece has an identifying mark or number so their place in the framework can be quickly determined. The predrilled holes can be easily aligned, allowing the construction crew to bolt them in place quickly and efficiently.
MK-12
FC-12

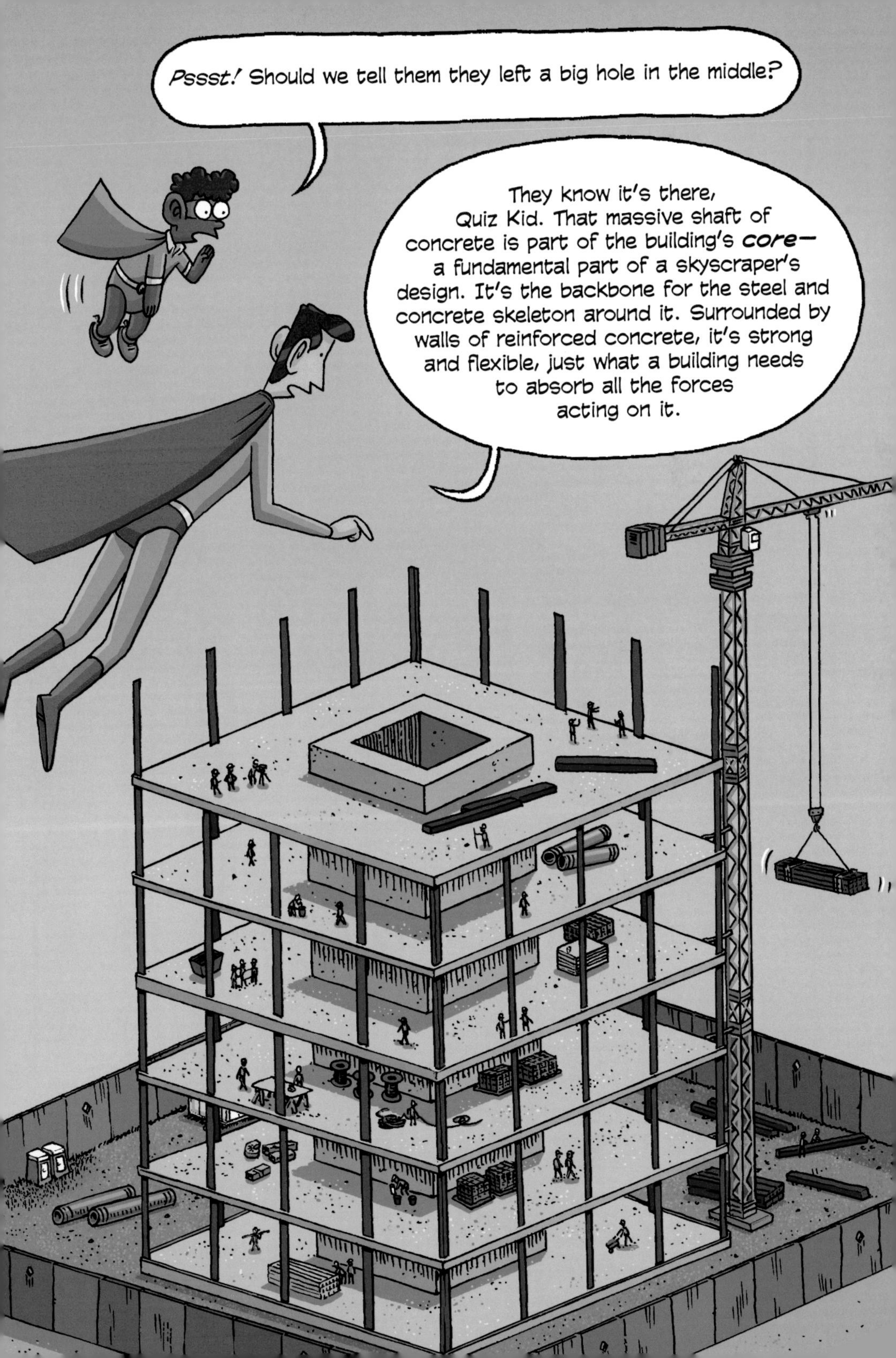
Pssst! Should we tell them they left a big hole in the middle?
They know it's there, Quiz Kid. That massive shaft of concrete is part of the building's ***core***—a fundamental part of a skyscraper's design. It's the backbone for the steel and concrete skeleton around it. Surrounded by walls of reinforced concrete, it's strong and flexible, just what a building needs to absorb all the forces acting on it.

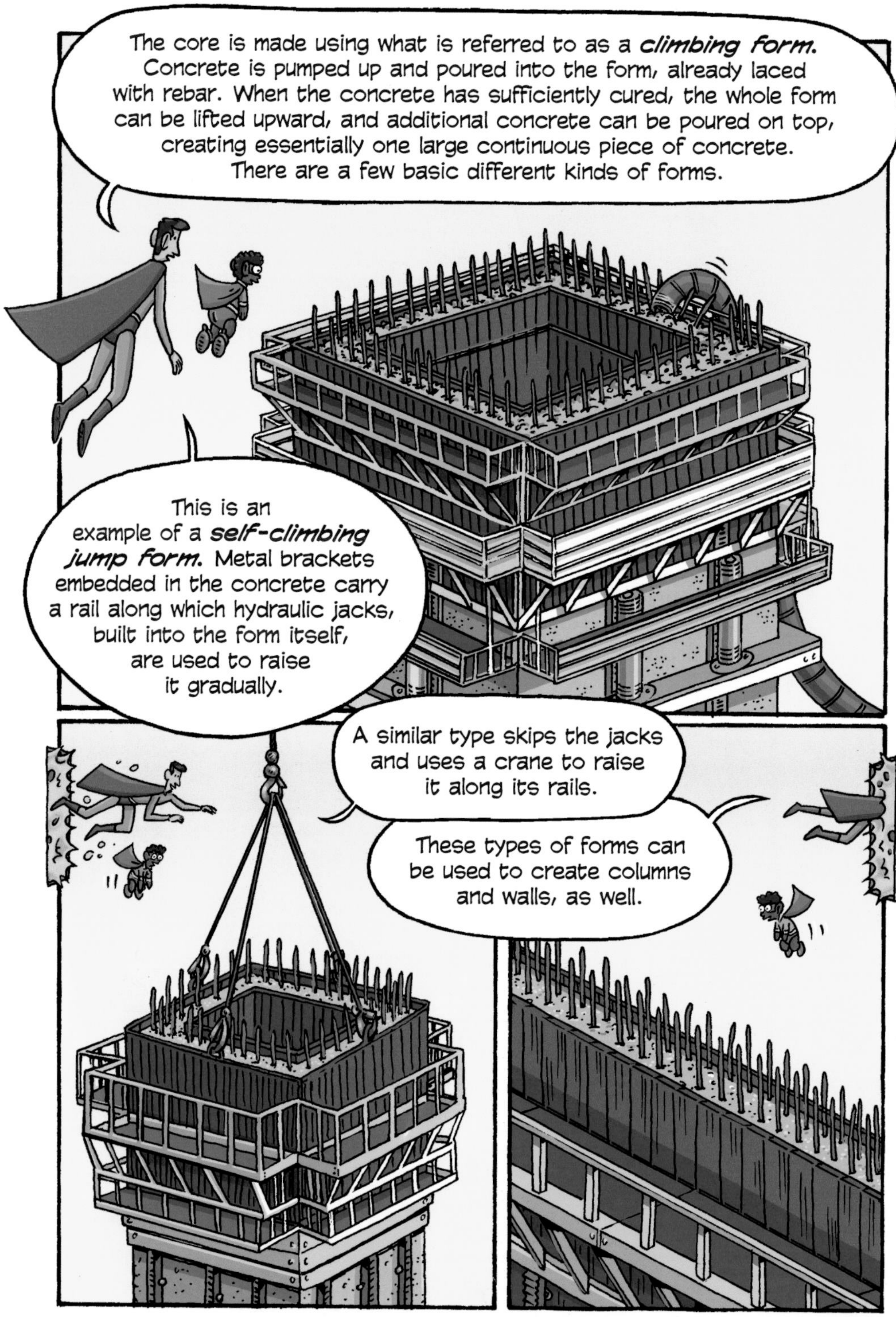
The core is made using what is referred to as a *climbing form.* Concrete is pumped up and poured into the form, already laced with rebar. When the concrete has sufficiently cured, the whole form can be lifted upward, and additional concrete can be poured on top, creating essentially one large continuous piece of concrete. There are a few basic different kinds of forms.
This is an example of a *self-climbing jump form.* Metal brackets embedded in the concrete carry a rail along which hydraulic jacks, built into the form itself, are used to raise it gradually.
A similar type skips the jacks and uses a crane to raise it along its rails.
These types of forms can be used to create columns and walls, as well.

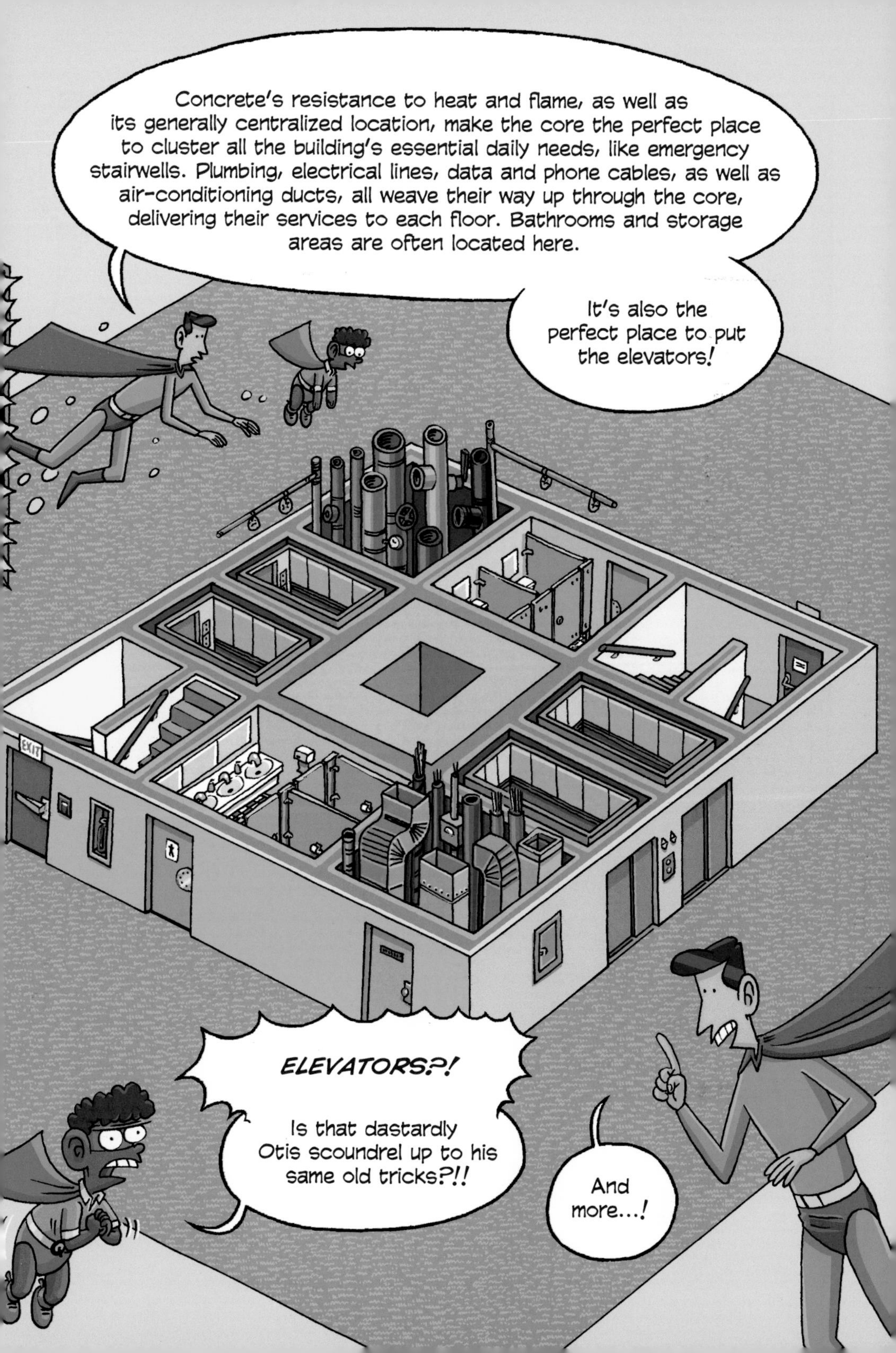
Concrete's resistance to heat and flame, as well as its generally centralized location, make the core the perfect place to cluster all the building's essential daily needs, like emergency stairwells. Plumbing, electrical lines, data and phone cables, as well as air-conditioning ducts, all weave their way up through the core, delivering their services to each floor. Bathrooms and storage areas are often located here.
It's also the perfect place to put the elevators!
EXIT
ELEVATORS?!
Is that dastardly Otis scoundrel up to his same old tricks?!!
And more...!

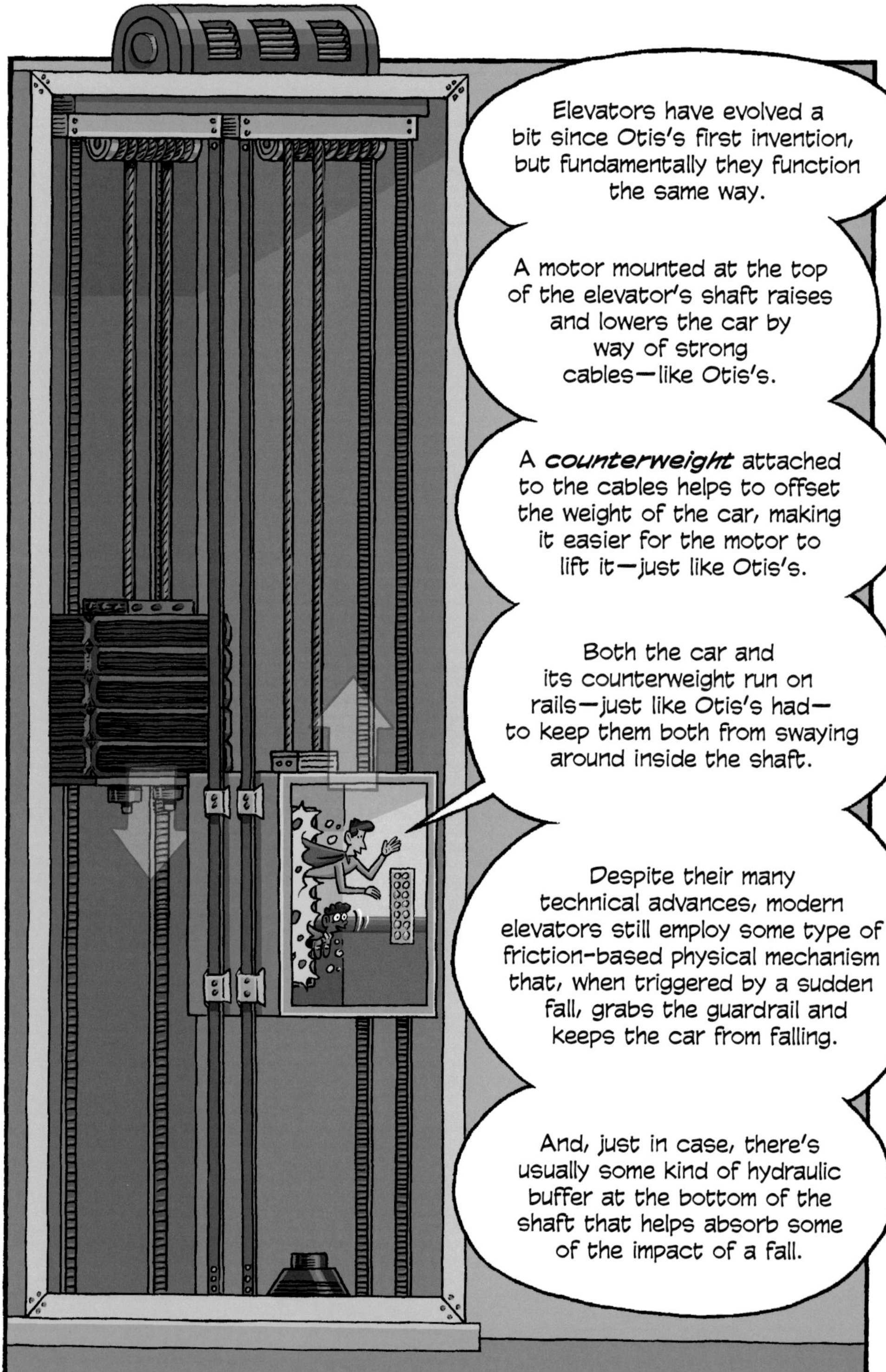
Elevators have evolved a bit since Otis's first invention, but fundamentally they function the same way.
A motor mounted at the top of the elevator's shaft raises and lowers the car by way of strong cables—like Otis's.
A ***counterweight*** attached to the cables helps to offset the weight of the car, making it easier for the motor to lift it—just like Otis's.
Both the car and its counterweight run on rails—just like Otis's had—to keep them both from swaying around inside the shaft.
Despite their many technical advances, modern elevators still employ some type of friction-based physical mechanism that, when triggered by a sudden fall, grabs the guardrail and keeps the car from falling.
And, just in case, there's usually some kind of hydraulic buffer at the bottom of the shaft that helps absorb some of the impact of a fall.

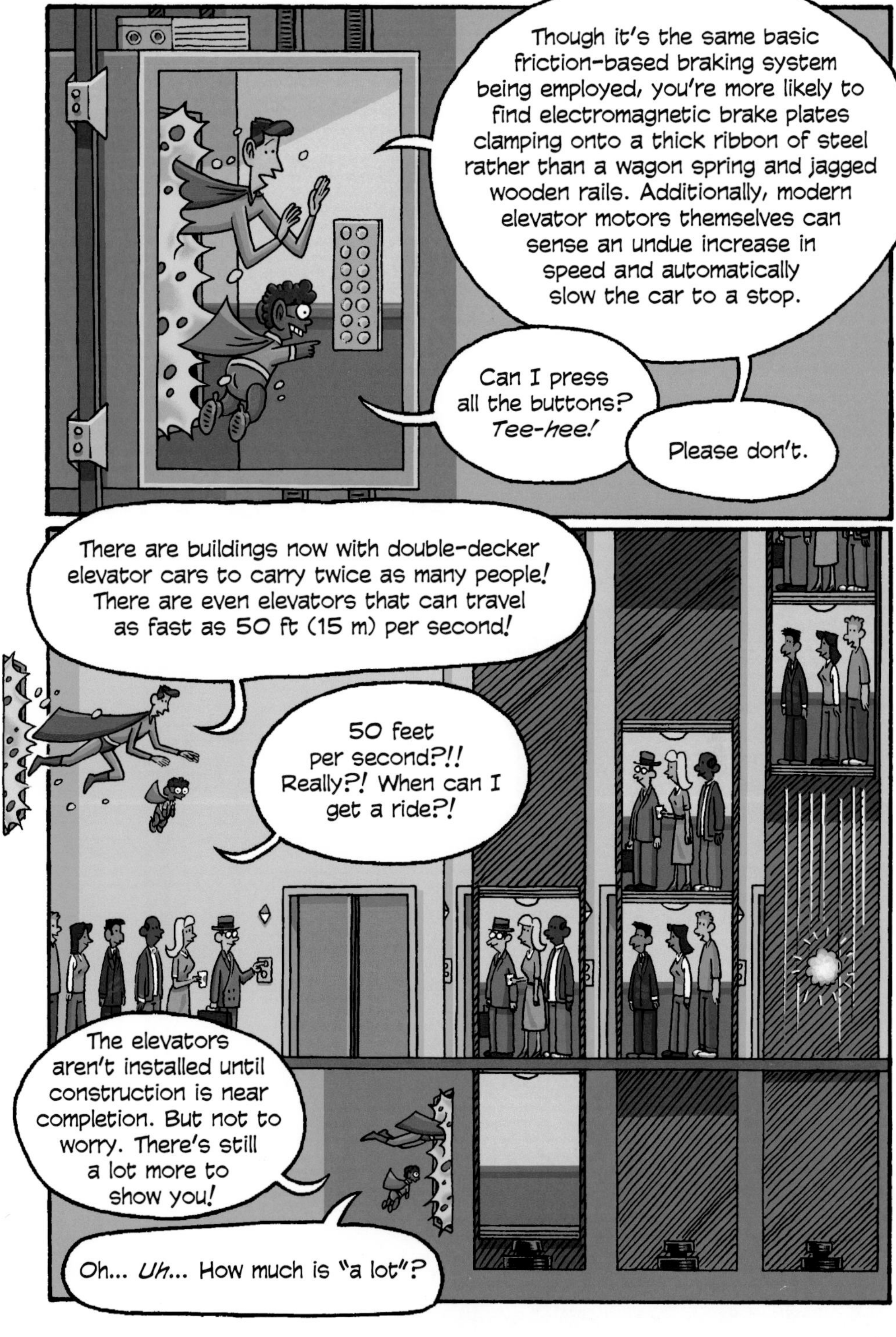
Though it's the same basic friction-based braking system being employed, you're more likely to find electromagnetic brake plates clamping onto a thick ribbon of steel rather than a wagon spring and jagged wooden rails. Additionally, modern elevator motors themselves can sense an undue increase in speed and automatically slow the car to a stop.
Can I press all the buttons? *Tee-hee!*
Please don't.
There are buildings now with double-decker elevator cars to carry twice as many people! There are even elevators that can travel as fast as 50 ft (15 m) per second!
50 feet per second?!! Really?! When can I get a ride?!
The elevators aren't installed until construction is near completion. But not to worry. There's still a lot more to show you!
Oh... *Uh*... How much is "a lot"?

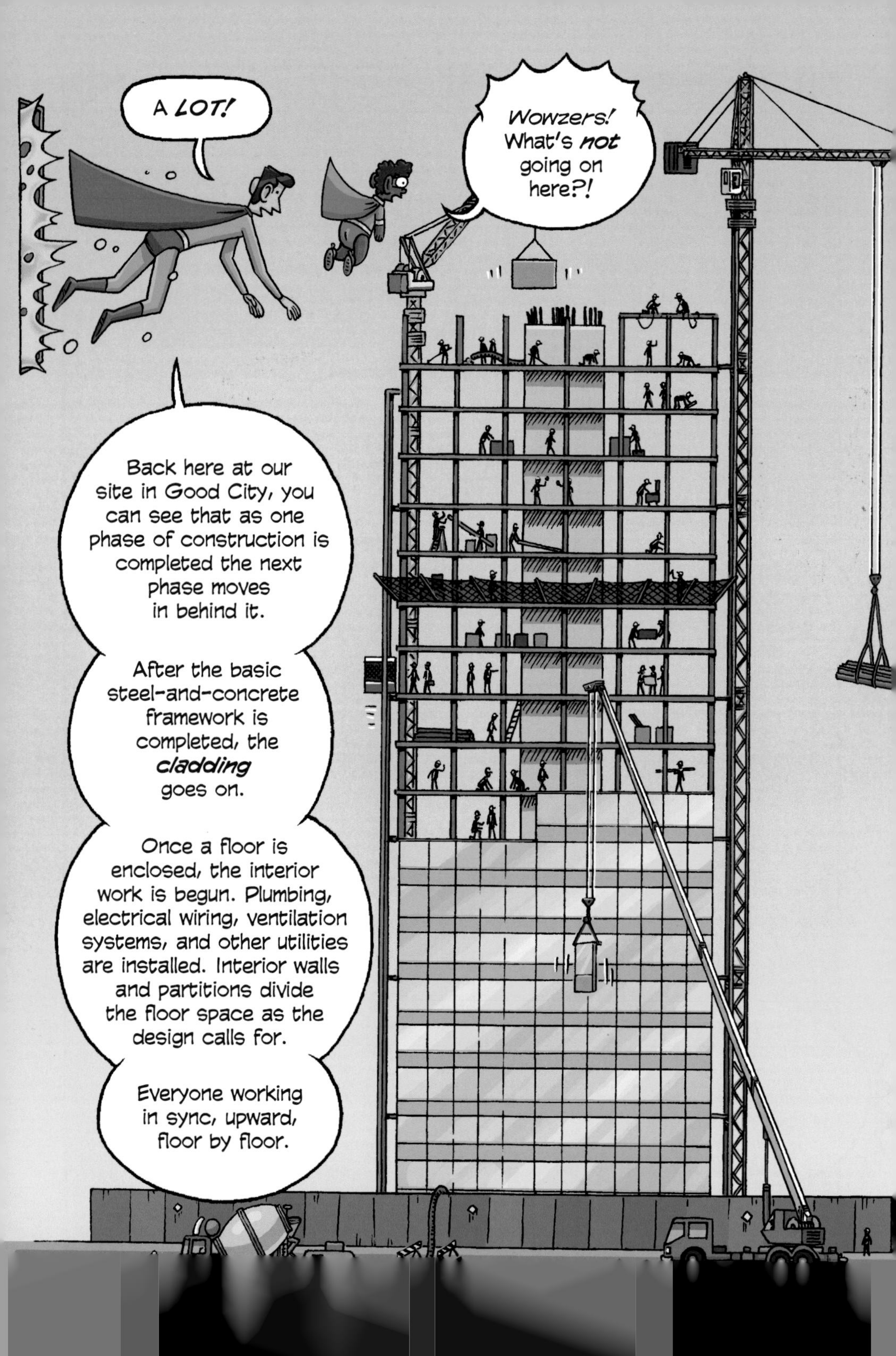
A *LOT!*
Wowzers! What's ***not*** going on here?!
Back here at our site in Good City, you can see that as one phase of construction is completed the next phase moves in behind it.
After the basic steel-and-concrete framework is completed, the ***cladding*** goes on.
Once a floor is enclosed, the interior work is begun. Plumbing, electrical wiring, ventilation systems, and other utilities are installed. Interior walls and partitions divide the floor space as the design calls for.
Everyone working in sync, upward, floor by floor.

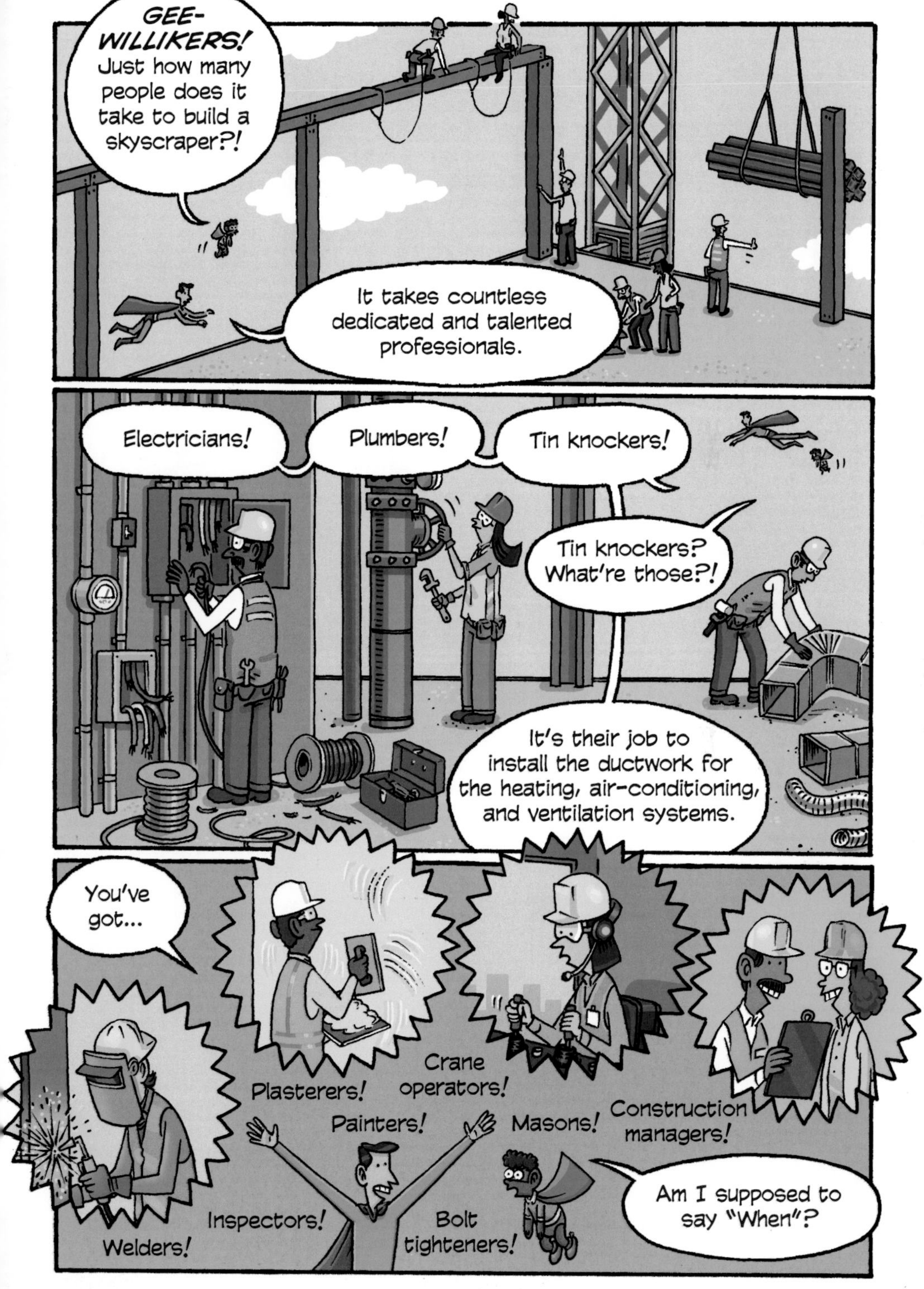
GEE-WILLIKERS! Just how many people does it take to build a skyscraper?!
It takes countless dedicated and talented professionals.
Electricians!
Plumbers!
Tin knockers!
Tin knockers? What're those?!
It's their job to install the ductwork for the heating, air-conditioning, and ventilation systems.
You've got...
Welders!
Plasterers!
Crane operators!
Construction managers!
Painters!
Masons!
Inspectors!
Bolt tighteners!
Am I supposed to say "When"?

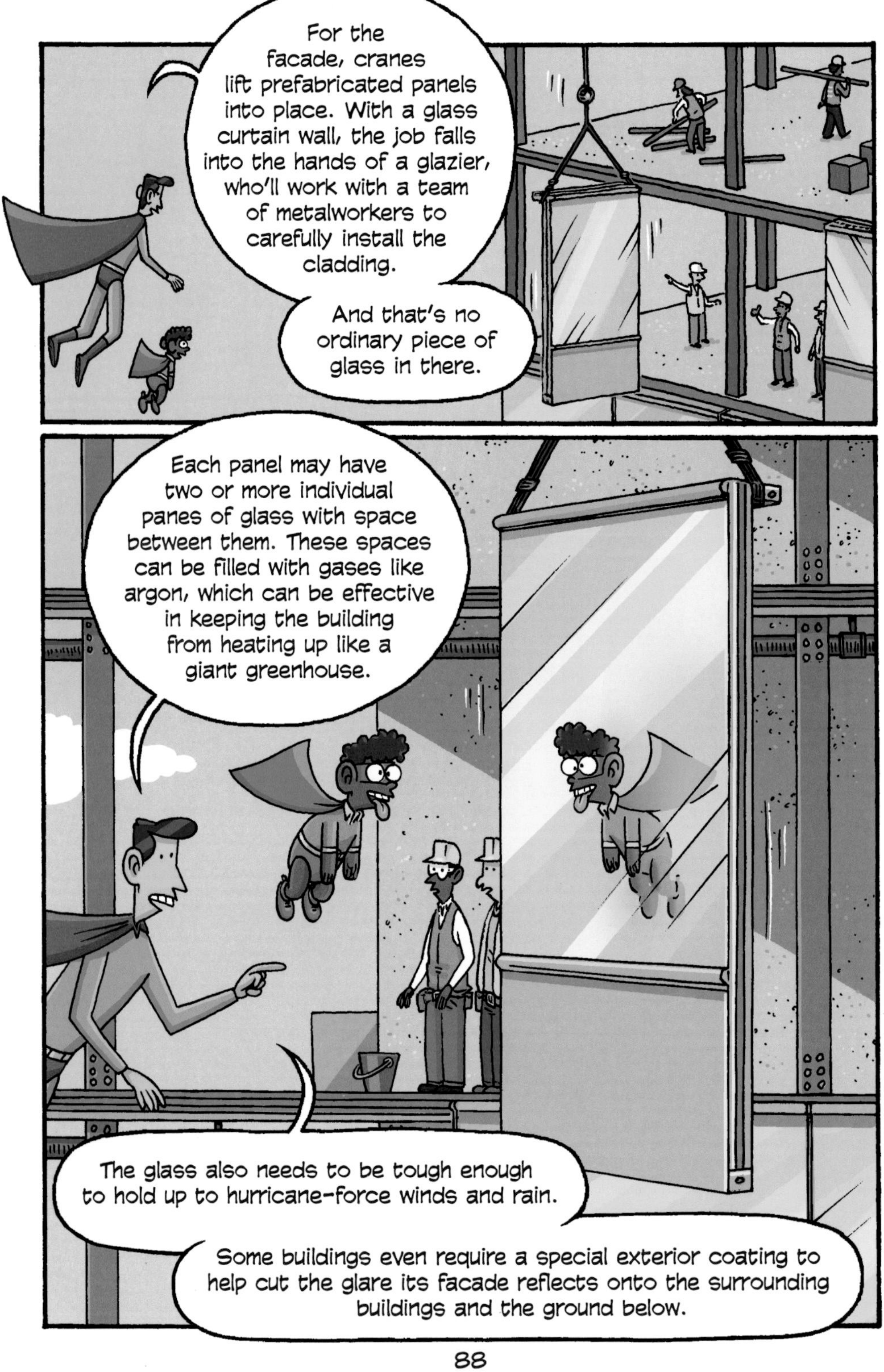
For the facade, cranes lift prefabricated panels into place. With a glass curtain wall, the job falls into the hands of a glazier, who'll work with a team of metalworkers to carefully install the cladding.
And that's no ordinary piece of glass in there.
Each panel may have two or more individual panes of glass with space between them. These spaces can be filled with gases like argon, which can be effective in keeping the building from heating up like a giant greenhouse.
The glass also needs to be tough enough to hold up to hurricane-force winds and rain.
Some buildings even require a special exterior coating to help cut the glare its facade reflects onto the surrounding buildings and the ground below.

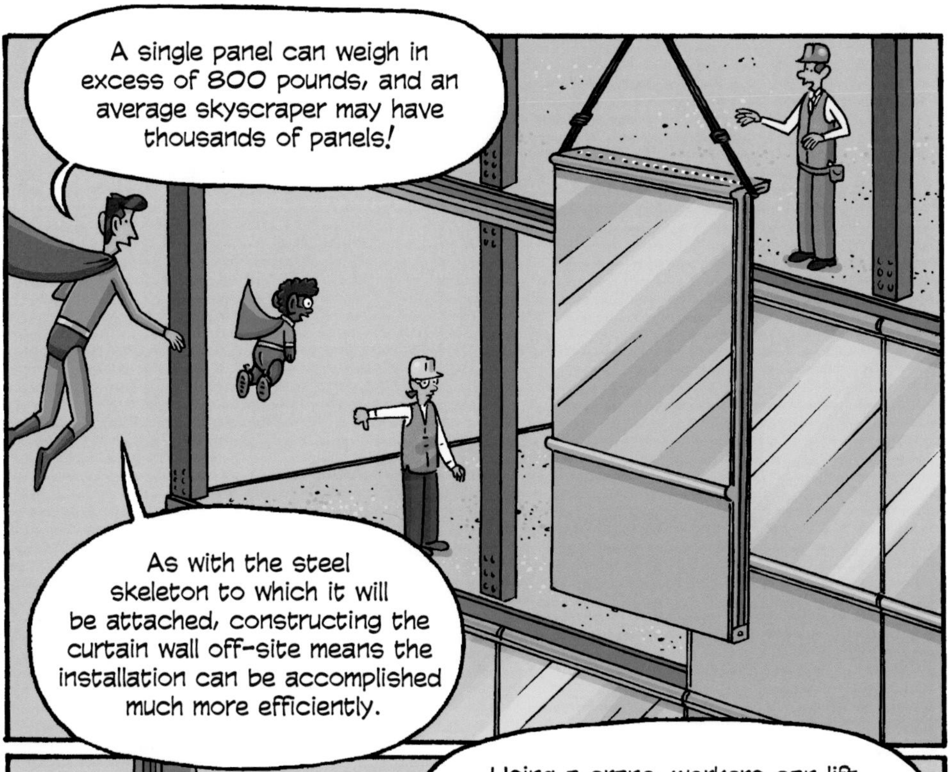
A single panel can weigh in excess of 800 pounds, and an average skyscraper may have thousands of panels!
As with the steel skeleton to which it will be attached, constructing the curtain wall off-site means the installation can be accomplished much more efficiently.

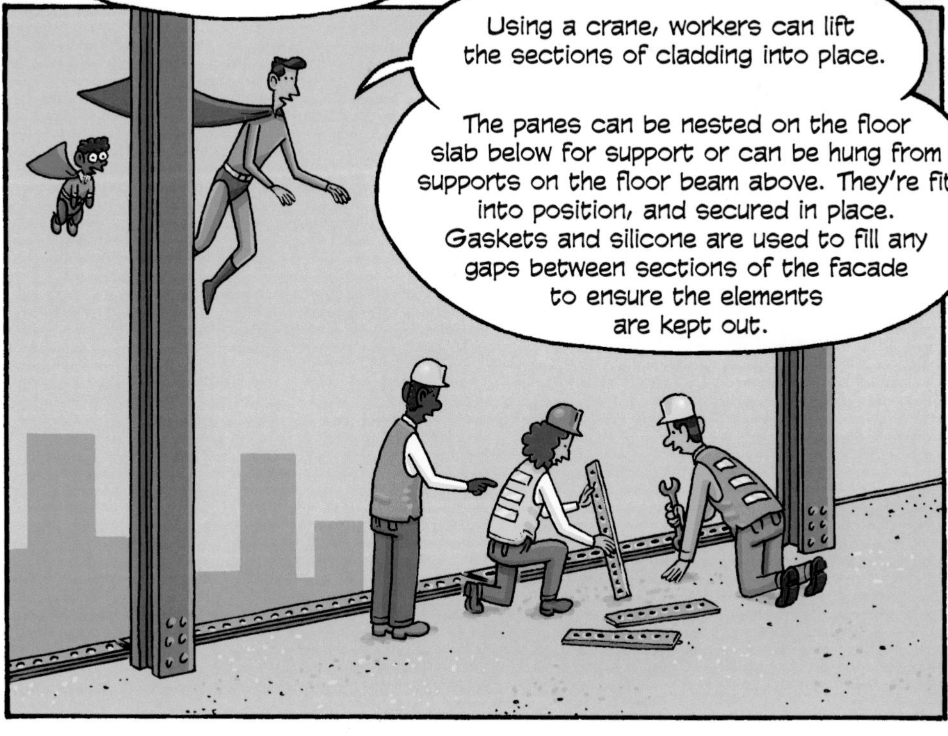
Using a crane, workers can lift the sections of cladding into place.
The panes can be nested on the floor slab below for support or can be hung from supports on the floor beam above. They're fit into position, and secured in place. Gaskets and silicone are used to fill any gaps between sections of the facade to ensure the elements are kept out.

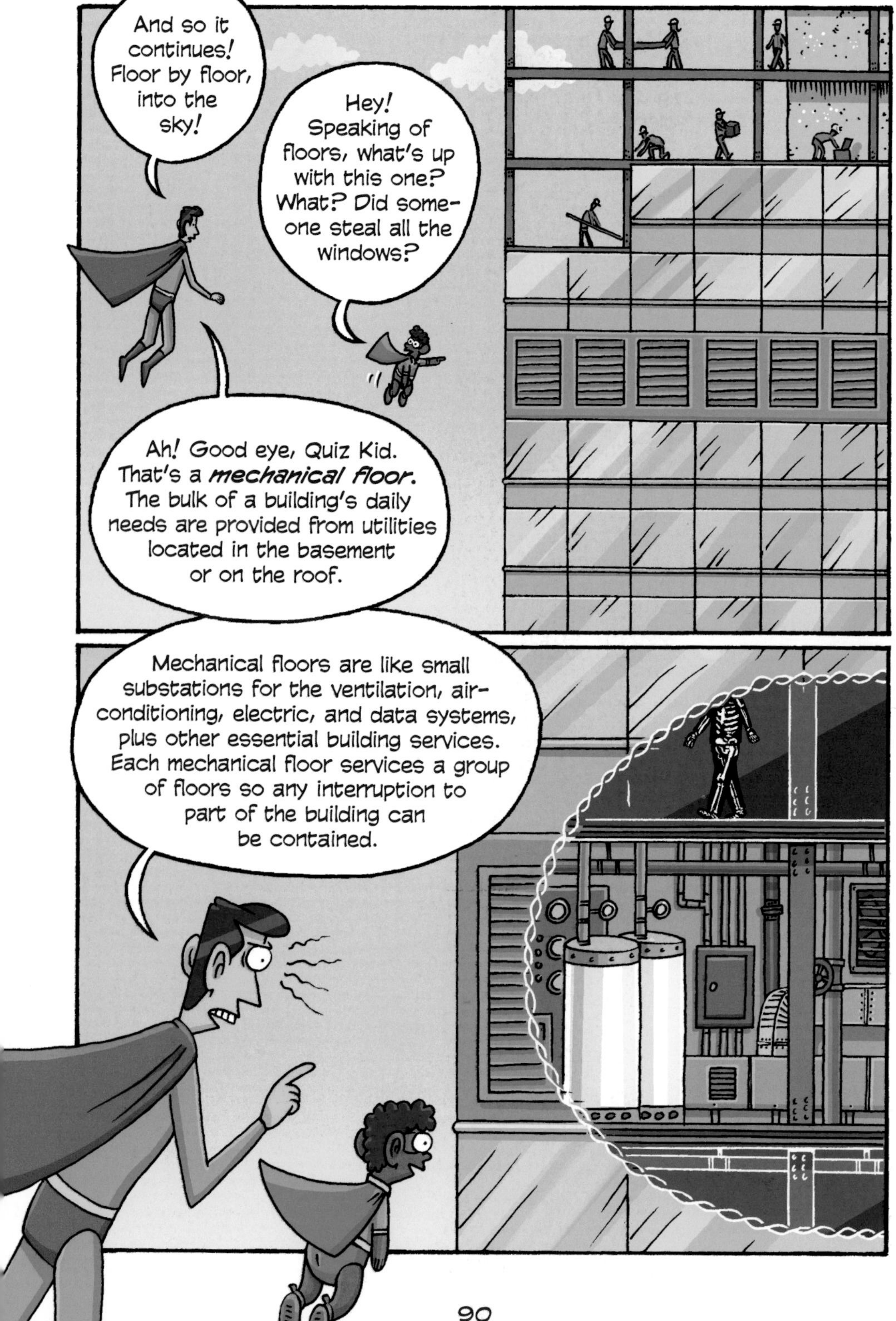
And so it continues! Floor by floor, into the sky!
Hey! Speaking of floors, what's up with this one? What? Did some-one steal all the windows?
Ah! Good eye, Quiz Kid. That's a ***mechanical floor.*** The bulk of a building's daily needs are provided from utilities located in the basement or on the roof.
Mechanical floors are like small substations for the ventilation, air-conditioning, electric, and data systems, plus other essential building services. Each mechanical floor services a group of floors so any interruption to part of the building can be contained.

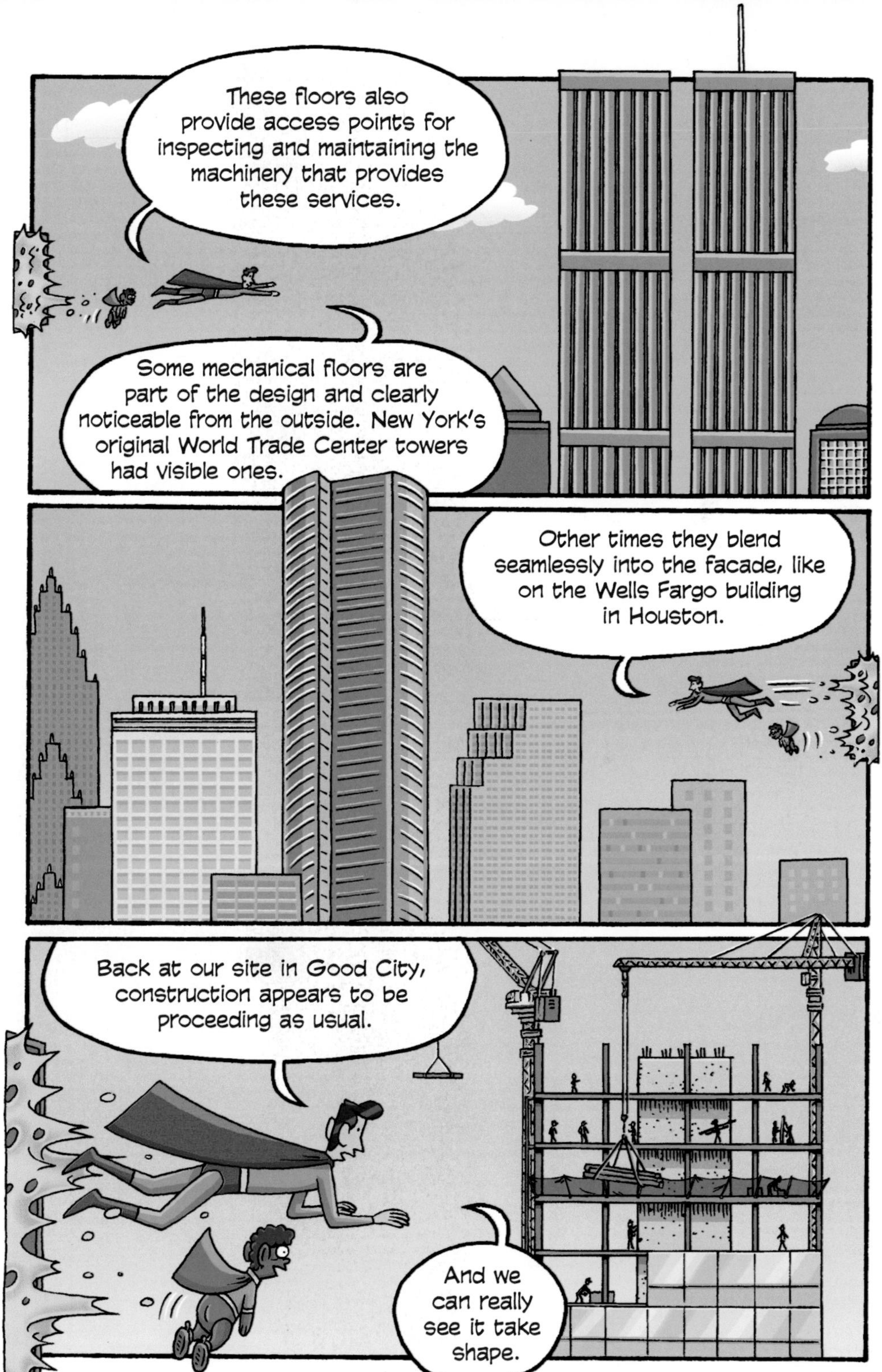
These floors also provide access points for inspecting and maintaining the machinery that provides these services.
Some mechanical floors are part of the design and clearly noticeable from the outside. New York's original World Trade Center towers had visible ones.
Other times they blend seamlessly into the facade, like on the Wells Fargo building in Houston.
Back at our site in Good City, construction appears to be proceeding as usual.
And we can really see it take shape.

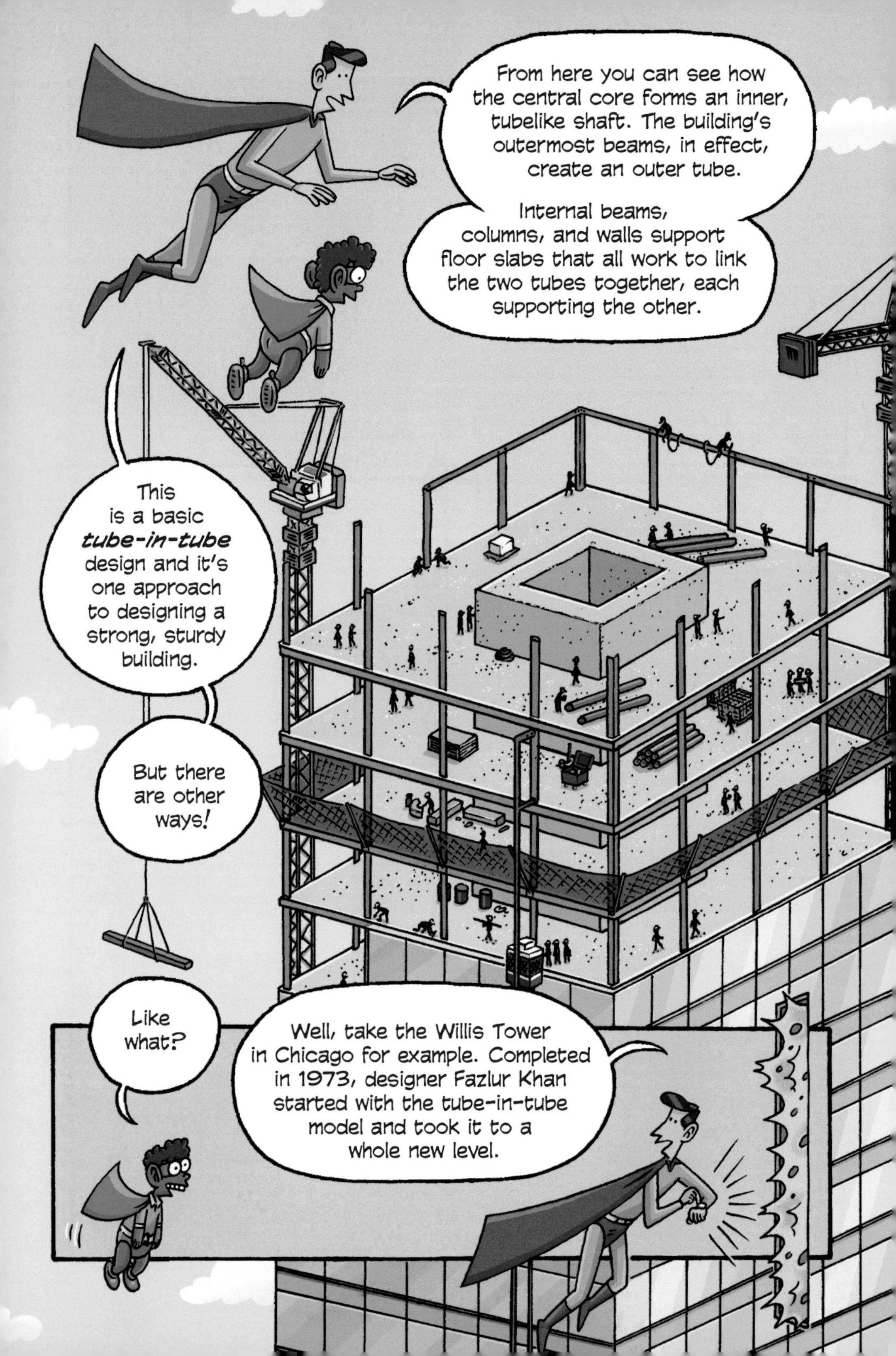
From here you can see how the central core forms an inner, tubelike shaft. The building's outermost beams, in effect, create an outer tube.
Internal beams, columns, and walls support floor slabs that all work to link the two tubes together, each supporting the other.
This is a basic ***tube-in-tube*** design and it's one approach to designing a strong, sturdy building.
But there are other ways!
Like what?
Well, take the Willis Tower in Chicago for example. Completed in 1973, designer Fazlur Khan started with the tube-in-tube model and took it to a whole new level.

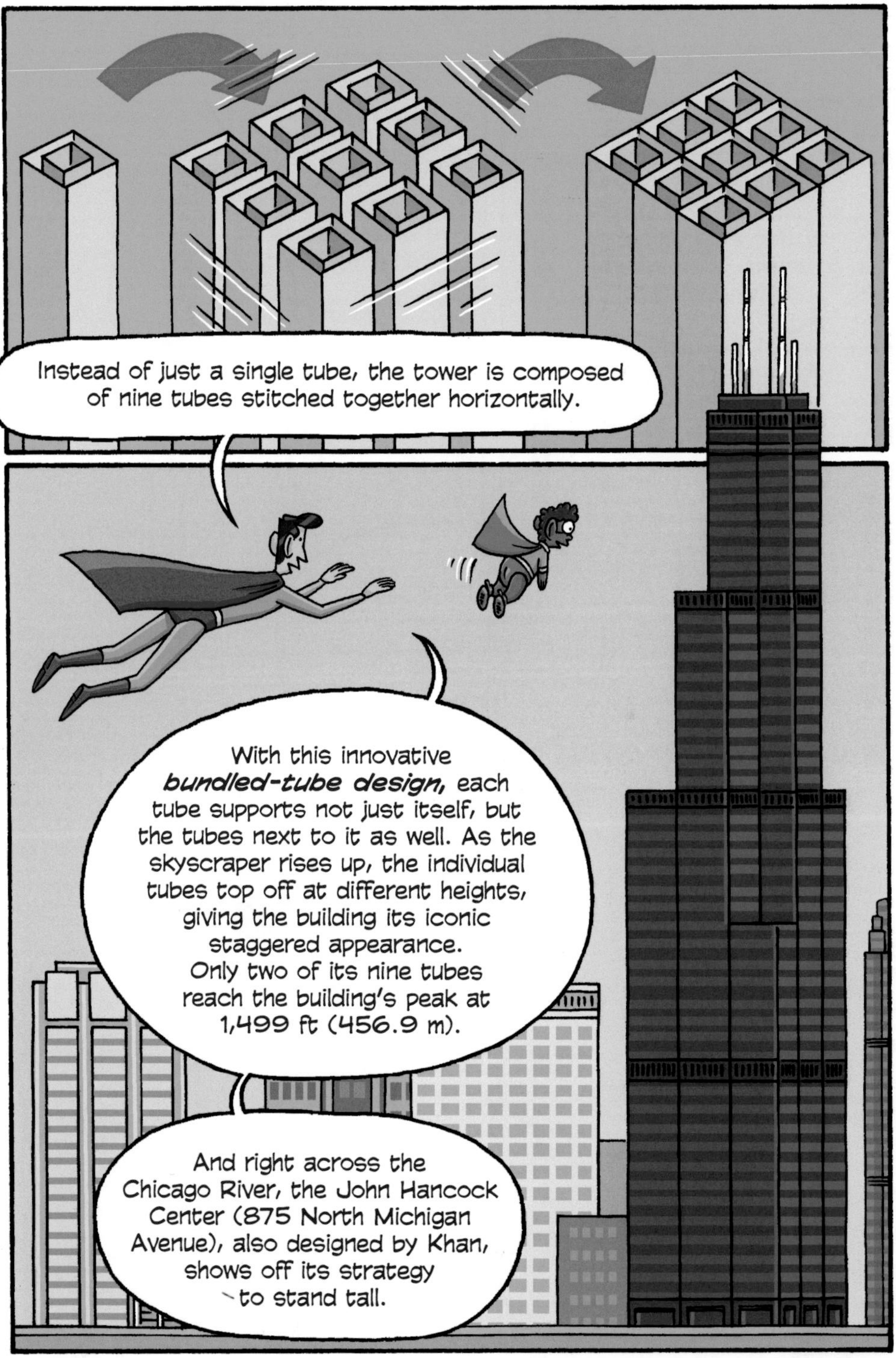
Instead of just a single tube, the tower is composed of nine tubes stitched together horizontally.
With this innovative ***bundled-tube design,*** each tube supports not just itself, but the tubes next to it as well. As the skyscraper rises up, the individual tubes top off at different heights, giving the building its iconic staggered appearance. Only two of its nine tubes reach the building's peak at 1,499 ft (456.9 m).
And right across the Chicago River, the John Hancock Center (875 North Michigan Avenue), also designed by Khan, shows off its strategy to stand tall.

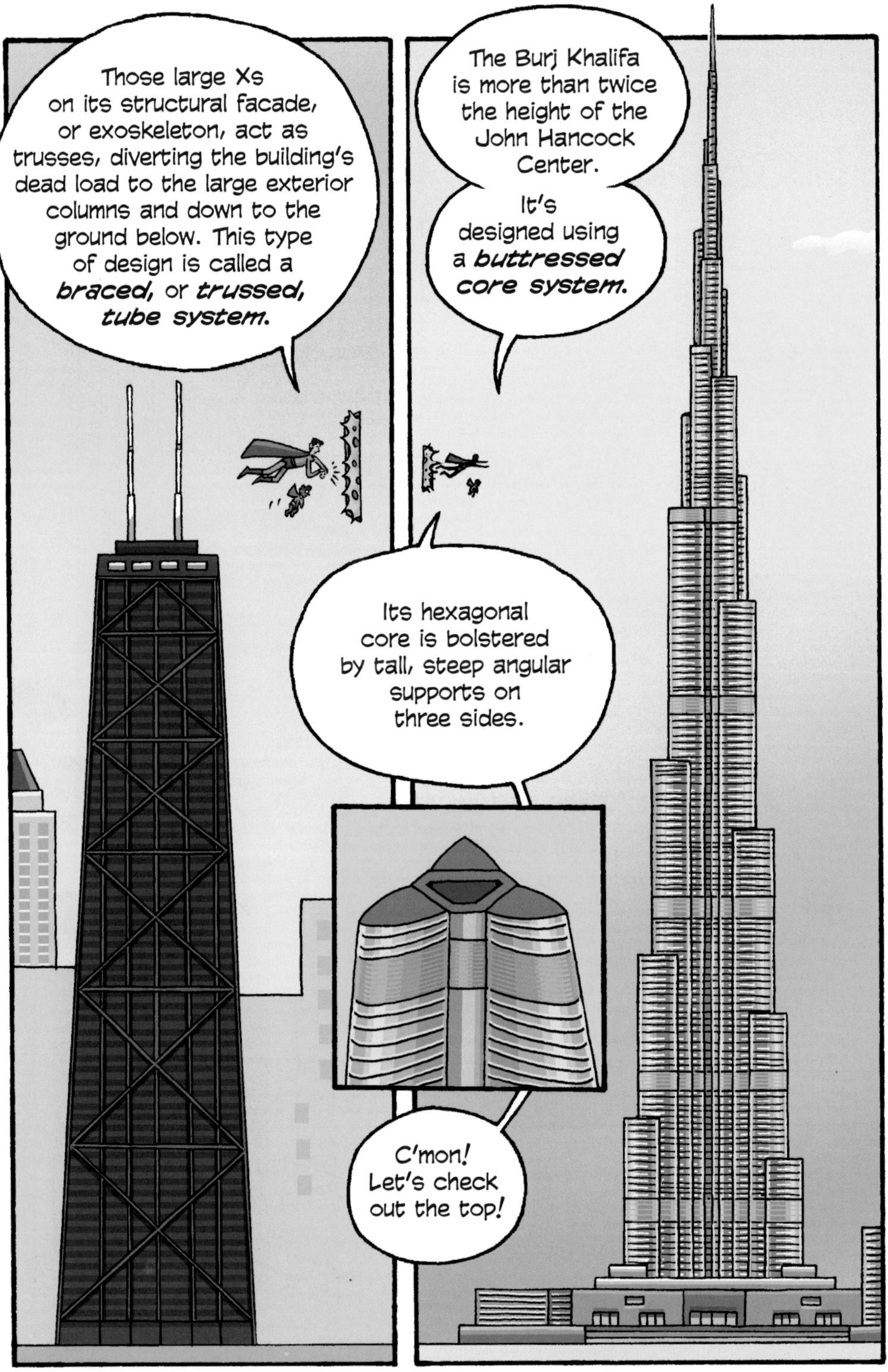

Those large Xs on its structural facade, or exoskeleton, act as trusses, diverting the building's dead load to the large exterior columns and down to the ground below. This type of design is called a braced, or trussed, tube system.
The Burj Khalifa is more than twice the height of the John Hancock Center.
It's designed using a buttressed core system.
Its hexagonal core is bolstered by tall, steep angular supports on three sides.
C'mon! Let's check out the top!

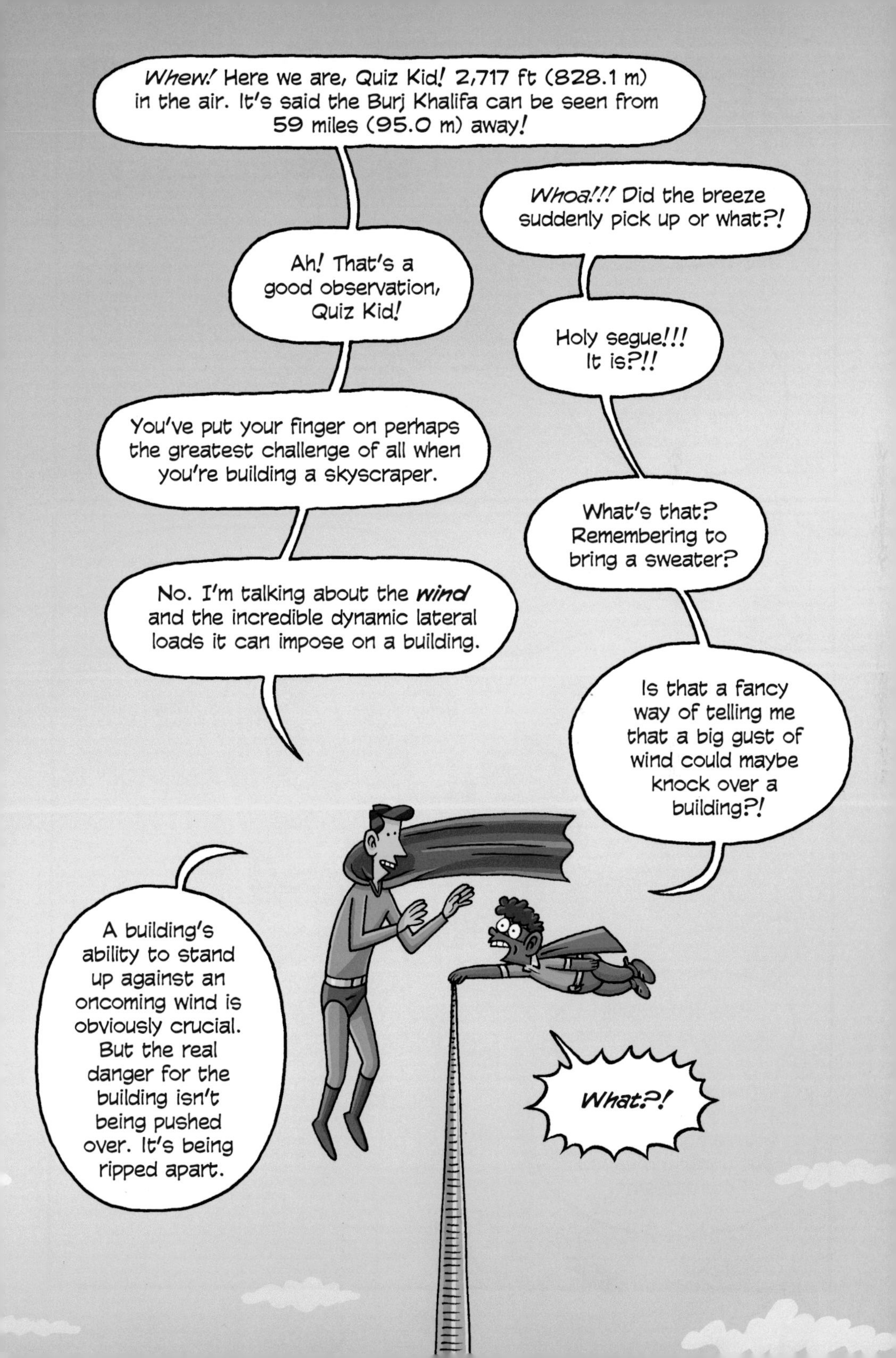
Whew! Here we are, Quiz Kid! 2,717 ft (828.1 m) in the air. It's said the Burj Khalifa can be seen from 59 miles (95.0 m) away!
Whoa!!! Did the breeze suddenly pick up or what?!
Ah! That's a good observation, Quiz Kid!
Holy segue!!! It is?!!
You've put your finger on perhaps the greatest challenge of all when you're building a skyscraper.
What's that? Remembering to bring a sweater?
No. I'm talking about the wind and the incredible dynamic lateral loads it can impose on a building.
Is that a fancy way of telling me that a big gust of wind could maybe knock over a building?!
A building's ability to stand up against an oncoming wind is obviously crucial. But the real danger for the building isn't being pushed over. It's being ripped apart.
What?!

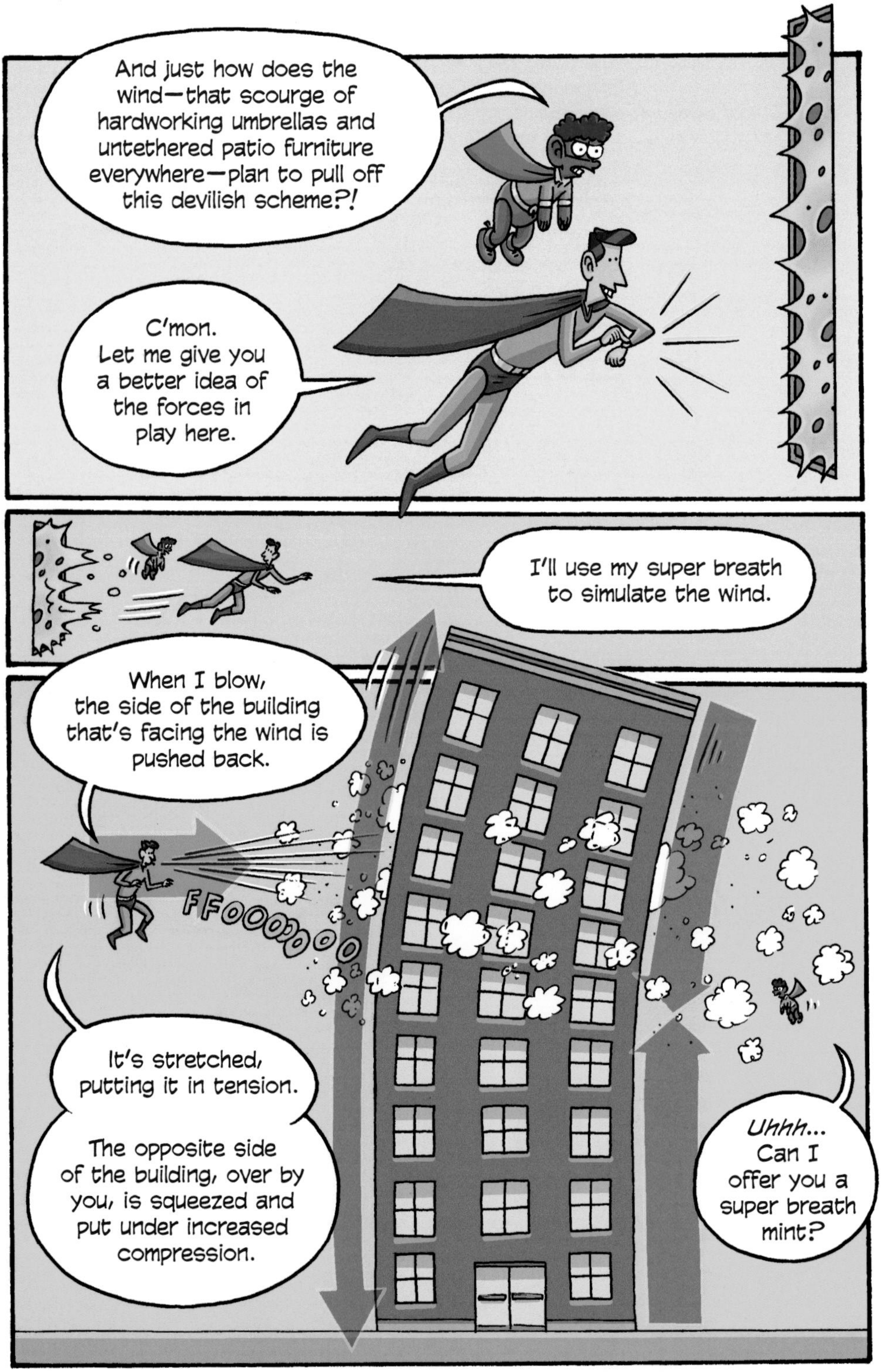

And just how does the wind—that scourge of hardworking umbrellas and untethered patio furniture everywhere—plan to pull off this devilish scheme?!
C'mon. Let me give you a better idea of the forces in play here.
I'll use my super breath to simulate the wind.
When I blow, the side of the building that's facing the wind is pushed back.
FFOOOOOOOO
It's stretched, putting it in tension.
The opposite side of the building, over by you, is squeezed and put under increased compression.
Uhhh... Can I offer you a super breath mint?

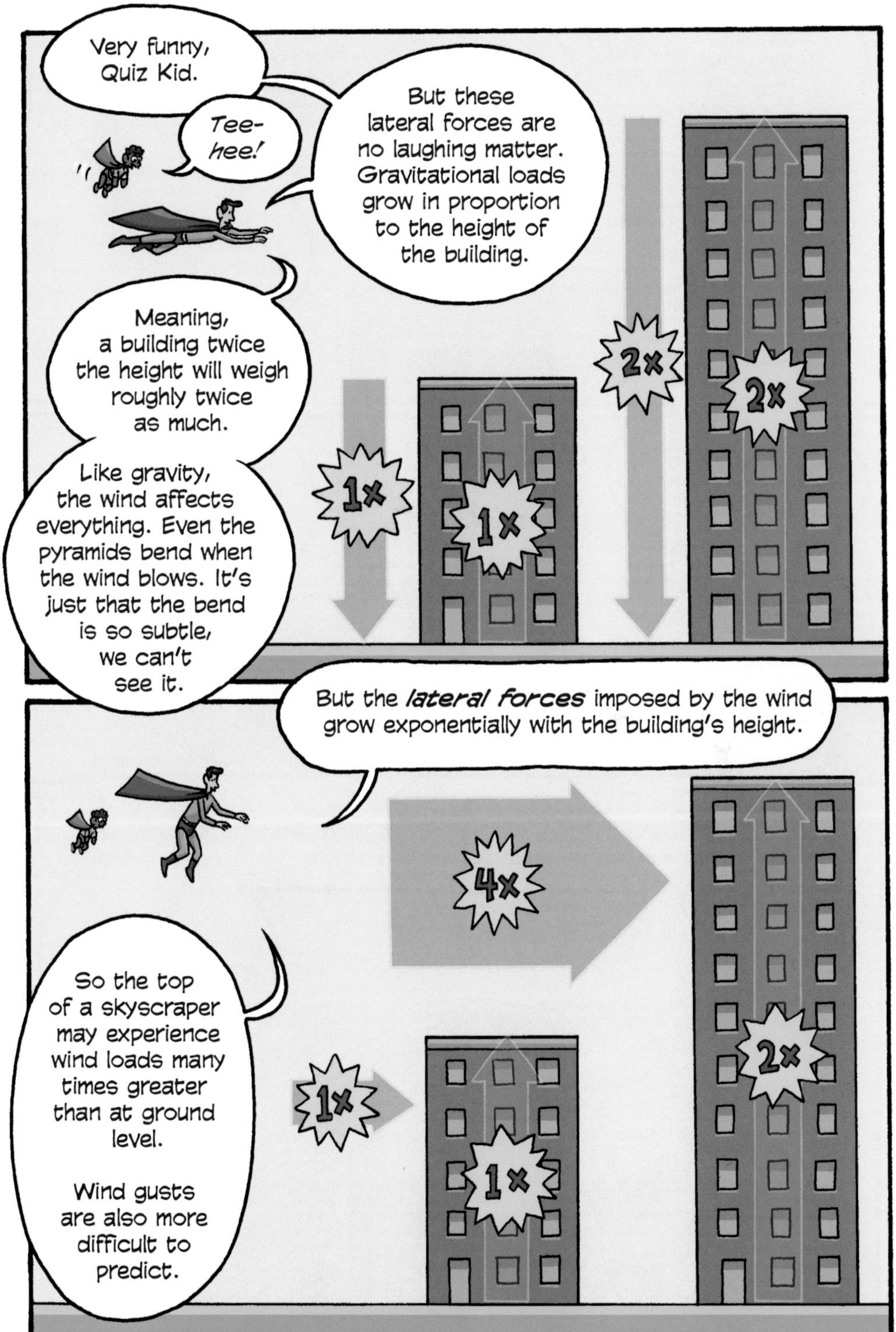

Very funny, Quiz Kid.
Tee-hee!
But these lateral forces are no laughing matter. Gravitational loads grow in proportion to the height of the building.
Meaning, a building twice the height will weigh roughly twice as much.
1x
1x
2x
2x
Like gravity, the wind affects everything. Even the pyramids bend when the wind blows. It's just that the bend is so subtle, we can't see it.
But the *lateral forces* imposed by the wind grow exponentially with the building's height.
4x
So the top of a skyscraper may experience wind loads many times greater than at ground level.
Wind gusts are also more difficult to predict.
1x
1x
2x

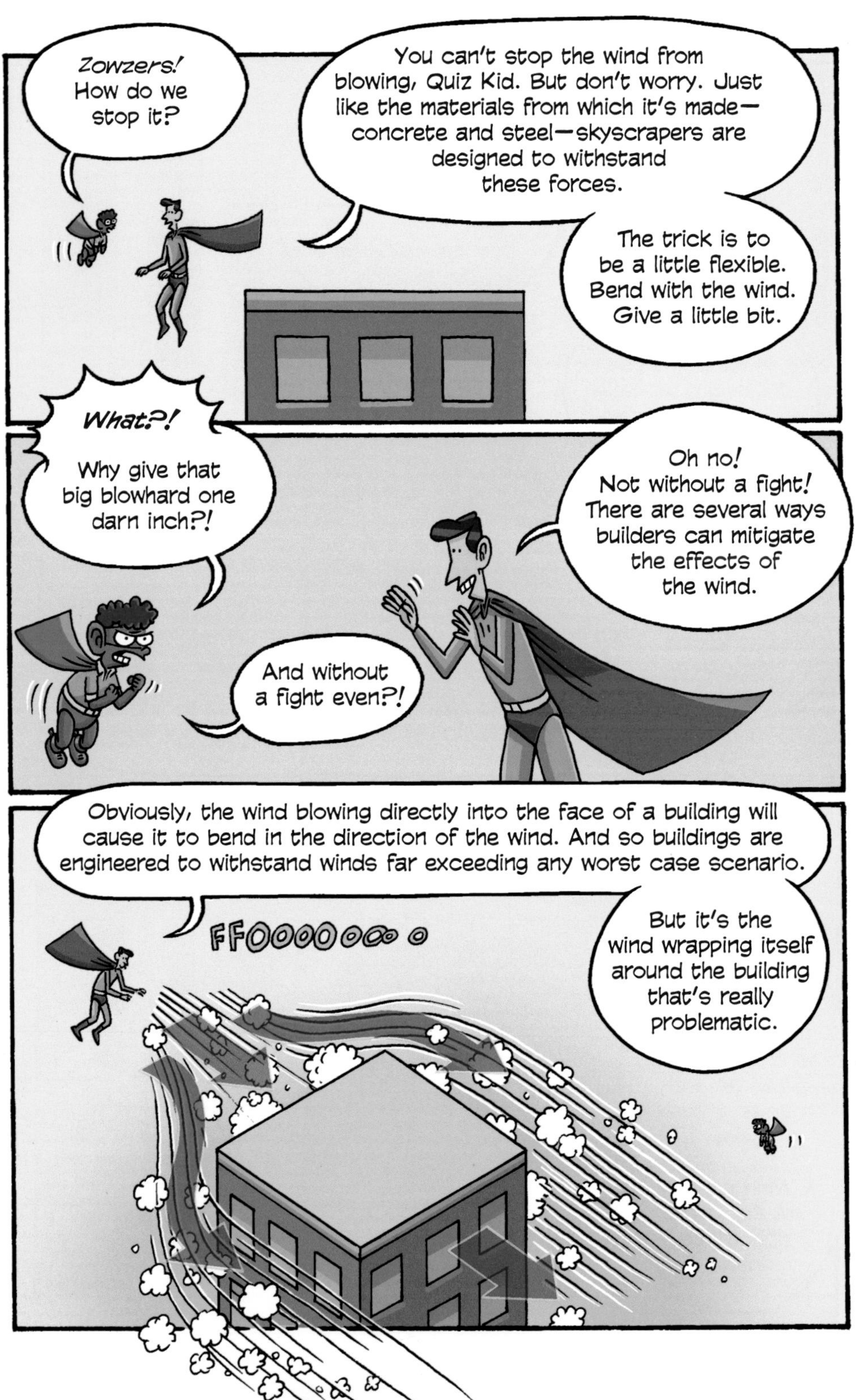
Zowzers! How do we stop it?
You can't stop the wind from blowing, Quiz Kid. But don't worry. Just like the materials from which it's made—concrete and steel—skyscrapers are designed to withstand these forces.
The trick is to be a little flexible. Bend with the wind. Give a little bit.
What?! Why give that big blowhard one darn inch?!
Oh no! Not without a fight! There are several ways builders can mitigate the effects of the wind.
And without a fight even?!
Obviously, the wind blowing directly into the face of a building will cause it to bend in the direction of the wind. And so buildings are engineered to withstand winds far exceeding any worst case scenario.
FFOOOOOOOO O
But it's the wind wrapping itself around the building that's really problematic.

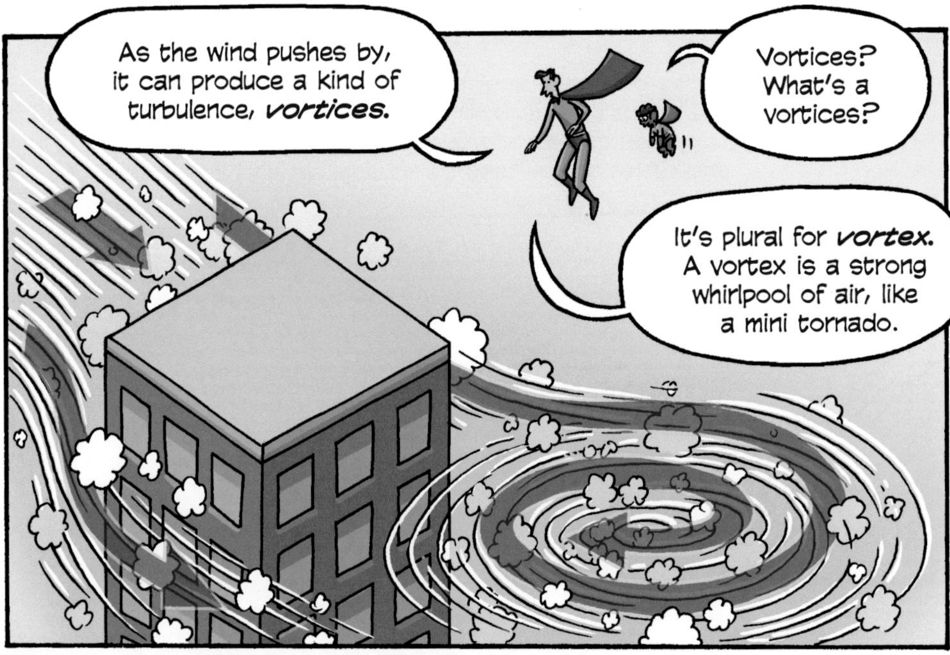
As the wind pushes by, it can produce a kind of turbulence, ***vortices.***
Vortices? What's a vortices?
It's plural for ***vortex.*** A vortex is a strong whirlpool of air, like a mini tornado.

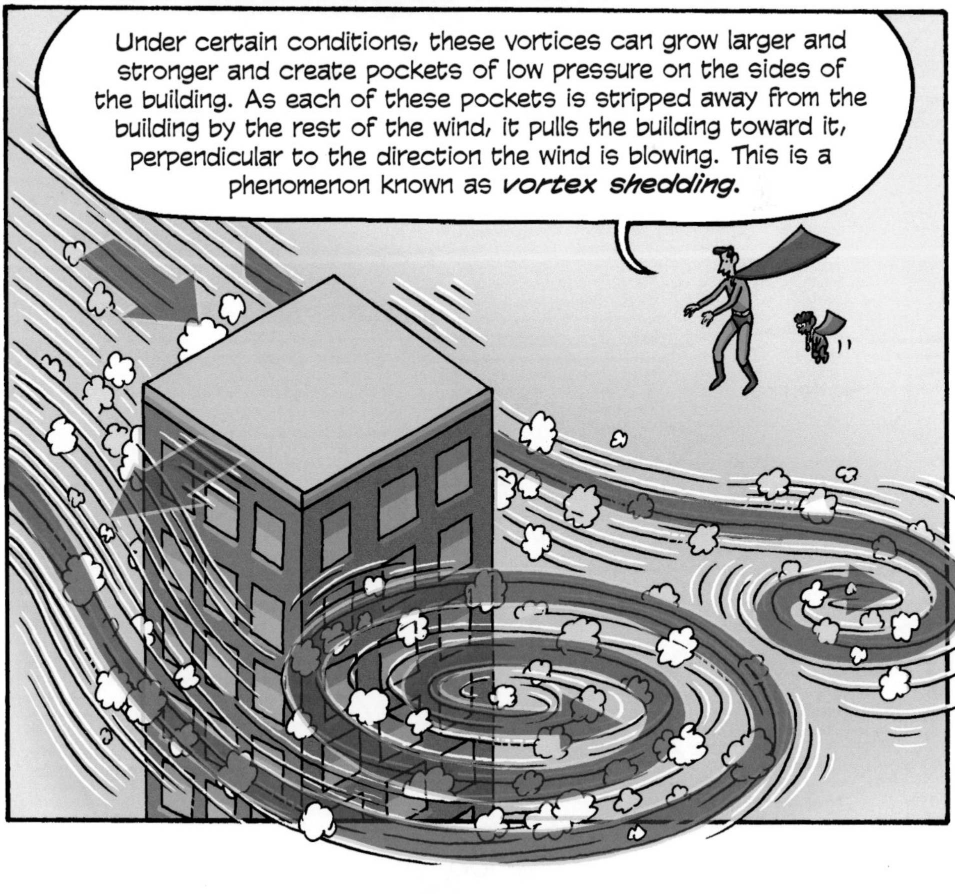
Under certain conditions, these vortices can grow larger and stronger and create pockets of low pressure on the sides of the building. As each of these pockets is stripped away from the building by the rest of the wind, it pulls the building toward it, perpendicular to the direction the wind is blowing. This is a phenomenon known as ***vortex shedding.***

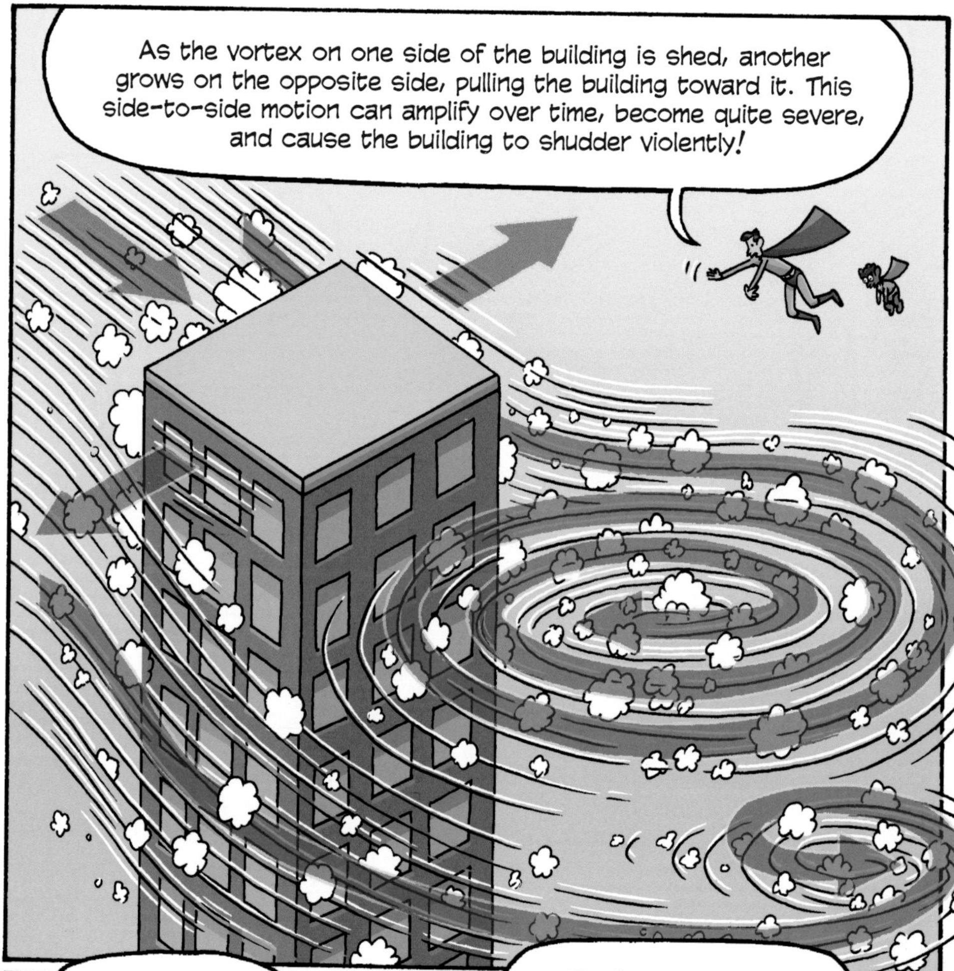
As the vortex on one side of the building is shed, another grows on the opposite side, pulling the building toward it. This side-to-side motion can amplify over time, become quite severe, and cause the building to shudder violently!

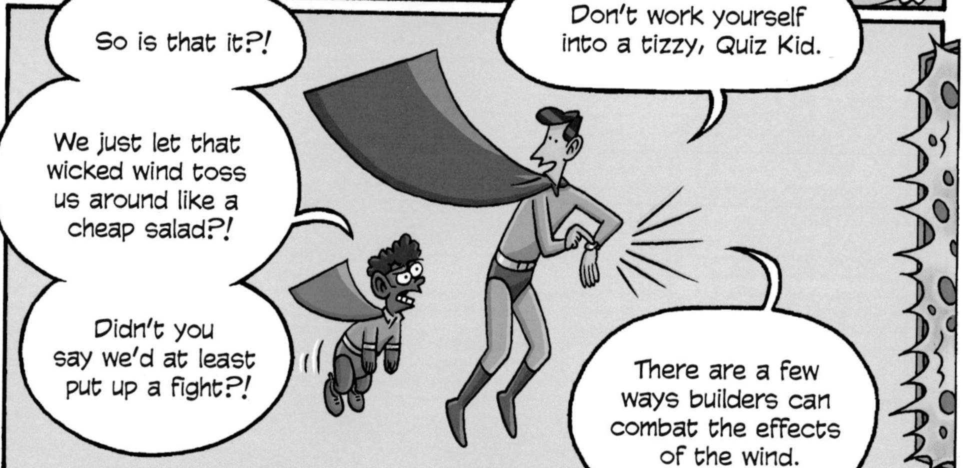
So is that it?!
We just let that wicked wind toss us around like a cheap salad?!
Didn't you say we'd at least put up a fight?!
Don't work yourself into a tizzy, Quiz Kid.
There are a few ways builders can combat the effects of the wind.

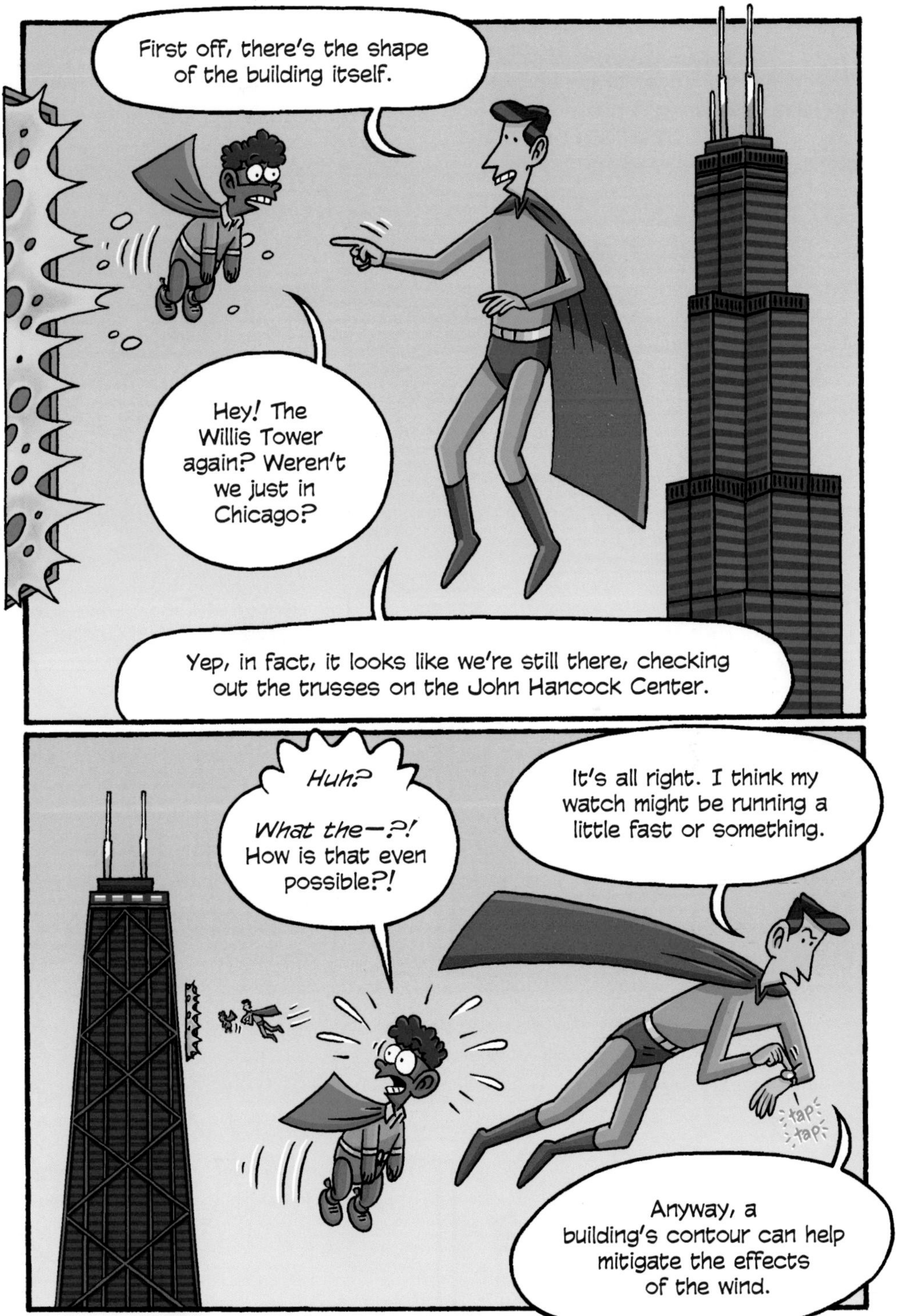
First off, there's the shape of the building itself.
Hey! The Willis Tower again? Weren't we just in Chicago?
Yep, in fact, it looks like we're still there, checking out the trusses on the John Hancock Center.
Huh?
What the—?! How is that even possible?!
It's all right. I think my watch might be running a little fast or something.
tap tap
Anyway, a building's contour can help mitigate the effects of the wind.

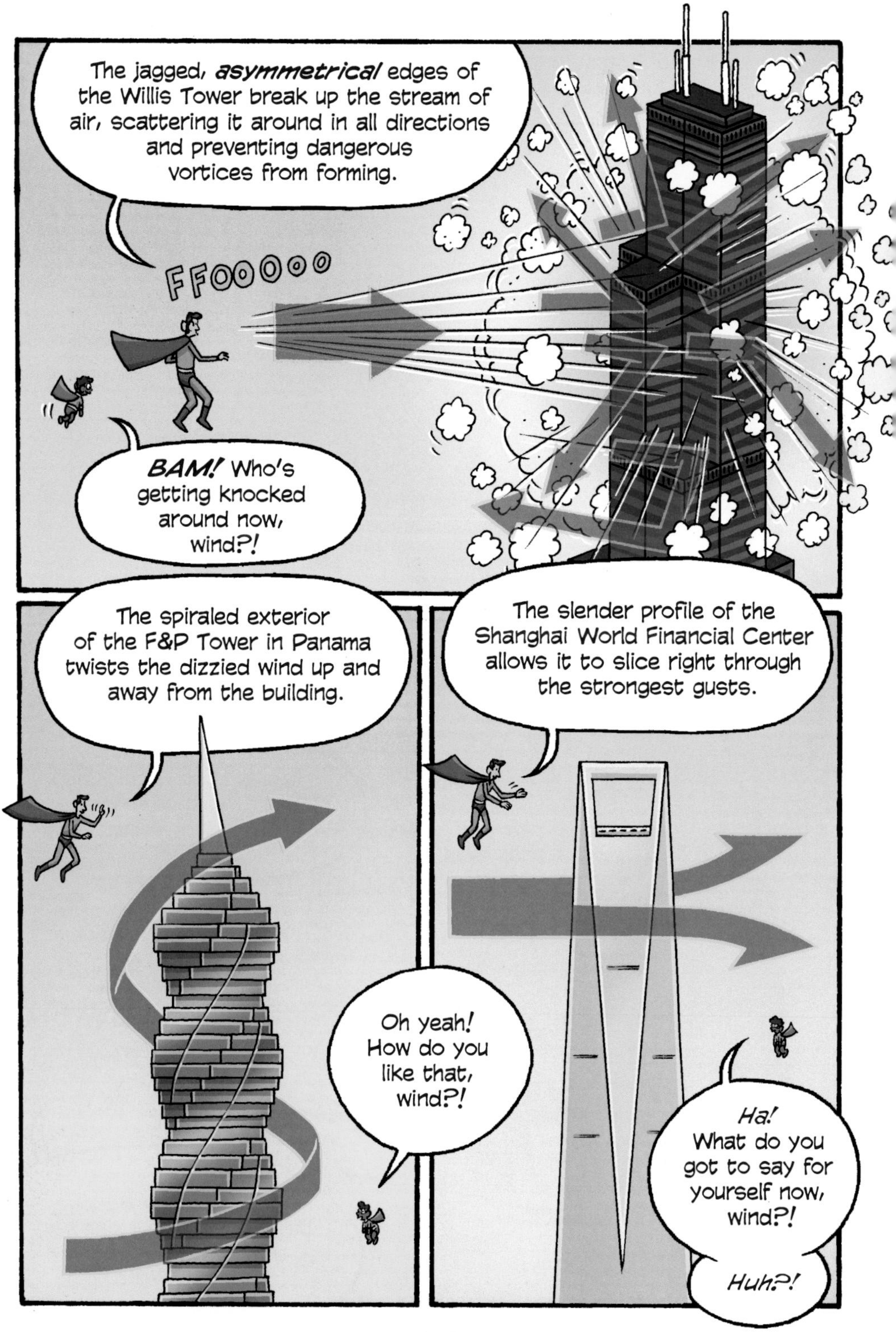
The jagged, ***asymmetrical*** edges of the Willis Tower break up the stream of air, scattering it around in all directions and preventing dangerous vortices from forming.
FFOOOOO
BAM! Who's getting knocked around now, wind?!
The spiraled exterior of the F&P Tower in Panama twists the dizzied wind up and away from the building.
Oh yeah! How do you like that, wind?!
The slender profile of the Shanghai World Financial Center allows it to slice right through the strongest gusts.
Ha! What do you got to say for yourself now, wind?!
Huh?!

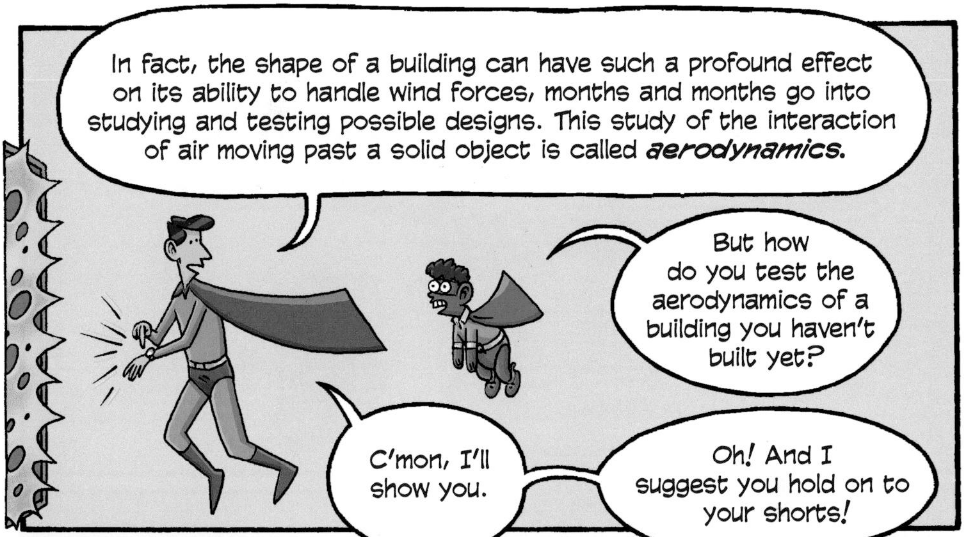
In fact, the shape of a building can have such a profound effect on its ability to handle wind forces, months and months go into studying and testing possible designs. This study of the interaction of air moving past a solid object is called *aerodynamics.*
But how do you test the aerodynamics of a building you haven't built yet?
C'mon, I'll show you.
Oh! And I suggest you hold on to your shorts!

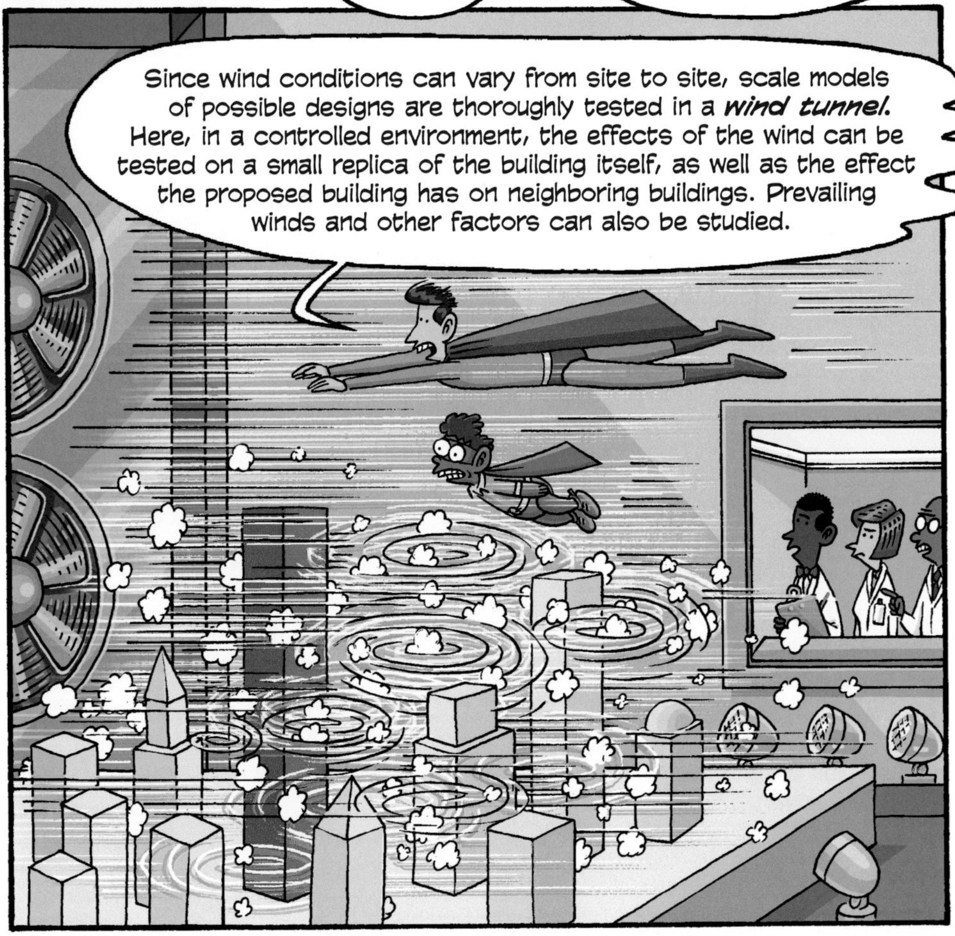
Since wind conditions can vary from site to site, scale models of possible designs are thoroughly tested in a *wind tunnel.* Here, in a controlled environment, the effects of the wind can be tested on a small replica of the building itself, as well as the effect the proposed building has on neighboring buildings. Prevailing winds and other factors can also be studied.

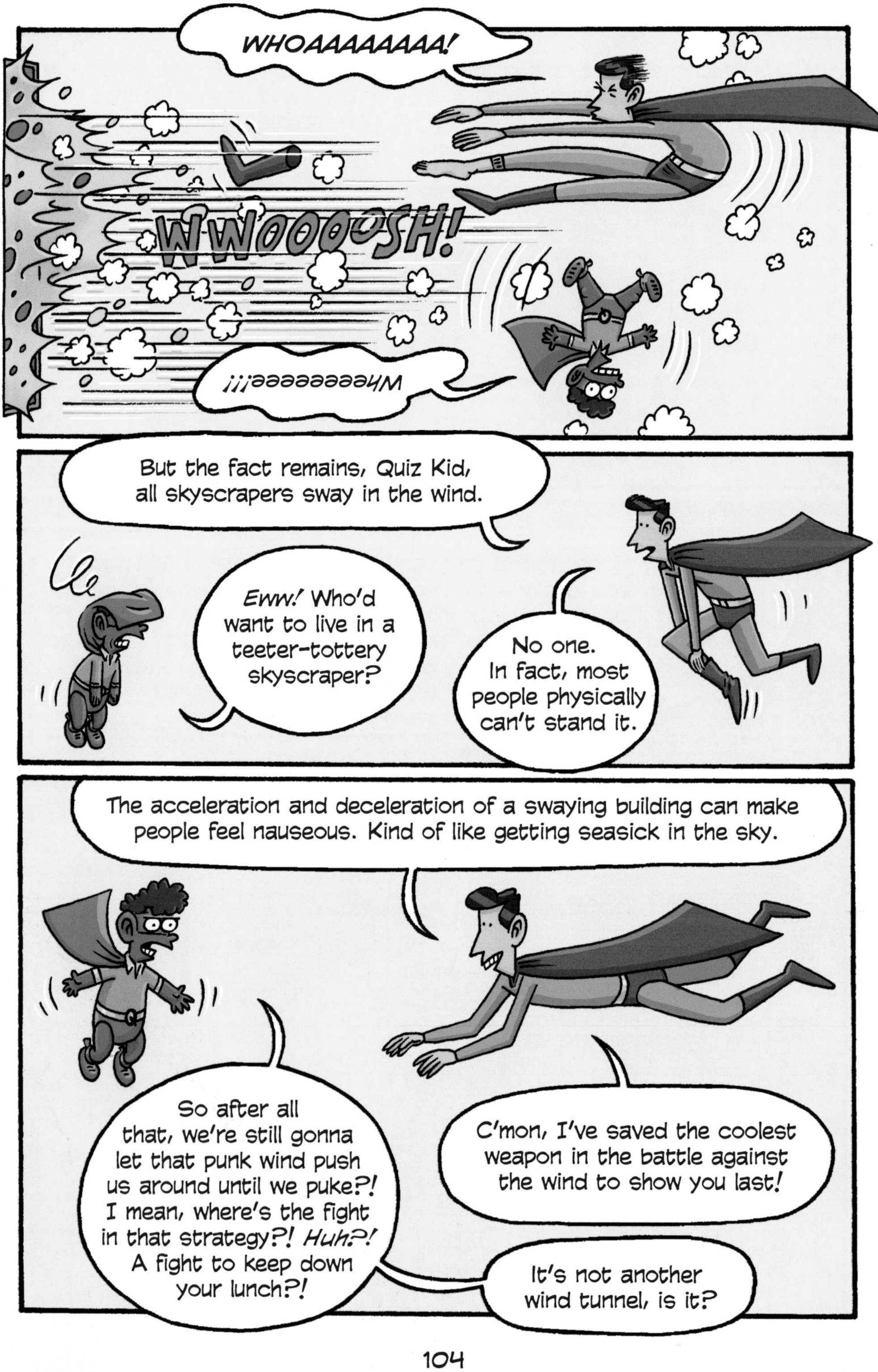
WHOAAAAAAAA!
WWOOOOSH!
Wheeeeeeee!!!
But the fact remains, Quiz Kid, all skyscrapers sway in the wind.
Eww! Who'd want to live in a teeter-tottery skyscraper?
No one. In fact, most people physically can't stand it.
The acceleration and deceleration of a swaying building can make people feel nauseous. Kind of like getting seasick in the sky.
So after all that, we're still gonna let that punk wind push us around until we puke?! I mean, where's the fight in that strategy?! Huh?! A fight to keep down your lunch?!
C'mon, I've saved the coolest weapon in the battle against the wind to show you last!
It's not another wind tunnel, is it?

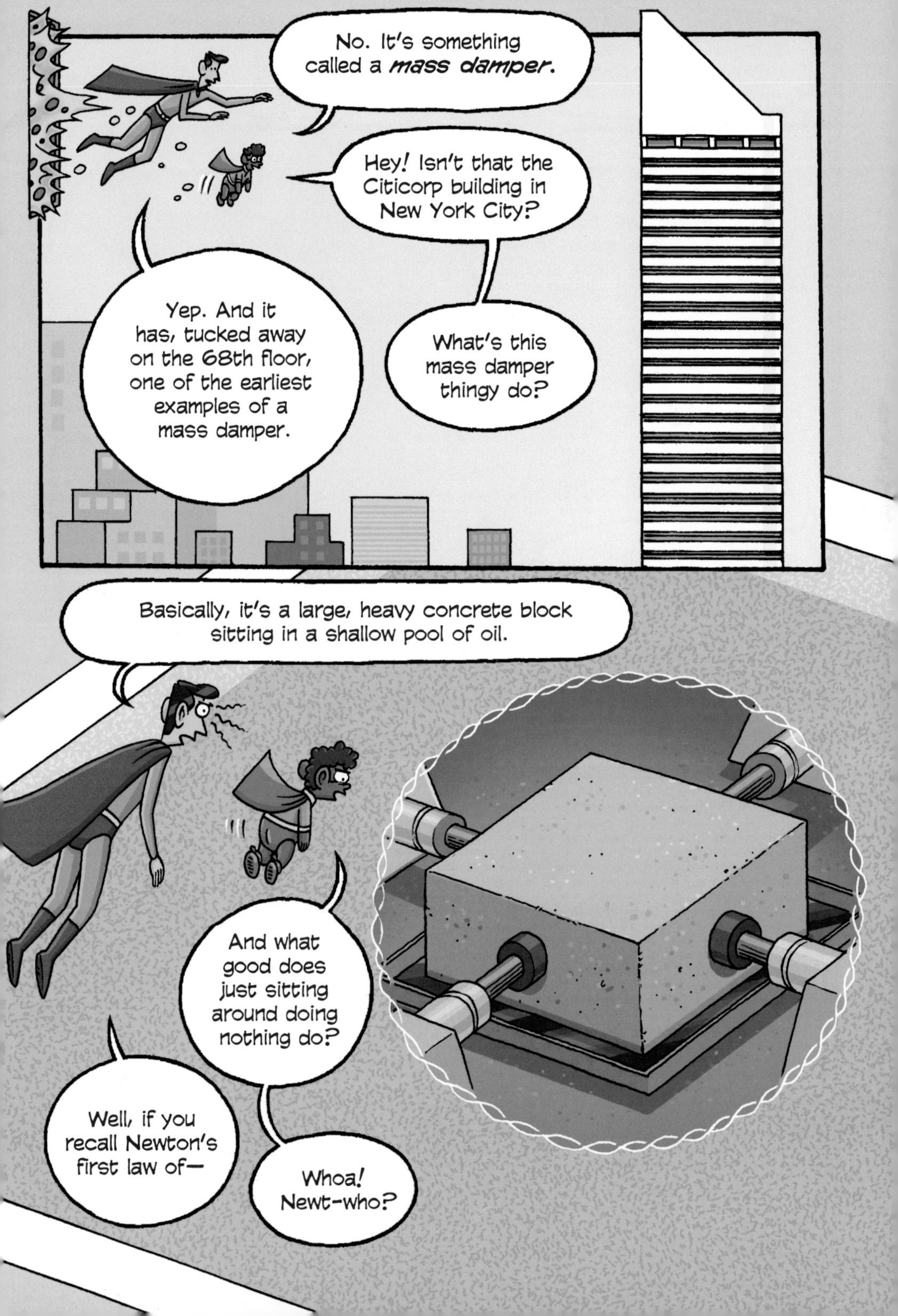
No. It's something called a *mass damper*.
Hey! Isn't that the Citicorp building in New York City?
Yep. And it has, tucked away on the 68th floor, one of the earliest examples of a mass damper.
What's this mass damper thingy do?
Basically, it's a large, heavy concrete block sitting in a shallow pool of oil.
And what good does just sitting around doing nothing do?
Well, if you recall Newton's first law of—
Whoa! Newt-who?

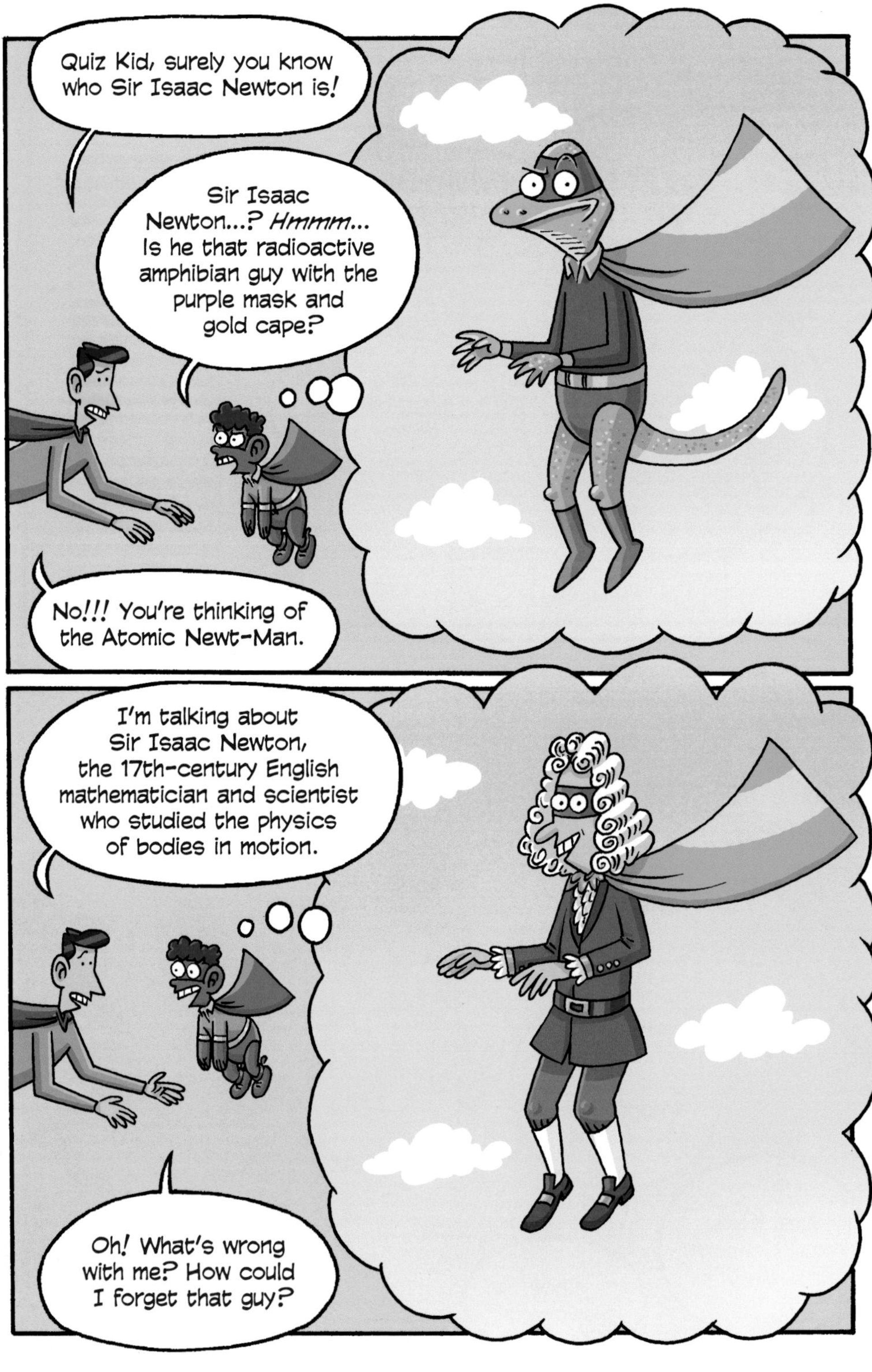
Quiz Kid, surely you know who Sir Isaac Newton is!
Sir Isaac Newton...? *Hmmm...* Is he that radioactive amphibian guy with the purple mask and gold cape?
No!!! You're thinking of the Atomic Newt-Man.
I'm talking about Sir Isaac Newton, the 17th-century English mathematician and scientist who studied the physics of bodies in motion.
Oh! What's wrong with me? How could I forget that guy?

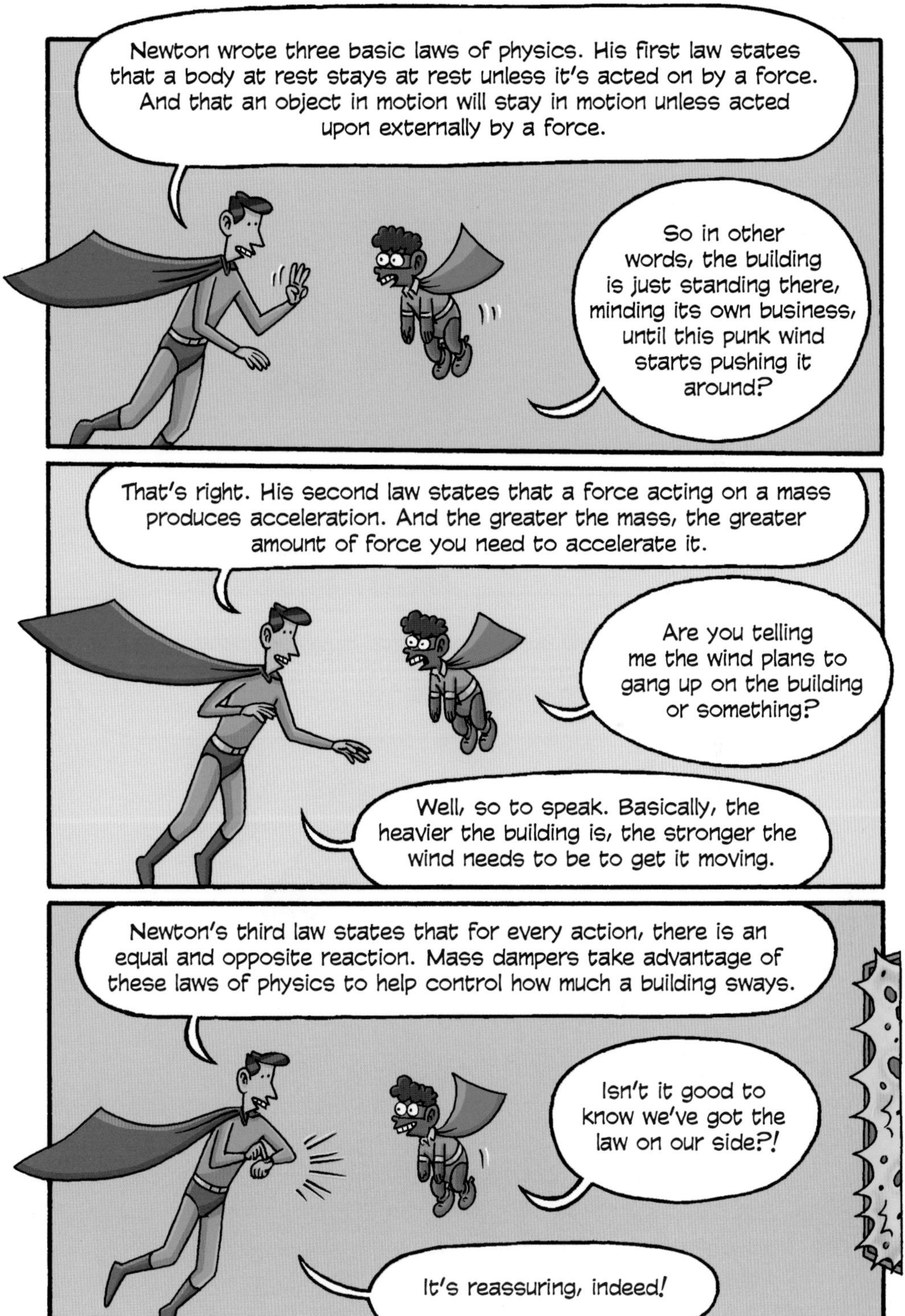
Newton wrote three basic laws of physics. His first law states that a body at rest stays at rest unless it's acted on by a force. And that an object in motion will stay in motion unless acted upon externally by a force.
So in other words, the building is just standing there, minding its own business, until this punk wind starts pushing it around?
That's right. His second law states that a force acting on a mass produces acceleration. And the greater the mass, the greater amount of force you need to accelerate it.
Are you telling me the wind plans to gang up on the building or something?
Well, so to speak. Basically, the heavier the building is, the stronger the wind needs to be to get it moving.
Newton's third law states that for every action, there is an equal and opposite reaction. Mass dampers take advantage of these laws of physics to help control how much a building sways.
Isn't it good to know we've got the law on our side?!
It's reassuring, indeed!

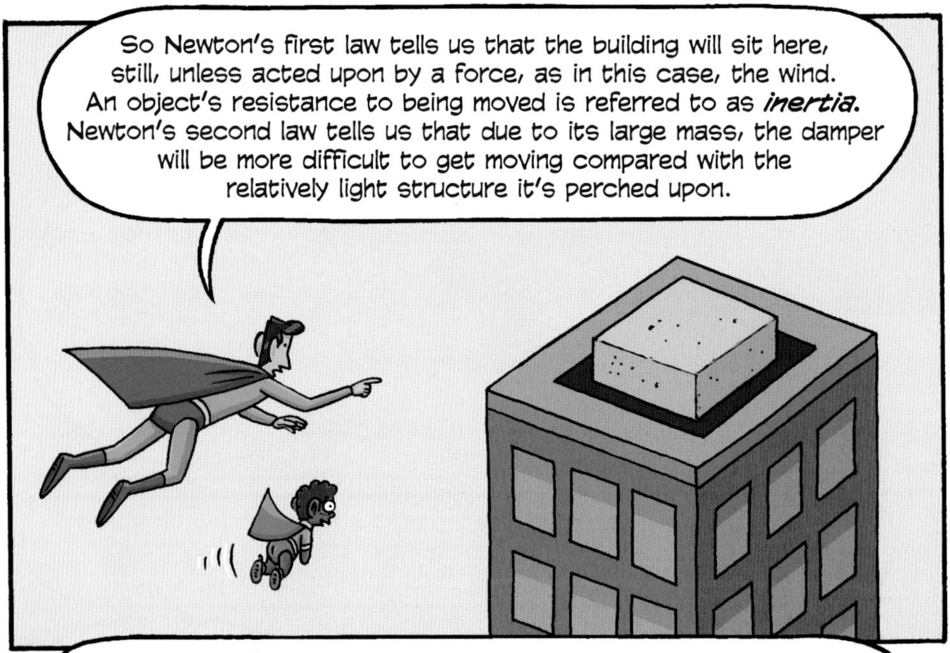
So Newton's first law tells us that the building will sit here, still, unless acted upon by a force, as in this case, the wind. An object's resistance to being moved is referred to as *inertia.* Newton's second law tells us that due to its large mass, the damper will be more difficult to get moving compared with the relatively light structure it's perched upon.

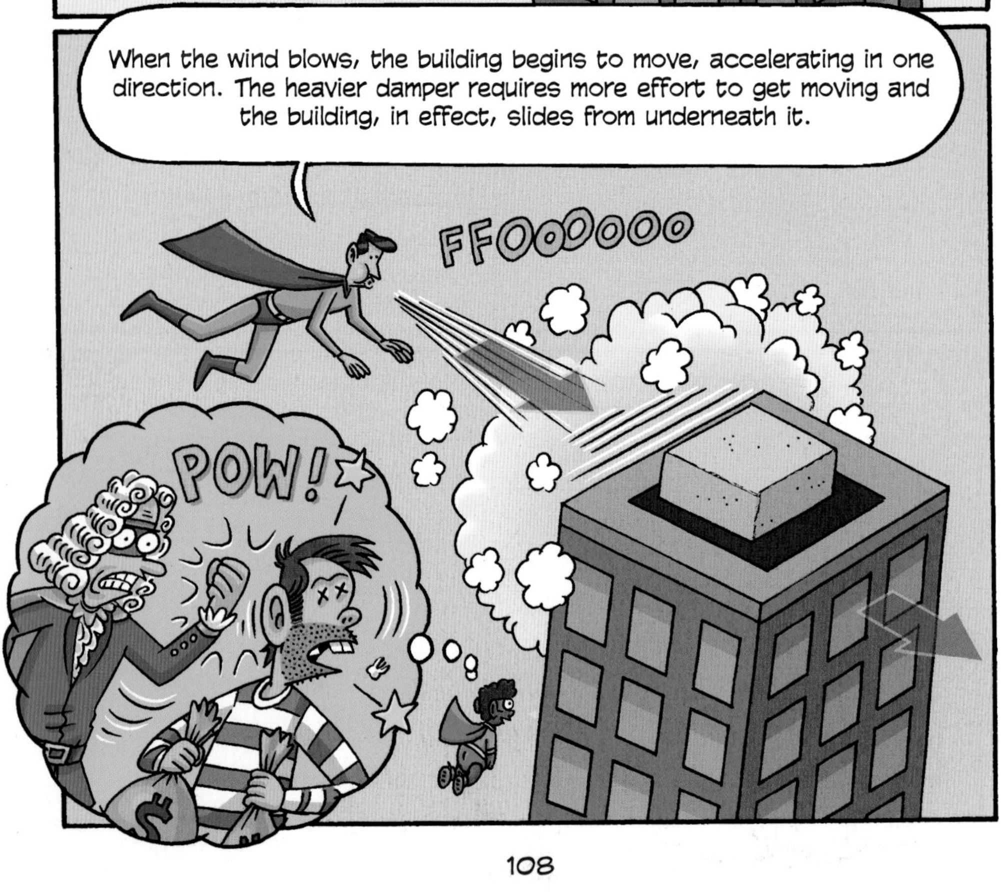
When the wind blows, the building begins to move, accelerating in one direction. The heavier damper requires more effort to get moving and the building, in effect, slides from underneath it.
FFOOOOOOO
POW!

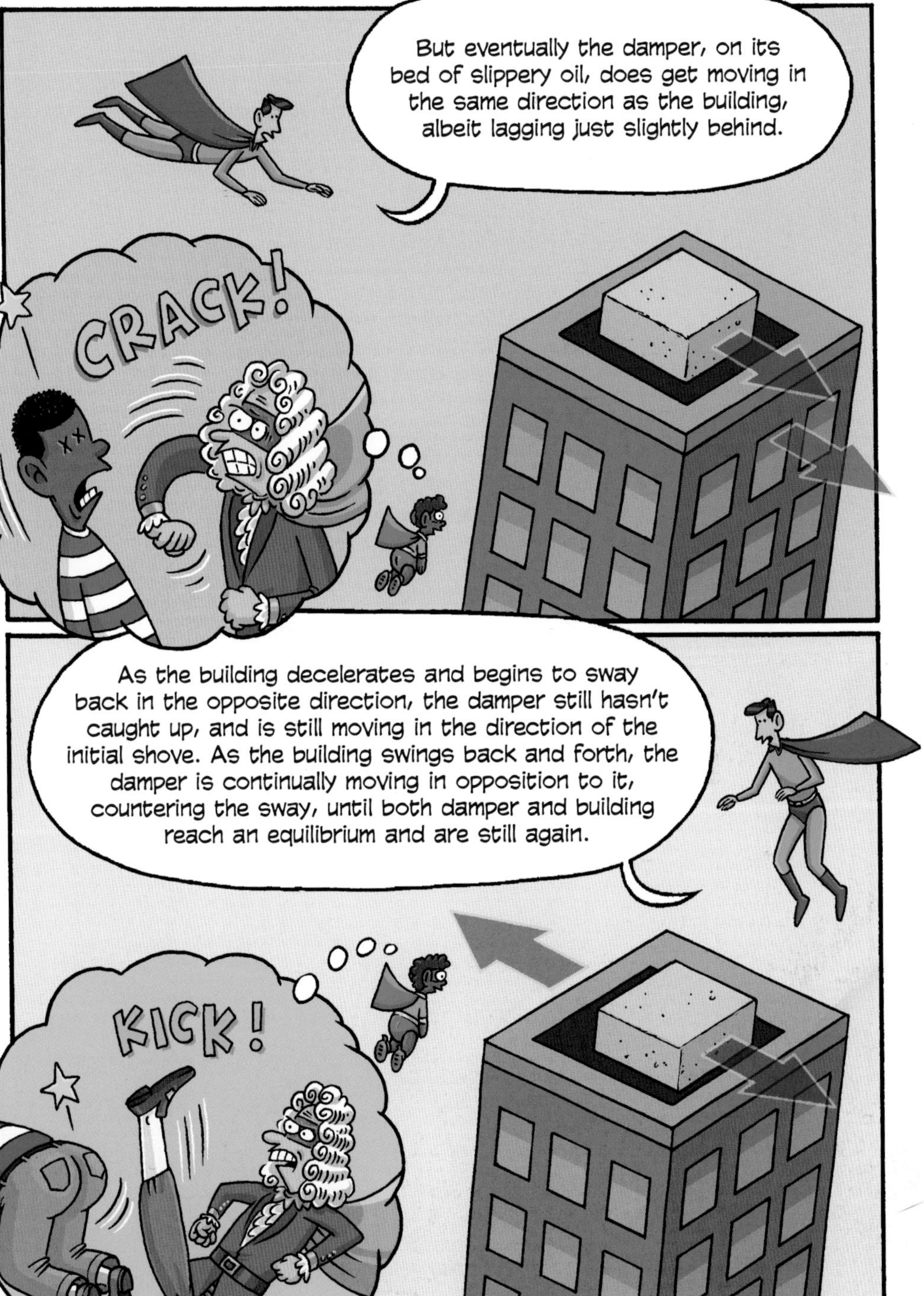
But eventually the damper, on its bed of slippery oil, does get moving in the same direction as the building, albeit lagging just slightly behind.
CRACK!
As the building decelerates and begins to sway back in the opposite direction, the damper still hasn't caught up, and is still moving in the direction of the initial shove. As the building swings back and forth, the damper is continually moving in opposition to it, countering the sway, until both damper and building reach an equilibrium and are still again.
KICK!

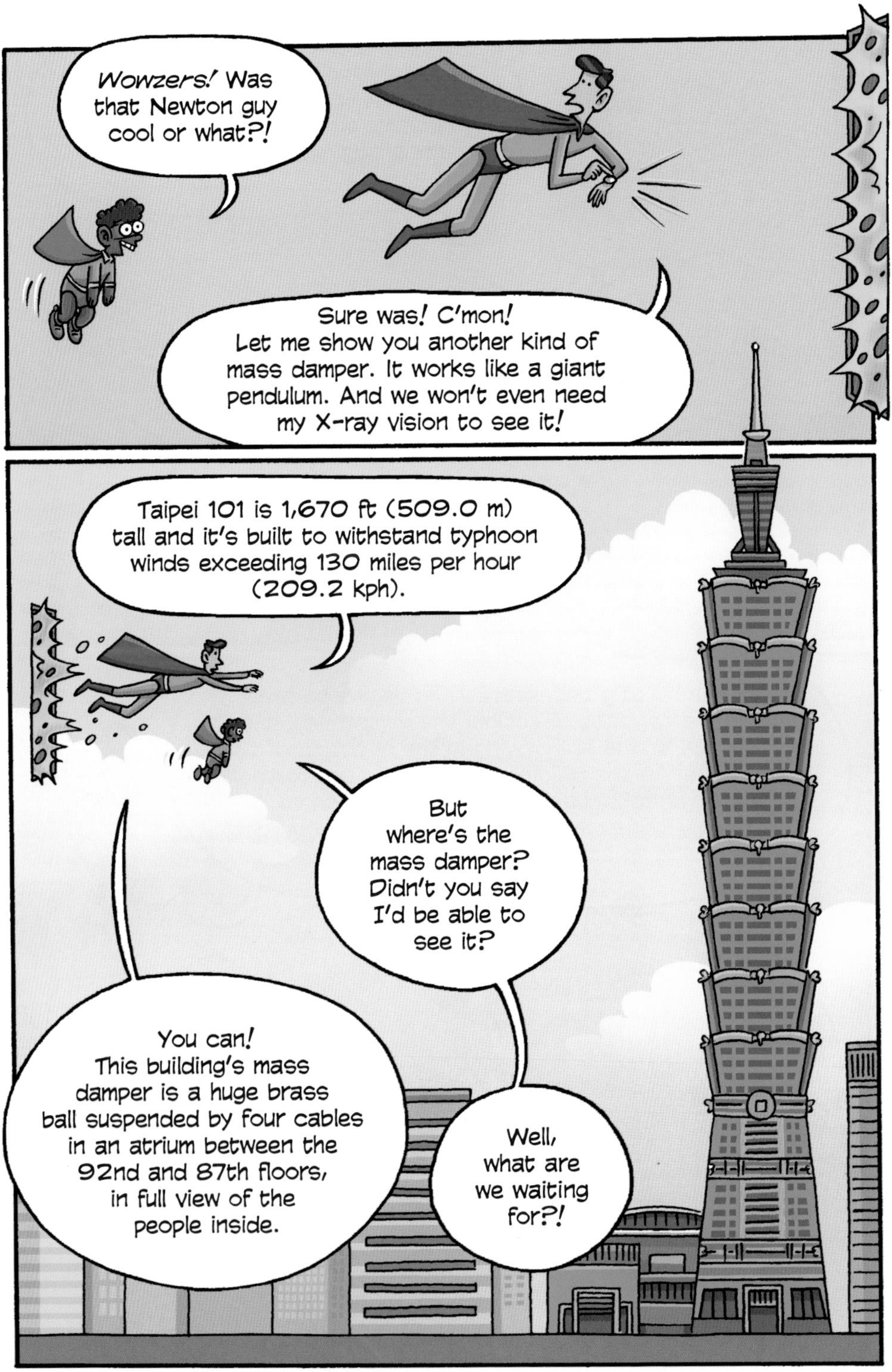
Wowzers! Was that Newton guy cool or what?!
Sure was! C'mon! Let me show you another kind of mass damper. It works like a giant pendulum. And we won't even need my X-ray vision to see it!
Taipei 101 is 1,670 ft (509.0 m) tall and it's built to withstand typhoon winds exceeding 130 miles per hour (209.2 kph).
But where's the mass damper? Didn't you say I'd be able to see it?
You can! This building's mass damper is a huge brass ball suspended by four cables in an atrium between the 92nd and 87th floors, in full view of the people inside.
Well, what are we waiting for?!

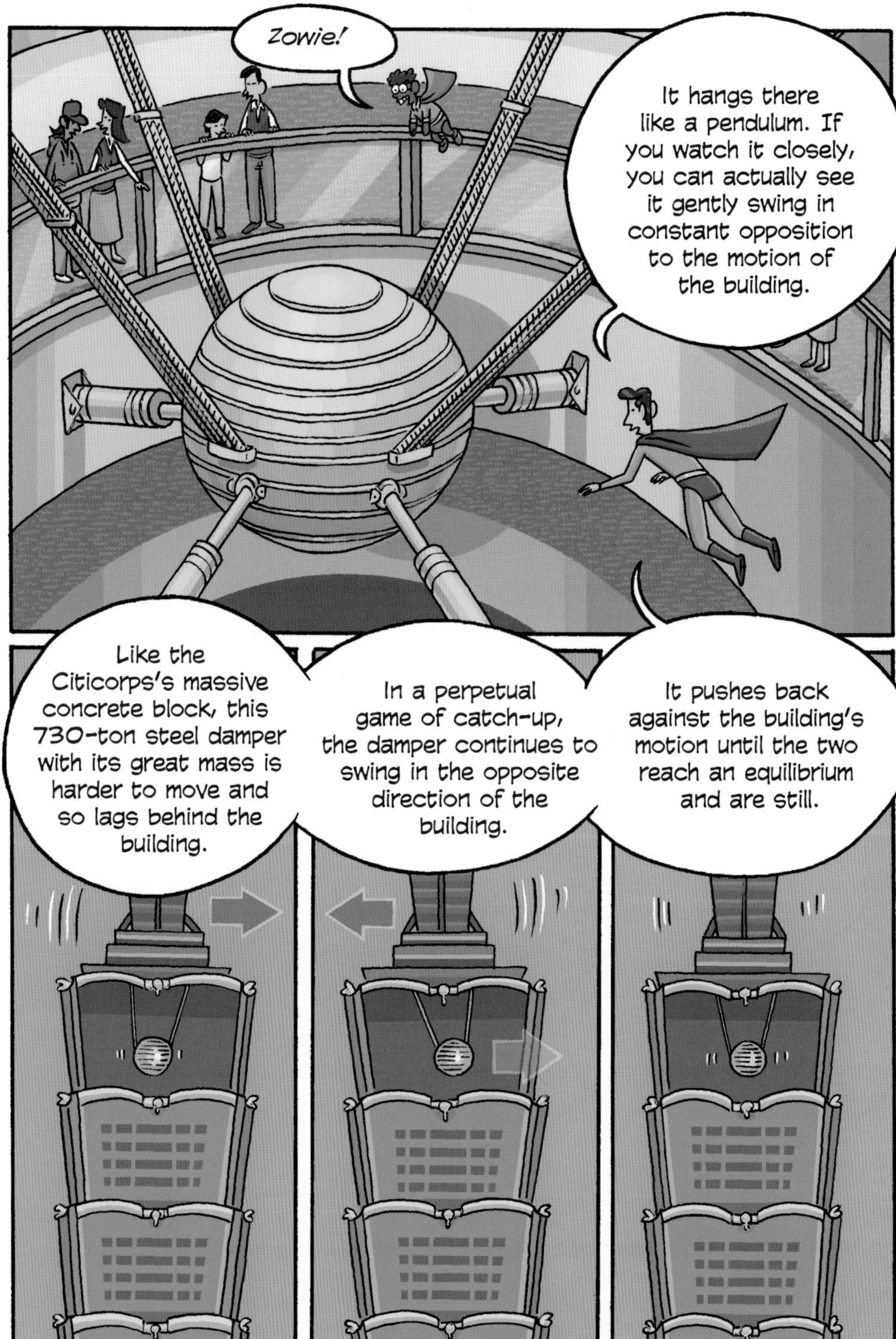
Zowie!
It hangs there like a pendulum. If you watch it closely, you can actually see it gently swing in constant opposition to the motion of the building.
Like the Citicorps's massive concrete block, this 730-ton steel damper with its great mass is harder to move and so lags behind the building.
In a perpetual game of catch-up, the damper continues to swing in the opposite direction of the building.
It pushes back against the building's motion until the two reach an equilibrium and are still.

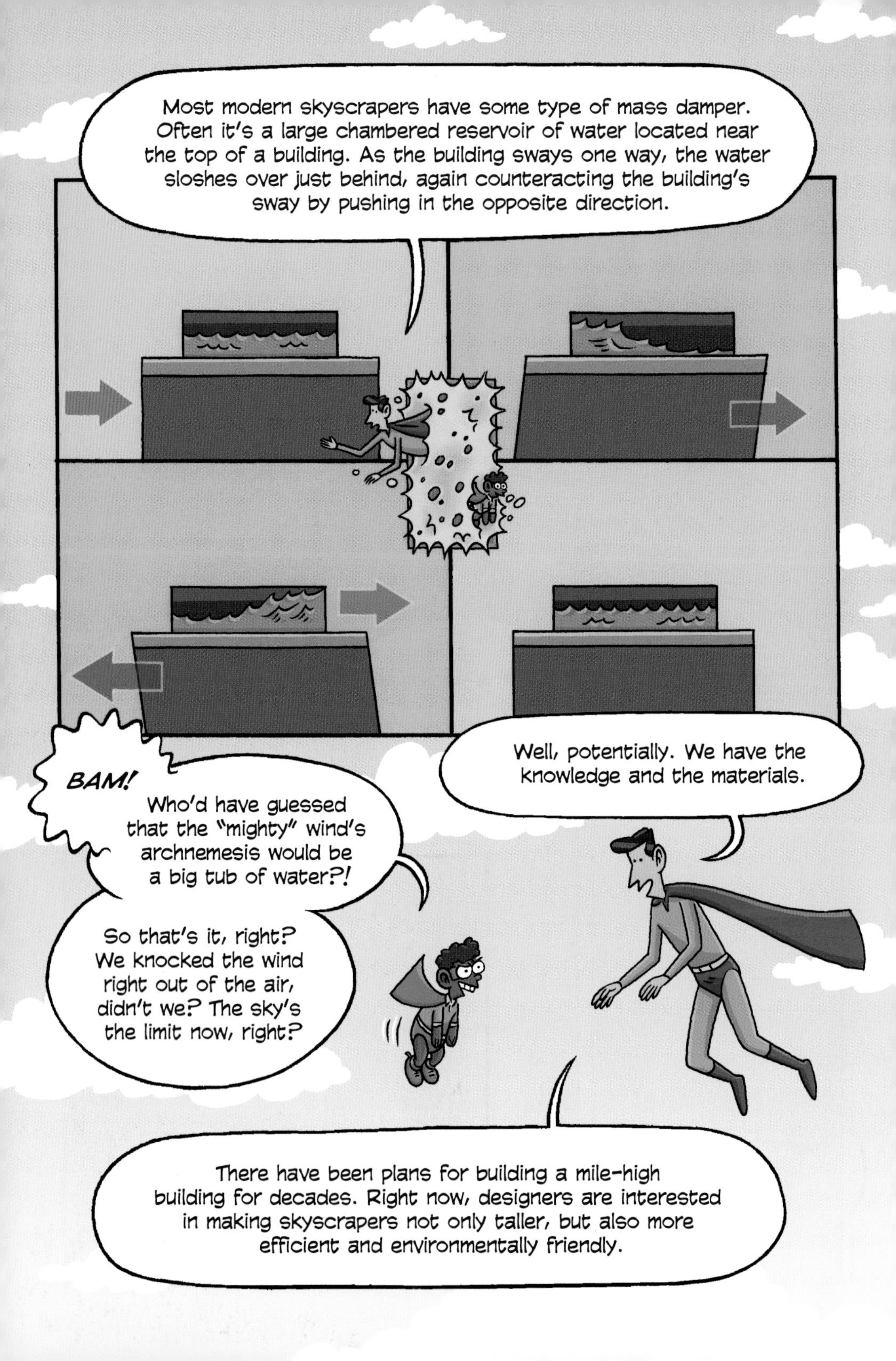
Most modern skyscrapers have some type of mass damper. Often it's a large chambered reservoir of water located near the top of a building. As the building sways one way, the water sloshes over just behind, again counteracting the building's sway by pushing in the opposite direction.
BAM!
Who'd have guessed that the "mighty" wind's archnemesis would be a big tub of water?!
So that's it, right? We knocked the wind right out of the air, didn't we? The sky's the limit now, right?
Well, potentially. We have the knowledge and the materials.
There have been plans for building a mile-high building for decades. Right now, designers are interested in making skyscrapers not only taller, but also more efficient and environmentally friendly.

The towers of the Bosco Verticale in Italy aren't overwhelmingly tall, but check it out—they're covered in more than 17,000 plants that help clean Milan's air and provide shade and natural insulation for the building.

The 787 ft (239.8 m) tall towers of the Bahrain Trade Center are connected by three skybridges with turbines attached, intended to harness the wind and use it to help power the building.

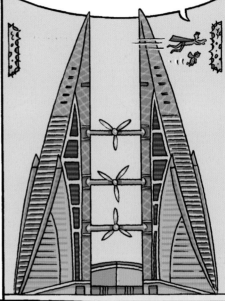

Wowzers! What will they think of next?

Well, unfortunately, my watch doesn't allow us to travel into the future or I'd show you some of what's on the horizon as far as the skyline is concerned.

Uh... Did I mention I was supposed to be home for dinner?

Oh my! And I've missed an entire day at work! I know! I'll set my watch to take us back to the beginning of the day, when we started our little skyscraper adventure.

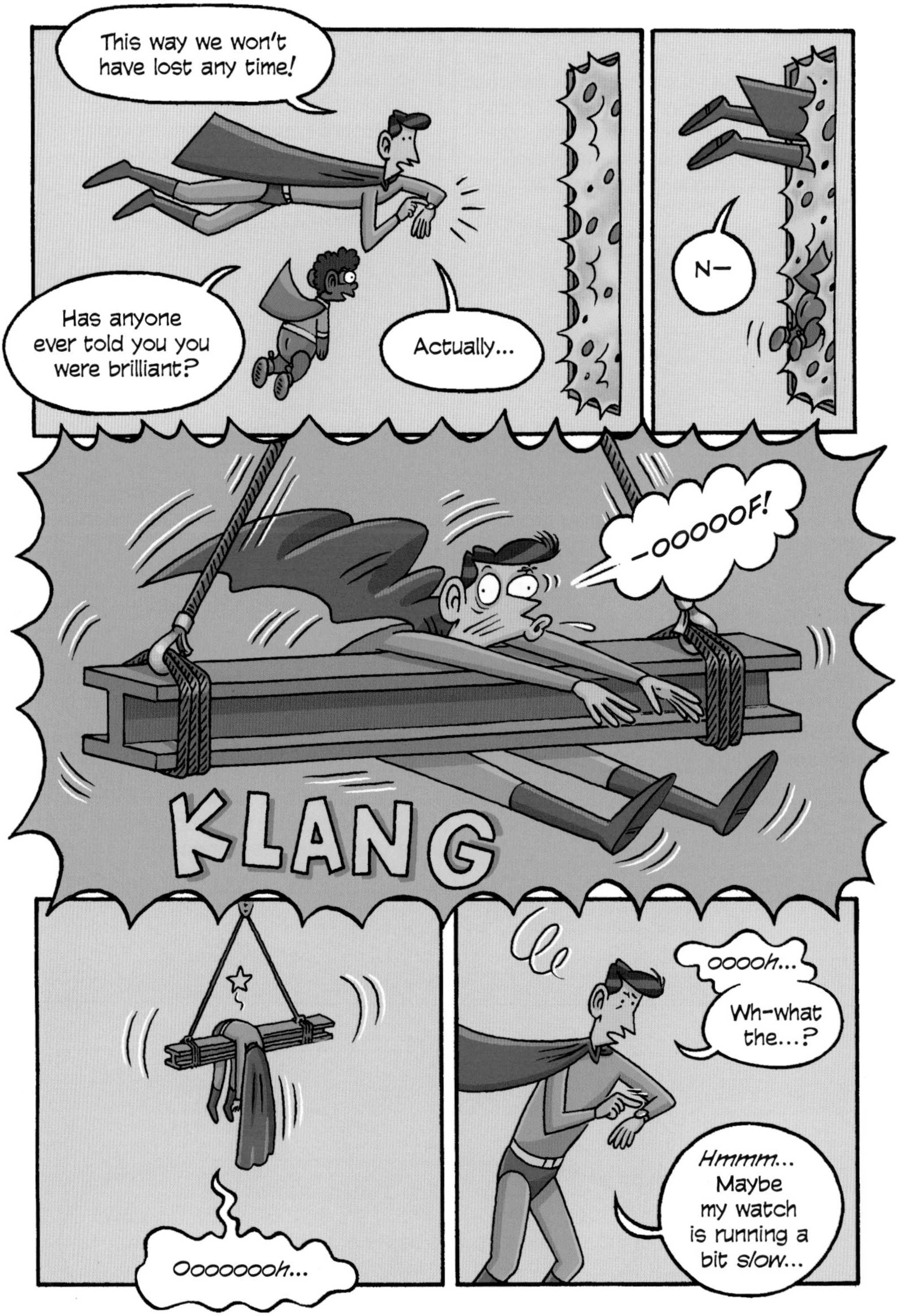
This way we won't have lost any time!
Has anyone ever told you you were brilliant?
Actually...
N—
-OOOOOF!
KLANG
Ooooooooh...
ooooh...
Wh-what the...?
Hmmm... Maybe my watch is running a bit slow...

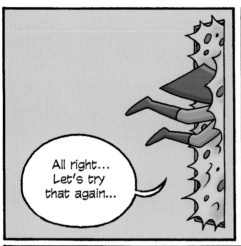

All right... Let's try that again...

Hey, Quiz Kid. Sorry about that.

What took you so long?

Umm... I'm not sure. I think it's time I took my watch in for servicing. But no big deal! I still have the whole day ahead of me. And so do you, Quiz Kid! Enjoy it! Now I've got to change into my secret-identity disguise and get to work! Gotta pay the bills, y'know!

Say, may I ask what you do?

Let's just say I work at a very prestigious architectural firm.

Anyway, Quiz Kid, it was really nice to—

Don'tcha just hate long goodbyes?

Huh!... What a curious kid...

SWOOOSH

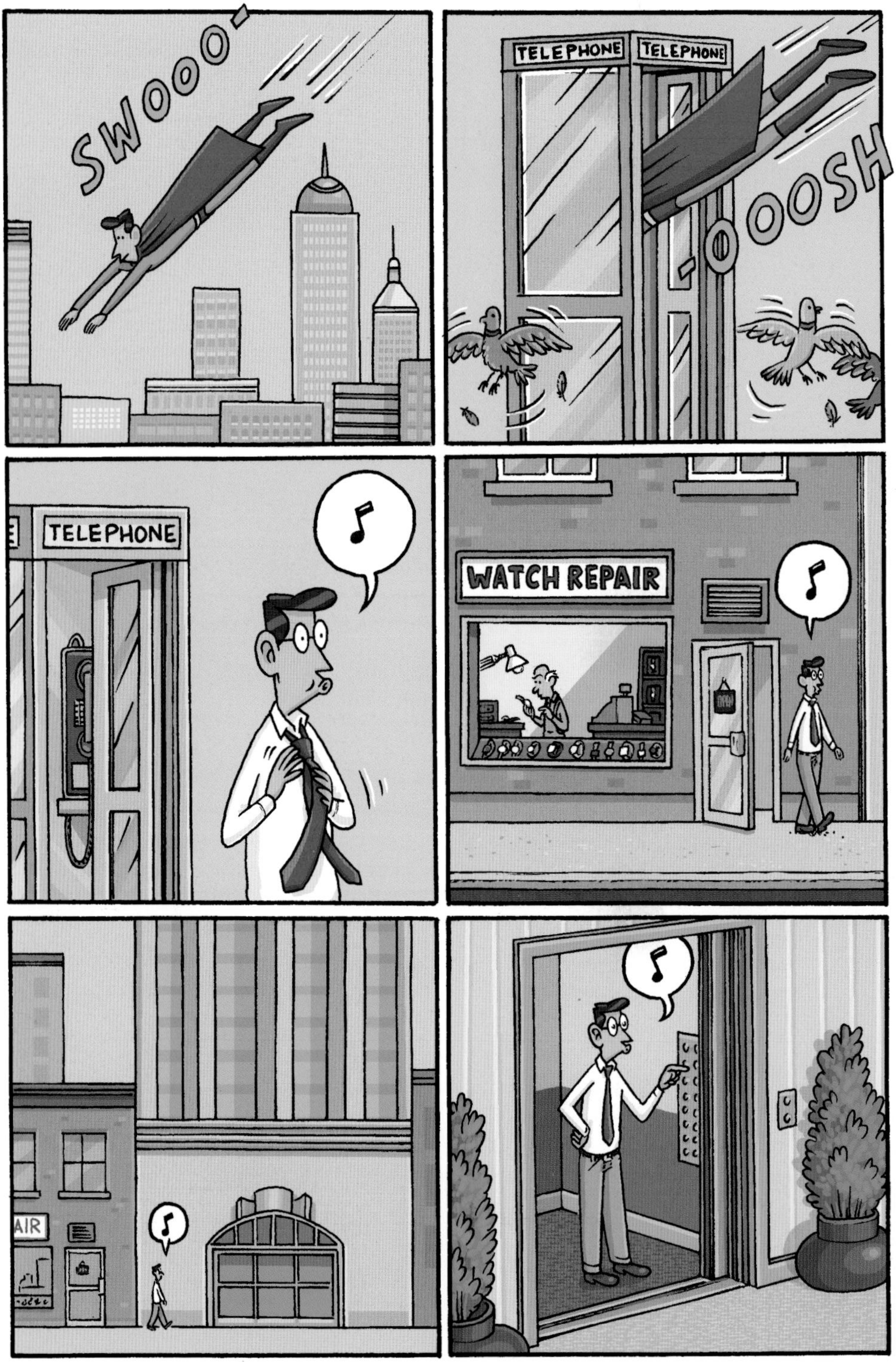
SWOOO-
TELEPHONE
TELEPHONE
-OOOSH
TELEPHONE
♪
WATCH REPAIR
♪
AIR
♪
♪

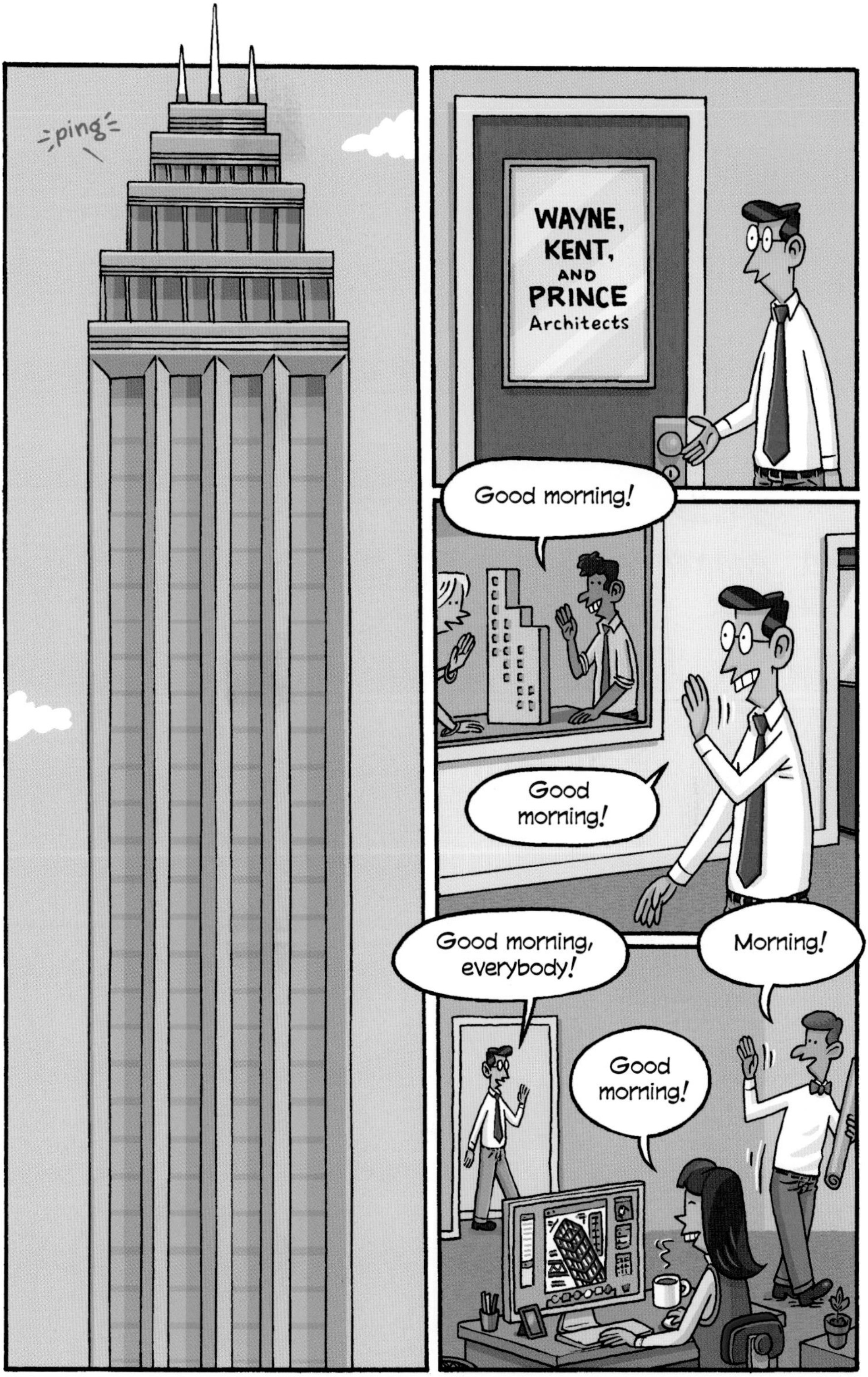
ping
WAYNE, KENT, AND PRINCE Architects
Good morning!
Good morning!
Good morning, everybody!
Morning!
Good morning!

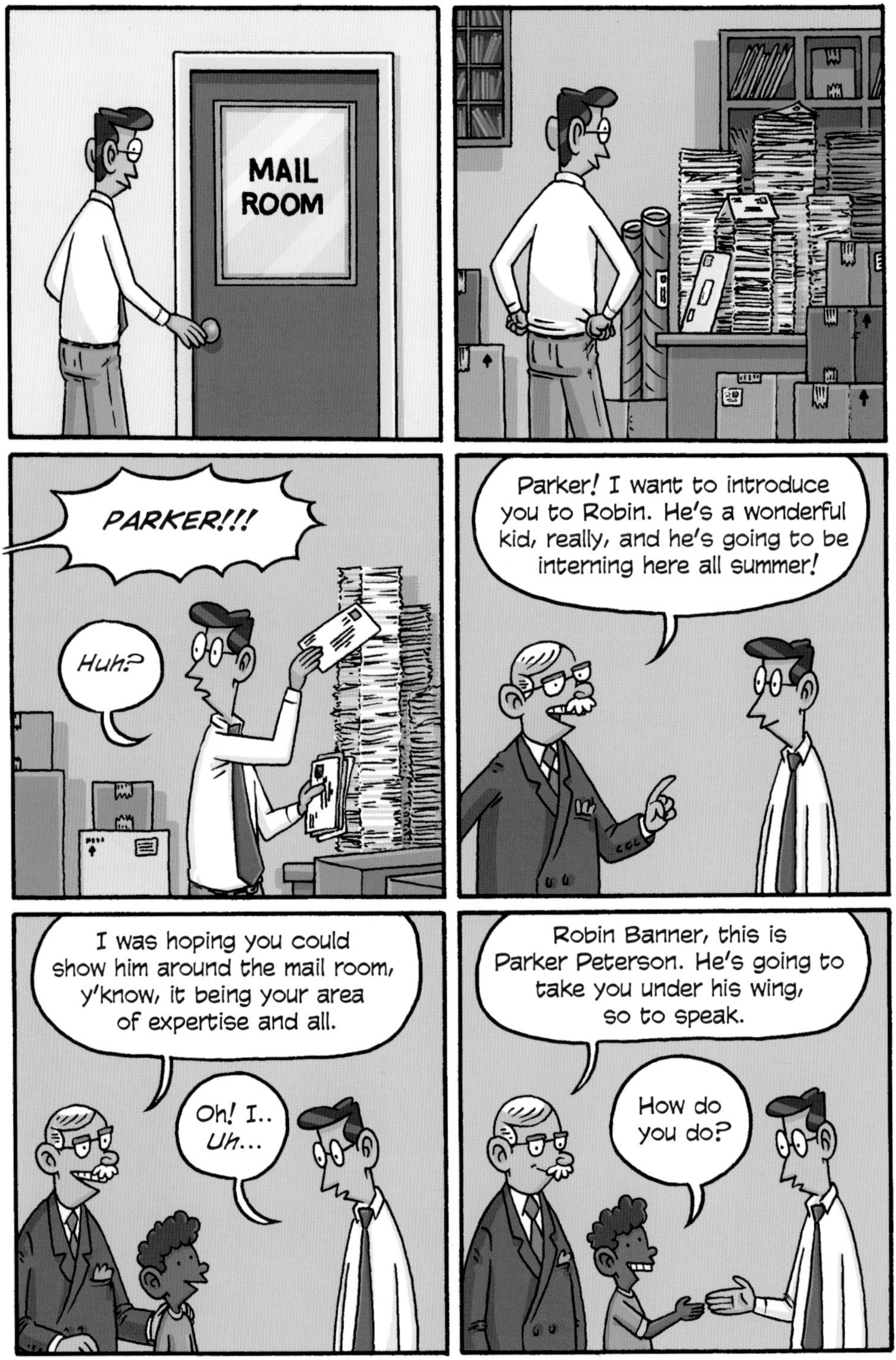
MAIL ROOM
PARKER!!!
Huh?
Parker! I want to introduce you to Robin. He's a wonderful kid, really, and he's going to be interning here all summer!
I was hoping you could show him around the mail room, y'know, it being your area of expertise and all.
Oh! I.. Uh...
Robin Banner, this is Parker Peterson. He's going to take you under his wing, so to speak.
How do you do?

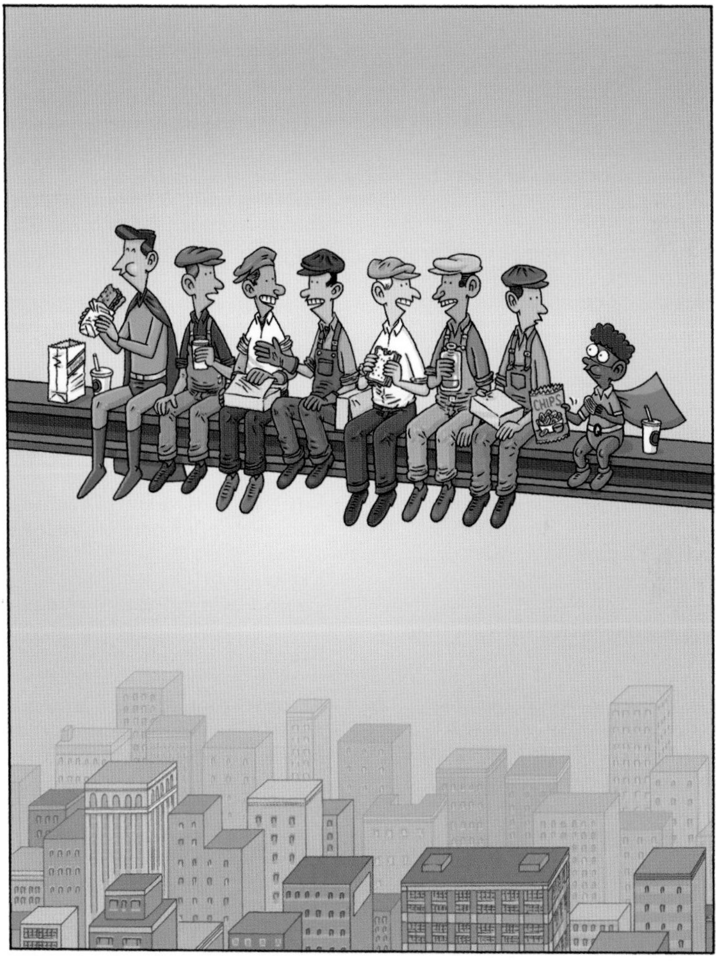
CHIPS

Glossary

Alloy A substance made by melting down and mixing metal with one or more additional elements.

Arch A curved opening.

Bedrock A solid layer of earth that is generally found hundreds of feet under the ground but can sometimes be found at the surface.

Buckling A sudden crumbling or crushing that occurs in an object when it is placed under more stress from compression than it is able to bear.

Caisson A type of pier or pile used to support a building.

Cast iron Iron that has been melted, poured into a mold to form a desired shape, and then cooled. It can be somewhat brittle.

Center of gravity The area of a mass where the force of gravity is greatest.

Cladding A material used for the external covering of a structure.

Climbing form A type of mold used for shaping poured concrete that can move vertically upward as it is filled to allow for additional concrete to be continually added.

Column A vertical support.

Compression A squeezing, crushing stress.

Core Typically the central area of a building that houses a building's daily essential needs, such as elevators, stairs, bathrooms, electrical equipment, storage space, and more. Structurally it acts like the backbone of a building, handling a large amount of a building load.

Corrugated Creased with alternating ridges and grooves.

Counterweight A weight that pulls in the opposite direction of an object being lifted in order to offset some of that object's weight, making it more stable and easier to lift.

Curtain wall A covering for a building that is wrapped around the exterior and is supported by the internal skeleton of the building. It is a nonstructural part of the building, and its main function is to keep the elements out and the people inside safe and comfortable.

Dead load The weight of the permanent, nonmoving elements of a building such as the walls and floors.

Equilibrium A state in which opposing forces or actions are balanced or stable.

Excavation Creating a cavity or hole in the ground by digging and removing earth.

Facade The exterior wall of a building.

Flange A tab or ridge projecting from the edge of an object and used to attach another object or to make it stronger.

Force A push or pull on an object.

Foundation Made of reinforced concrete, it's the underground part of a building on which the entire structure sits.

Friction pile Part of a building's foundation, it is a type of jagged pile that is held in place by the compression of the soil surrounding it.

Girder A particularly large steel or concrete horizontal support beam.

Gravity An invisible force that draws one mass toward every other object. The greater the mass, the greater its force of gravity.

Hardpan A compacted layer of earth underlying softer top soil. It is dense and largely impermeable to water and roots.

Hexagonal Having six sides.

I-beam A steel girder so called due to its distinctive shape.

Inertia The resistance of an object to move or change direction without the influence of an outside force.

Keystone The topmost, wedge-shaped stone in an arch. It locks all the other blocks in the arch together.

Lateral force An exponential force that acts against a structure horizontally, parallel to the ground, typically due to the wind or an earthquake.

Limestone The sedimentary rock that is processed via high heat to create lime, a vital ingredient in cement and concrete.

Lintel A horizontal beam.

Live load The weight of a structure's contents such as furniture, people, and other temporary or movable objects. Also, the forces created by the elements such as wind, rain, and earthquakes.

Load A force that a structure must be able to withstand without failing, including the weight of the building itself and its contents due to the force of gravity as well as the forces imposed by the wind or earthquakes.

Masonry A structure made from smaller pieces, usually stone or brick, that are bonded together using cement or mortar.

Mass A measure of how much matter is in an object regardless of its size.

Mass damper A mechanism, generally installed near the top of a building, that reduces the sway of a building caused by the wind by moving in the opposite direction of the building.

Mat A type of foundation consisting of a large, thick, level slab of reinforced concrete on which a building can sit.

Mortar A building material made from water, sand, lime, and cement. It is used to hold bricks or stones together in a masonry structure.

Pendulum A weight hung from a fixed point that allows it to swing freely to and fro under the influence of gravity.

Permeability The ability of a substance to allow another substance to pass through it.

Pig iron A crude form of iron produced in a blast furnace after the first reduction of iron ore. Brittle and riddled with impurities, it is further refined to make cast and wrought iron, as well as steel.

Pile A vertical column of concrete poured and cast in place, or a large steel beam driven deep into the ground that functions similarly to a pier or caisson in dispersing a structure's load over a greater area.

Pile driver A machine used to hammer piles into the earth.

Rebar A long, thin, rugged steel rod that can be bent or welded into any shape. It can be embedded into wet concrete, adding tensile strength to the concrete after it has cured.

Safe bearing capacity A measure of the ground's ability at a site to support the weight of a building.

Sedimentary A type of rock that is formed by the accumulation of mineral and organic particles deposited by wind, water, and ice.

Silica A compound of silicon and oxygen found in sand, quartz, and flint. It can be used to make glass and cement.

Skeleton frame A grid work of steel columns and beams that serves to support the walls and floors of a building.

Spire A tall structure that tapers to a point on top, usually found on the top of buildings.

Steel An alloy of iron and carbon that is hard and strong. It can be shaped, bent, or formed into any shape as required for a particular use.

Stress The pressure or tension exerted on an object by a force.

Substructure The part of a building that is beneath ground level.

Superstructure The part of a building that rises up from the foundation and into the sky.

Tension A stretching force that pulls a material outward.

Terra-cotta A hard, fired brownish-red clay.

Truss A rigid support crafted from many smaller diagonal pieces.

Turbine A machine used to produce power by harnessing the fast-moving flow of air (or another fluid) as it passes a special wheel or spindle with blades or vanes affixed.

Turbulence The irregular, sometimes violent movement of air, water, or other fluid.

Ventilation The process of removing stale indoor air and replacing it with fresh outside air.

Vortex A mass of whirling air (or another fluid) that spins so fast that it pulls objects into its center.

Vortex shedding A phenomenon where, as wind flows past a building, vortices form and then pull away from alternating sides of the structure, which can cause the building to shake and sway violently, perpendicular to the wind.